Teatime
in the Northwest
THIRD EDITION

THE NORTHWEST'S BEST TEA ROOMS,
TEA PARTIES & EVENTS, AND
RECIPES FOR TASTY TEA TIME TREATS.

By

Sharon & Ken
Foster-Lewis

SPEED GRAPHICS
SEATTLE, WASHINGTON

About the authors

Ken and Sharon Foster-Lewis live on a quiet corner of Camano Island in Washington State.

Ken hails from Liverpool, England where his life experience was as varied as jumping out of airplanes with the British Parachute Regiment and working as a dancehall bouncer during The Beatles' early days. He has also lived in New Zealand, where his adult daughters Jennifer and Amanda and grandsons Connor and Elih live.

Sharon grew up on the Oregon Coast and received her education at Linfield College and University of Oregon before moving to Alaska. She met Ken in Alaska in 1978 where she was working for the airline on which he was a passenger.

They own and operate TeaTime, a national wholesale distributor of tea and tea-related gifts and are working on a new book. A shared love of nature, history, animals and travel carried them around the world before settling in the home Ken built for them overlooking the teatime sunset on the sparkling waters of Puget Sound.

Front cover photograph of "Teatime on Jones Island" Copyright ©2000 by Ken Foster-Lewis.

Printed in the United States of America.
ISBN 1-929258-01-1

For Jennifer Jayne
and Amanda Ann
with love

Introduction

Recently two English tourists stopped in at the Seattle Chamber of Commerce and asked where they might find a good Afternoon Tea. After some ruminating, paper shuffling and murmurs of desperate discourse behind the counter, the clerk returned and answered brightly, "The Empress Hotel!"

Within this third edition of **TeaTime in the Northwest** are more than 150 ways to find and enjoy good tea in Oregon, Washington and British Columbia. No matter where your travels take you in this beautiful Pacific Northwest, you're likely to find a peaceful haven and a pot of good tea when you get there. And while few would dispute that The Empress Hotel is indeed a bright spot in the region's tea scene, you won't ever find it on a walking tour of Seattle, even with sensible shoes.

So whether you're in the mood to be pampered and steeped in elegant formality, to relax in the sweet charms of the Victorian era, or to savor the simplicity of the Pacific Rim influence in tea, you'll find it here.

"Come for tea!" The simple three word invitation rings with welcoming hospitality. Nestled there within its letters is the word 'comfort.' We wish you all of the hospitable comforts TeaTime in the Northwest has to offer.

Many happy teatimes,
Sharon and Ken

Foreword

Dear Sharon:

I love this book! I guarantee that anybody who loves tea–and the Pacific Northwest–is sure to love it too. I think we should buy several copies each to pass out to the pleasure-deprived. Thank you for your very valuable work.

You show how we who love the Pacific Northwest as well as infusions of Camellia sinensis continue to multiply. You give the names and addresses of our preferred gathering places–nay, you reveal the secret names of our TEAS! An earlier time might have declared that these are acquired tastes, and not to be advertised at large–but YOU!!! You tell all, Sharon, ALL!

You can tell tea drinkers from coffee drinkers in traffic by the way tea drinkers motion others to enter lanes of traffic ahead of them, you say. If you give recipes, Sharon, you also give us a notion of the sort of woman you are–contemplative and thoughtful, stylish, particular, and liking nothing more than to sink into that silence of observation so cherished by the tea sages.

How daring of you, dear Sharon, to bring to those coffee-swallowing multitudes of your native Northwest news of a kinder, gentler beverage, more ancient and more ennobling! Times for tea are the silk in the fabric of life at the places Sharon shows us in this guide.

We happy few–the region's tea lovers–are all your beneficiaries and bow in thankful homage!

Your Admiring Colleague–

James Norwood Pratt

Special Thanks

About halfway through creating this third edition of TeaTime in the Northwest little voices in our heads whispered smugly, "Tsk,tsk,tsk- you've really bitten off more than you two can chew this time, haven't you?" Fortunately, for every time that little naysayer injected doubt, there were three or four louder voices of friends, family, tea room owners, booksellers and readers of prior editions, all expressing confidence and enthusiasm for this new book. With their support "the more than we could chew" started getting broken into little dainty bites, until the plate was clean.

Could it be that one of the reasons we like Afternoon Teas so much is that the treats are almost always bite-size?

Heartfelt thanks go to those louder, cheerier voices of Mom and Dad, Chuck Hill, Ian Clyde, Emily-Mum, Susan Creighton, Sue Graves, Maureen O. Wilson, Claire Winget, Irene Moody, Auntie Marwayne, Monica and Maria-lynn Olsson, Angel Lady Marilyn, tea room proprietors in the Northwest, and all of you kind readers who took time to write to us. A special thank you to James Norwood Pratt, a national treasure, who graces the tea scene with wisdom, humor, kindness and generosity of spirit.

For her good taste and appreciation of fine things, we thank Irene Moody for her loan of the Royal Doulton tea service which appears on the cover of Teatime in the Northwest, Third Edition.

On our back cover is the tea room photo "Afternoon Tea" courtesy of Butchart Gardens, Ltd. See page 160. The photo of Campbell House on page 34 is by our friend Anne Nisbet, author of The Gourmet's Guide to Northwest Bed & Breakfast Inns. Thanks, Anne.

TABLE OF CONTENTS

A note about this new edition:

We've learned from tea room owners that there are now roving tea parties out "tea-touring," guided by the earlier editions of this book. Knowing what a thrill it is for us to be asked to sign books made us think it might be fun for you to collect the autographs of the tea room proprietors in this new edition when you visit. These hospitable folks are what make Northwest teatime so special. Their livelihoods are dedicated to providing peaceful havens for all of us to enjoy a bit of solitude or connect with friends over a pot of good tea. Because many of these places are cozy, family-run businesses, (there are many mother-daughter teams in this new edition) we encourage you to call ahead and confirm the days and hours of operation to avoid surprises if a schedule has changed since going to print. Thank you for letting us share these special places with you.

 The symbol at left appears next to establishments that offer teas or events by arrangement. If you want someone to serve an Afternoon Tea at your home or arrange a child's tea party for a birthday, look to these experts who offer a variety of themes and menus.

A Brief History
of the World's Oldest
Beverage

Like the thick fogs that often shroud our Pacific Northwest coastline, so too has the origin of tea been clouded through time by myth and legend.

Scholars seem to agree that in the year 2,737 BC, there existed an enlightened Chinese emperor named Shen Nung. It's on his silk-clad shoulders my favorite version of tea's origin rests. Shen Nung was revered as a horticulturist and a bit of a health nut. His understanding of hygiene was so advanced for the day that he was even predisposed to boil his drinking water. One windy day, while working in his garden, several glossy, green leaves drifted into his cauldron of hot water. Glancing up, he noted that it came from a tree bearing a lovely pure white flower. As he bent over his cauldron with a ladle to remove the leaves, Shen Nung noticed a delicate and pleasant aroma was being emitted. Instead of using the ladle to fling the serrated leaves from the pot, he dauntlessly lifted it to his lips and sipped. Not only did he find the taste fresh and delightful, but he noted too that the beverage gave a lift to his flagging energy. Detailed instructions were issued throughout the land on the care and cultivation of this plant Camellia sinensis, a distant cousin of those welcome harbingers of Pacific Northwest spring, our camellia bushes.

India and Japan also lay claim to the discovery of tea, I just happen to like gardening stories. It's safe to say that the plant was growing all over Asia as it's native to semitropical and tropical climes, as well as the light air over 5,000 feet elevation. If left untrimmed, the plant grows to treelike proportions of 40 feet and more and lives a good 70 years. There are some fun legends about irate monkeys plucking branches from the trees in the wild and throwing them down at humans bent on annoying

. . . At the fifth cup I am purified;
The sixth cup calls me to the realms of the immortals.
　　Lu T'ung

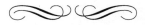

Drink tea that your mind may be lively and clear.
　　Wang Yu Cheng
　　Sung Dynasty

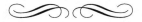

them. Shame to lose that legend, but I can only deal with one at a time. It didn't take early gardeners long to see the advantage for harvesting if the plant was kept trimmed to a bush of 3 or 4 feet in height, probably because you couldn't count on mad monkeys all the time.

By the 5th century AD tea had become as popular a trade commodity as vinegar, rice and noodles, making its way along established trade routes to Persia by sure-footed caravan. The subtle shift had begun from considering tea as a medicinal elixir to a pleasurable social beverage and major bartering tool.

By 780 AD, enterprising tea merchants sought a forum to promote their product. In commissioning Lu Yu to create the masterpiece essay Ch'a Ching or The Classic of Tea they had found a means to formalize the cultivation, preparation, and enjoyment of tea. The book had far-reaching social effects, some of which could not be anticipated by the tea merchants. Government revenue officials, tirelessly sniffing out ways to augment their coffers, levied the very first tea tax. A unified cry of outrage arose, as tea had become so deeply ingrained in the culture by this time. Revenue officials retreated grudgingly from implementing the tax for more than a decade.

So who was this Lu Yu? He was an orphan found wandering and taken in as a child by a Buddhist monk. The austerity of his adopted father's calling held no appeal for Lu Yu, so he went to the opposite extreme and ran away and joined the circus as an acrobatic clown. While performing in the provinces Lu Yu met a benefactor who introduced him to books and culture and provided him with an education. So it was that Lu Yu, orphan and clown, became revered as a scholar, author, cultural celebrity and friend to an emperor. So poetic and detailed are the instructions set forth in Lu Yu's essay that they have survived for more than 1,200 years. Today they form a basis for the ritualized Japanese Tea Ceremony Chanoyu, in which the very essence of religious thought of the day has been embodied beautifully and simply.

We shape clay into a pot, but it is the emptiness inside that holds whatever we want.
Tao-te Ching

At about the time that Juan de Fuca's ship was plying the waters of Puget Sound, and Shakespeare was seeking funding in England for A Midsummer Night's Dream, boatloads of Portuguese Jesuit priests were on the move too. Riding anchor in a teeming harbor of China, a Dutch navigator of one of those Portuguese ships, Jan Hugo van Lin-Schooten now had time on his hands. In letters to his wife back in the Netherlands, Jan Hugo wrote of the wonders of the Orient and described in glowing prose his encounter with a new beverage - tea. In 1595, after Mrs. van Lin-Schooten had succeeded in having her husband's letters published in Holland, the public demand for tea was high. The Dutch wasted no time in establishing a trading base in Java, to which more than 60 round-trip trading voyages would be made in the first seven years.

By 1610, the first Chinese teas were shipped to Europe by the Dutch, where it was introduced to Holland, Britain, France, Germany, Scandinavia, Russia and North America. The Germans and the French were quick to shrug off the new beverage, returning instead to the comfortable familiarity of their ales and wines. While the other countries adopted tea as a beverage of daily consumption, it had virtually entered the bloodstream of England. Reminiscent of later day "infomercials", advertising bulletins in England called "broadsides" attributed almost magical virtues to tea, and they couldn't get enough. The Dutch held a tight grip on trade and kept the price so high that for the first 50 years, tea was kept under lock and key in the parlors of the upper crust. In a unique combination of bloodshed and diplomacy the British grasped control of the tea trade, and by 1700 affordable tea was reaching the tables of England. Smug in their abilities to grow anything, the British failed in their attempts to introduce the plant to their soil. Nonetheless, the infusion into their lives was complete, tea had made the transition from being a nectar for the exclusive enjoyment of emperors, tsars, and kings, to the daily table of the common man.

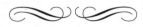

We had a kettle; we let it leak.
Our not repairing it made it worse.
We haven't had any tea for a week . . .
The bottom is out of the Universe.
Rudyard Kipling

The celebrated tea clipper Cutty Sark

There are few hours in life more agreeable than the hour dedicated to the ceremony known as afternoon tea.

Henry James,
Portrait of a Lady

Late in the 1700s British tea merchants commissioned American shipbuilders to develop and construct a class of sailing ship designed specifically for the tea trade. The clippers, as they were called, were three-masted, graceful and fast. Capable of transporting one million pounds of tea each trip, their speed dramatically improved the bottom line. Fortunes were made.

Meanwhile in America, dissatisfaction was growing in the colonies proportionate to the increased taxes being heaped upon them by Britain. While diplomacy resulted in the repeal of the taxes on many goods imported, the three pence per pound tax on tea was completely beyond discussion. In 1773 American colonial housewives formed the first consumer group boycott, uniting under the banner "Mistresses of the Families." It was widely suspected by this group that the British were not only guilty of price-gouging, but compounding the sin by shipping inferior grade tea to the colonies. This scandalous "uprising" of uppity colonial women set tongues wagging over teacups in the gentile parlors of London and planted the seeds for an even larger rebellion.

The high taxation and shortsightedness of the English government was not limited to the colonies, however. Within England the duties and taxes added to tea had raised the cost for a pound of tea to four times the average man's weekly wage. Finally reaching 120%, much of the revenue was earmarked to save the financially beleaguered and poorly managed British East India Trading Company.

High duty and high demand for tea combined to make tea smuggling a lucrative vocation in England. The intricate coves and hidden inlets that make the southern England coastline so charming also made it ideal for the clandestine off loading of tea. Small vessels plied the moonlit waters to meet the large commerce ships, most of them Dutch, silently riding the swell offshore. At one point nearly 50% of the tea in England was contraband, and a farm labor shortage resulted from able-bodies young men seeking their fortunes under cover of darkness.

Meanwhile back in the colonies, another group of able-bodied young men was determined to make a more visible and dramatic protest. On December 16, 1773, disguised as American Indians "The Sons of Liberty" swarmed the docks in Boston and dumped 340 large chests of tea into the harbor. British Parliament was swift in meting out punishment and repression. In the colonies the kettles of revolution simmered and bubbled and the First Continental Congress convened. Tea had started a revolution.

It was American Captain Gray's explorations in the Pacific Northwest that led to the fledgling country opening trade gates of its own. He had succeeded in generating a lucrative trade with the North Coast Indian tribes to acquire the lush pelts of otter, mink and beaver, all prized highly in China. These furry denizens of the Pacific Northwest became the link that allowed trade directly with the world for tea and other products, transported directly to North America on its own ships.

Afternoon Tea began as an English institution in 1840 when Anna, the 7th Duchess of Bedford's stomach began to growl. The Duchess was a society trendsetter who was also a snacker, being unable to get by on the twice-daily big meals of the time. Around four or five in the afternoon she summoned for cakes and sandwiches, bread and butter, and whatever little goodies the kitchen could provide to accompany her pot of tea. Legions of closet-snackers followed the trend-setting duchess and teatime upon tea party the custom grew. It was adopted by manual and farm workers in the form of "high tea," a more substantial meal that included meats and cheeses and more robust fare. This was often the laborer's main meal of the day.

In 1848 an English gentleman with the providential name of Fortune disguised himself in the robes of a Chinese merchant. Carried around the Chinese countryside in a curtained sedan-chair under cover of darkness, Robert Fortune, who was later knighted for his efforts, conducted early industrial espionage on tea cultivation. Surreptitiously this horticulturist garnered soil samples, tea cut-

And freedom's teacup
still o'erflows
With ever-fresh
libations,
To cheat of slumber
all her foes
and cheer the
wakening nations!
Oliver Wendell
Holmes
*Ballad of the Boston
Tea Party*

Teatime in the Northwest

tings and processing techniques in areas of China that were off-limits to foreigners. His purloined knowledge enabled the British to establish large tea plantations in India, known as "gardens" that thrive to this day.

Queen Victoria declared tea to be the national beverage of England. Not encouraged by her nanny to have tea as a young princess, she outfitted her vacation retreat with a small scale table and plush chairs embroidered with her own children's names to invite them to share the custom early. Teatime indulgences emerged in the general marketplace. Pottery makers sensed the demand and began competing with each other for novel teapot designs. Suddenly merchants shelves were awash with tea paraphernalia.

In 1864, the enterprising manager of ABC, Aerated Bread Company in London wheedled some unused space from her employer in order to offer tables for tea and baked goods. Business thrived. Society's approval of tea had created the very first public place a lady could actually go unchaperoned. While they would not win the right to vote for another 40 years, tea drinking ladies were heady with their new found freedom. Tea rooms and women's liberation both flourished.

Today, those initial endeavors have engendered a harvest of public tea rooms in Oregon, Washington and southern British Columbia. As varied as the inhabitants of this beautiful area are, we are united by our sense of how special our Pacific Northwest is and by our desire for pleasant havens for tea. From the ivy-mantled, hushed tone, tinkle of silver on bone china tea rooms to the countrified, casual, or eclectic tea rooms, the Northwest has a special place for you to linger over "the cup that cheers."

Lu Yu Explains Tea

Imagine, if you will, that Lu Yu is given one day back on 20th century earth and he must spend it in the Pacific Northwest. Closing his eyes and randomly dialing numbers in a phone booth, he calls your home. It's Saturday morning, you have some free time, so you arrange to pick him up since he doesn't drive.

Lu Yu is easy to spot near the phone booth in the colorful silk brocade jacket which he has gathered around him to ward off the misty Northwest chill. As he shifts from foot to foot to stay warm, you note with concern the small splash his sandals make in the puddle. "The first stop will be Eddie Bauer and Nike," you ruminate thoughtfully, "then a good cup of tea to set things right." (Fortunately, you had the presence of mind this morning to bring along your copy of Teatime in the Northwest.) "An 8th century tea philosopher should enjoy a good 'cuppa'."

The shelves of the cheery tearoom are a feast for the eyes! The colorful tins and shiny boxes glisten in the morning light with colors to rival the richness of Lu Yu's silk jacket, (which you feel a little guilty thinking would look good with your black slacks). After apologizing for the weather on the drive over, you realize that with the topic of tea you've struck a pleasant chord for conversation.

"So many teas . . ." his eyes caress the crowded shelves with delight, lingering over the myriad of green teas like one recognizing an old friend. He makes his choice, and the pot is delivered to your table. With his waterproof Eddie Bauer jacket draped casually over the back of his chair, and the aromatic beverage creating a mystic aura over your table, Lu Yu once again takes on the mantle of an 8th century tea philosopher. As you make a mental note to remove the price tags and extra button packet hanging from his new jacket, he begins:

"All teas come from the leaves of one bush, the Camellia sinensis. It is in the processing of the tea leaves that the three different teas are created." His new Nikes squeak on the floor under the table and appear to startle him.

Tea tempers the spirit and harmonizes the mind, dispels lassitude and relieves fatigue; awakens thought and prevents drowsiness.
     Lu Yu

"Three different teas? There must be thousands," you assert, perhaps a little too strongly. You may not be a tea philosopher, but you do know your retail tea merchants' shelves. "Perhaps Lu Yu is a little out of touch with what's happened in the last 12 centuries," you decide to yourself.

"Three teas," he patiently restates, his voice underlining the importance of this very basic piece of tea information, "black tea, green tea, and oolong. It is the processing that determines their differences. There are dozens of varieties of each of these three, usually named for the region in which they are grown, and then literally thousands of different tea blends."

"What is this 'process' that the tea leaf undergoes?" you query, realizing this person really does know his tea.

Lu Yu inhales the aroma of the tea. He fumbles a moment with the handle on the cup, decides to simply avoid it, and holds it gently in his two hands like one would a small bird. The warmth is a welcome comfort to his cold palms. "The process is either three or fourfold depending on the type of tea. First, withering removes as much moisture as possible from the leaves. Then they are rolled or manipulated to partially rupture the leaf tissue. This step releases naturally-occuring enzymes that begin the process of fermentation. It is the degree of fermentation that determines which of the three tea types you are producing. That is what distinguishes them from each other," he says matter-of-factly.

Suddenly you flash back to a wine appreciation class you took from a local wine expert. "Fermentation?" you ponder, "Like in the production of a good wine?"

"No," he says simply and patiently like speaking to a child. "Like in the production of a good tea. The term fermentation actually is a slightly misleading technical term for the process of oxidation - the exposure of the leaves and the released enzymes to air. Finally, they are dried or fired, which stops the fermentation process and dries the leaves evenly." "Naturally" he adds, "there are numerous variations on this general process de-

The goodness is a decision for the mouth to make.
Lu Yu
The Classic of Tea

pending on the source of the leaves and also the country in which the final tea is manufactured. Darjeeling, Keemun, Assam and Ceylon are all black teas for example. Black teas are subjected to all four of the steps, Oolongs are lightly withered and rolled and only partially fermented before being dried."

"And your favorite, the green tea?" you probe.

"Ah, green tea," he rolls his eyes skyward in remembered delight, "green tea is not fermented at all. The leaves are steamed or heated rather than withered, then rolled and dried. The leaves remain green because they do not oxidize. A green tea is light and clear with a delicate, very flavorful taste." He smiles and nods toward the pot between us, "But I must say I am enjoying this black tea! As I say in my book, 'the goodness is a decision for the mouth to make'. You have read my book, haven't you?"

Avoiding his stare over the rim of his cup you assure him that it was your fond intention to read the whole book, and one day soon you certainly would, that you had been a bit busy lately. You are relieved to notice that this seems to satisfy Lu Yu.

" What a delightful experience it has been for me to see how far tea has come in 1,200 years." he actually smacks his lips after tipping his cup for the last taste and rises. "But now I really must be getting back. Do you have any other questions for me before I go?"

"Well, I read somewhere that you actually were an acrobatic clown in a travelling circus in China. Is this true?" You had been longing to ask that question all through the morning but did not want to seem impertinent nor to interrupt the wondrous flow of tea knowledge. Slipping the embroidered silk jacket from his shoulders, he folds it gently, caressing the fine brocade, and hands it to you with a slight bow saying "Please accept this humble gift as appreciation of your kind hospitality," and with a smile, Lu Yu executes two perfect backflips out the door of the tearoom and disappears into the Pacific Northwest mist.

I am in no way interested in immortality, but only in the taste of tea.

Lu T'ung

The first European teacups evolved from Oriental tea bowls and were without a handle. To avoid burned fingers, Europeans poured a sip of tea into the saucer to cool. A single handle was added to the cup in the mid-18th century.

Types of Teas

My Aunt Marwayne knows the night sky. With unbridled delight she will rock back on her heels, throw her gray head back, and enthuse, "Oh look, there's Venus in Taurus! Ah, Jupiter's moving through Gemini." From the sky she can tell the seasons of the year. From the sky she can tell the seasons of a person's life. The night sky in her company seems a friendly place, populated by stars with which you are on a first name basis. I admire that wealth of knowledge and the comfort of that familiarity.

Before I got to know much about tea I had a general feeling it must all be pretty much like the teabag variety. My expectations were minimal, and the brew I made met these limited expectations nicely. It would be brownish. It would burn my tongue if I wasn't careful. It was okay. The idea of subtle varietal differences in tea had not entered my thoughts.

The following varieties of the three main types of tea (Black, Oolong, and Green) are provided simply as a starting point for your own exploration. Within these varieties are literally thousands of variations based on country of origin and even the blending techniques of various tea companies. Experimentation will help you find your personal favorites, and even to create your very own blends:

Black Teas

Assam - from northeast India, this is a robust and hearty tea with a strong malty flavor and rusty color, grown at low altitude, and used in Irish Breakfast Tea. Good served with milk.

Ceylon - from Sri Lanka, golden color, a strong full taste and delicate fragrance. Good served throughout the day.

Darjeeling - makes an excellent after-dinner tea, rich in flavor, with a flowery bouquet. This tea is grown high in the foothills of the Himalayas of north India, and is an expensive tea.

Earl Grey - a 19th century British statesman the Second Earl Grey, was given this recipe in appreciation from the Chinese for his diplomatic work. Typically drunk in the afternoon, Earl Grey has a pungent, flowery fragrance and delicacy owing to Oil of Bergamot sprayed on the tea.

English Breakfast - often either a blend of Indian and Ceylon teas or a Keemun based blend, this popular morning tea is full-bodied, strong, and aromatic. Its rich flavor is enhanced with milk.

Keemun - a fine quality Chinese tea originating in the Anhui Province of southern China, this is a full-bodied tea with a haunting nut-like quality to its taste. Serve with milk for maximum enjoyment.

Lapsang Souchong - the leaves are smoked over embers to create this rich exotic tea. Redolent of campfires, its distinctive aroma reminds both Ken and me of the smell of Admiral Nelson's ship moored in Portsmouth, England. We don't know why, but we find a tarry, nautical quality to this unusual tea experience.

He loved happiness like I love tea.
Eudora Welty

Oolong Teas

Formosa Oolong - almost all Oolong comes from Taiwan. This tea has a refreshing, fruity aroma and sparkling nature, and has been anointed "the philosopher's drink". Oolongs are created in other countries, but Formosa Oolong has been given the nod by most tea experts as the best.

Green Teas

Gunpowder - when Europeans first arrived in Zhejiang Province of China and were shown the pellets of rolled young or medium-age leaves that constitute this tea, it is said that they named it because of the resemblance to lead ball shot. Low in caffeine, it has a delicate yet penetrating flavor.

Gyokuro - one of Japan's most highly revered green teas made from only the tender top buds. Mild and sweet, as its name "Pearl Dew" would imply, it is one of Japanese teas that have become known collectively as "the white wines of teas."

Hyson - green tea from China or India; fragrant, light, and mellow.

Mattcha - Japan's ceremonial powdered tea, less than 1% is exported.

Hoochow - the first of the annual crop of green tea from China, a light and sweet tea.

In the early 1900s, Mr. Thomas Sullivan, a tea merchant in New York City accidentally created the teabag. Attempting to stimulate sales by mailing samples of the tea wrapped in silk cloth to potential customers, many who received it simply poured boiling water over the bag rather than opening it as the vendor had originally intended. Hemp gauze soon replaced the silk to make the teabag cost effective.

When is tea not tea?

While the question may sound like a riddle emanating from the head of the Mad Hatter's table, it does require some consideration.

It is important to remember that true tea is a beverage created by the infusion of boiling water and the leaves of only one specific plant, the Camellia sinensis. Western cultures, however, have embraced the term 'tea' to encompass healthful herbal, root, fruit, tree bark, and seed brews in rapidly growing varieties and blends. Well-known examples, all of which are caffeine-free, are chamomile, rose hip, burdock, ginseng, cardamom, and a wide array of mints. The French call these refreshing herbal infusions "tisanes" to distinguish them from tea.

Imbued by traditional folklore of all cultures, (and more recently medical research), to possess beneficial properties, the herbal infusions constitute a whole separate world of steeped beverages. The varieties deserve study, respect, appreciation and experimentation. There are many excellent books on the topic.

Chai

The word cha is the original word for tea in China. In India, where milk and spices were added, the word became chai (rhymes with high). Now at least four Northwest companies are creating Chai. Three Oregon companies: Oregon Chai and Xanadu Teas in Portland, and Sattwa Chai in Newberg are succeeding in introducing the spicy tea drink to the North American taste buds, as is The Chai Guy (a.k.a. Jan Drabeck) in Seattle, Washington.

As Chaimeister Jan Drabek asserts, "Chai is like chocolate chip cookies or lemonade, everyone has their own way of doing it." Usually Chai is created from varying combinations of the following: black tea, hot milk, vanilla, honey, ginger, cinnamon, clove, nutmeg, cardamom, sometimes crushed almonds and even pepper (yes, pepper). A highly individual drink, it varies from household to household in India. Invigorating, refreshing and rich, many predict that Chai will gain converts from the latte crowd in rapidly growing numbers. See our recipe section for a version of chai made from individual herbs and spices.

How to brew a perfect pot of tea

Bring freshly drawn, cold water to a rolling boil in your kettle, allowing about 3/4 cup water per serving. Do not allow the water to boil too long as this tends to diminish the end flavor through insufficient aeration. Never reheat water. By the way, if you do not like the taste of your tap water for drinking, you will not like it any better in tea. In that case, use commercially bottled waters.

Use a spotless ceramic or glass teapot that has been warmed by filling with hot tap water for a few minutes. Drain that water completely out of the teapot.

Into the warmed teapot place one rounded teaspoon of a good quality loose tea per six-ounce cup that you are making.

Pour the boiling water over the tea in the teapot, stir, and allow to brew for five full minutes. Time the brew. The single most common cause for poor tea is not following this step and erroneously attempting to judge the brew by its coloration. Use this time to get your cups, milk, sugar, and/or lemon slices ready.

Separate the spent leaves from the brew. This is especially easy if your teapot has a removable leaf basket, use a strainer, or decant into a warmed serving pot. Stir the brew to even it out.

Serve it fresh. If you like your tea less strong, add hot water after the tea has brewed. Brewing another pot, if everyone wants more, is the tastiest idea.

The custom of pouring the milk into the cup before the hot tea dates back to seventeenth century England. Until then, the British had only known pewter and earthenware mugs for drinking ale, and were afraid that hot tea poured into newly introduced fine porcelain cups would crack them. The custom continues to this day as a matter of personal choice. Queen Elizabeth adds milk after the tea is poured.

"Sun Tea" advice

Iced tea was invented at the St. Louis World's Fair by an enterprising British tea vendor on a hot day when he became tired of watching customers pass his booth to get free samples of ice-cold soft drinks and lemonade.

Make special ice cubes for your iced tea by freezing a raspberry, blackberry or mint leaf in each cube.

Maybe it's because the Northwest doesn't see as much sun as other parts of the country that we're immediately charmed by a beverage made with solar power. Maybe it's the memories for many of us of our first sip of the brew in the 1960s with gentle folk music playing in the background. Whatever the reason, "sun tea" followers attach the same seasonal significance to placing the jar on the windowsill that many bird lovers attach to the return of the swallows. Summer just can't be far behind.

Health care professionals recently have raised several unsettling questions regarding the possibility of bacteria forming during the regular "sun tea" brewing conditions. Tea authorities recently have pointed out that the flavor of the tea will never be at its height since the water never really gets hot enough for maximum flavor. As charming a ritual as a jar of water and teabags on a sunny windowsill may seem, all signs seem to indicate that there is now a better way.

Harney & Sons Fine Teas recommends the following: for 1 quart of tea, place 7 tea bags or 3 T. loose tea in a heatproof 1 quart container. Bring 1 cup of cold water to a rolling boil and pour over the tea. Stir, cover, and let stand for 15 minutes. Add 3 cups of cold water and stir. Remove the tea bags or strain the loose tea and serve over ice. Adding a cinnamon stick, lime or orange slices, or a split vanilla bean while the tea steeps lends a light natural flavor.

So give the sunny windowsill back to your cat so she can watch the return of the swallows to your yard, and raise a healthy glass to summer.

Tea Dyed Fabrics and Old Time Advice

"Everything old is new again," the old song professed, and with the return of tie-dyed shirts and bell bottoms that point is driven home. Taking it one step further and harking back to the early 1900s, tea-dyed fabric has once again become fashionable. Validated by the "Shabby Chic" cult, embraced on the pages of Martha Stewart's magazine, and adorning well-dressed soft cushions everywhere, the subtle coloration of tea-dyed fabric makes a clear and comfortable fashion statement.

My own dear mother didn't pass down to me a wealth of practical domestic instruction, (except not to store bananas in the refrigerator, which doubled as her sex-education chat as I recall), but I did come away with a 900-page tome on domesticity that has been passed from woman to woman in our family, Mrs. Curtis's Household Discoveries and Cookery Book published in 1908. Yes, 1908, which may explain a lot about my housekeeping, you can't just run out to Costco and buy boot-black and whale oil you know.

The industrious Mrs. Curtis urges us to spotclean our black silk ballgowns with raw potato juice and tea, to drop an oyster shell in our tea kettles to soften the water, to save money on flypaper by using sweetened tea to catch the little pests, to clean our mirrors with it, and to win the adoration of our families by spreading wet tea leaves on our rugs prior to sweeping. (Don't try any of this at home and then blame me! Remember Mrs. Curtis has been gone a long, long time, and she took her battalion of liability attorneys with her!)

Mrs. Curtis also recommended tinting your lace doilies with an infusion of strong tea. This good idea has been revived, and today is a popular treatment of all light-colored fabric to achieve a vintage coloration. The following instructions are updated for us millennium women:

If dying one-yard pieces of fabric for pillows or placemats, use a 16-quart stainless steel pot and 3

I hope the next time we meet we won't be fighting each other. Instead we will be drinking tea together.

Jackie Chan
Rumble in the Bronx

gallons of tap water. While you are bringing the water in the pot to a full boil, fill your sink with cold water and thoroughly soak the fabric that is to be dyed. The fabric needs to be uniformly wet to accept the dye process evenly.

To the boiling water add 8 ounces of loose black tea, either in a muslin bag or thrown in loose to be scooped out later with a big strainer. Boil the tea leaves for at least half an hour or longer. The strength of the dye will be determined by the length of the boiling. Remove from heat, add 1/2 cup white vinegar, and extract the muslin bag or scoop out the tea leaves with a strainer. Wring out the soaking fabric and add the damp fabric to the infusion and allow it to steep for several hours, agitating occasionally to insure even dyeing and checking regularly to see if the color you desire has been achieved. When the fabric has reached the desired color (and remember that wet fabric will dry to a lighter color,) use tongs to remove it from the tea bath. Rinse under cold running water until it runs clear. Wring out the fabric and dry on a rack away from sunlight. It's always advisable to keep any pots and tongs used for dyeing separate from your cooking utensils.

Nestled there in Mrs. Curtis's book of housewifery, amid the unrelenting drudgery of scrub-board washing and rug-beating is a glimpse of grace: "Have in one corner of the room a small, low table with an alcohol lamp and suitable tea things for making a cup of tea," Mrs. Curtis urges, "This simple expression of hospitality gives a note of good cheer that is much needed in modern social life. There need be no formality suggested by a cup of tea offered to a caller even in the most quiet neighborhoods, and having all the needful things at hand gives the serving of tea an air of grace and naturalness." Here's to you, Mrs. Curtis!

. . . they had a Very Nearly Tea, which is one you forget about afterwards, and hurried to Pooh Corner, so as to see Eeyore before it was too late to have a Proper Tea with Owl.

A. A. Milne
The House at Pooh Corner

Peering through the leaves into the future

Old West outlaw and gunslinger Jesse James was married to a tea leaf reader. History doesn't chronicle if Mrs. James saw bad omens m her teacup the morning that her husband was ambushed, or whether her husband, in a hurry to go out and rob some more banks simply dismissed her dire predictions. He was, after all, a coffee drinker. This simply proves that history, like tea leaf reading, is more of an art than an science.

It is widely suspected that fortune telling from tea leaves, like the beverage itself, began with the Chinese and spread from there throughout civilization. Cultural variations developed, with Scottish ladies adding much to the lore. In the highland of Scodand, the tea leaf reader was called the "spae-wife" (or spywife) because every morning she could spy into the day's events without leaving her breakfast table.

To indulge yourself with a tea leaf reading, make the tea in a pot that has no strainer. Pour the brewed tea into a cup, preferably one with a plain white interior. The fate seeker drinks the tea, holding in mind a question or wish, until only a teaspoonful or less of the tea remains. The seeker then turns the teacup upside down on the saucer and turns the cup around three times counterclockwise with her left hand ending with the handle of the cup facing the tea leaf reader. Gently, holding the saucer with her left hand and the bottom of the cup with her right, the tea leaf reader rights the cup and replaces it on its saucer. The shapes the tea leaves have formed are studied and analyzed. Sometimes combinations of images and symbols will have developed, and the skillful reader will intuitively discern the meanings.

The handle of the cup represents the questioner. Like a written page, the reading begins at the left of the handle and proceeds around the entire cup. Patterns close to handle indicate something ahout home and family life. If the leaves lie opposite the

A tea leaf in cockney rhyming slang is a thief.

Matrons, who toss the cup, and see
The grounds of fate in grounds of tea.
    Alexander Pope

handle, the indications are for strangers in the seeker's life or events away from home. Leaves near the brim indicate the near future, but the leaves on the bottom of the cup indicate a more distant future.

The following pictures are linked through folk-lore to specific meanings and portents. Maybe a few have been tweaked just for fun:

Tea will always be the favored beverage of the intellectual.
Thomas
DeQuincey

angels	always means wonderful news!
bell	good news, especially if near the top of the cup
birds	messengers of favorable news except if you just washed your car
boat	a friend will visit, maybe from an island
camel	a burden to be patiently borne
cannon	good fortune, unless you're being shot out of it
cigar	a new friend, one who smokes those icky, smelly things outside hopefully.
clock	better health (more tea, fewer cigars)
clouds	if the general formation is light and fluffy looking, a happy surprise will be coming. If the clouds are dark and dense, then maybe the surprise is of a more serious nature, or you have serious doubts.
dagger	danger from self or others - watch your step and don't run with scissors please.
deer	quarrels and disputes, missing apples from your trees
door	an odd event, be sure to open it before going through.
dog	a dear friend. If positioned at the bottom of the cup, this pal may be in need of your help. Spay or neuter.
duck	money is coming
egg	a new little bundle of joy maybe? A good omen.
elephant	wisdom or strength.
envelope	good news - maybe that money from the duck arrives

frog	success in love. We've all kissed a few.
grapes	happiness, especially so after that bottle of wine
hammer	hard work ahead
house	shelter and security is coming
iceberg	danger, or maybe Leonardo DeCaprio will drop by
kite	your deepest wishes come true for you!
ladder	look for a gradual rise to a new level or promotion, especially if employed in house painting or window washing.
leaf	a completely new life for you!
letters	initials of significant people or events
monkey	deception in love matters. That big ape.
mountain	your goals are in sight, but require a lot more effort
octopus	danger, especially so if scuba-diving is your thing
pig	greed
question mark	signals worry in general. Stop that!
raven	bad news, especially at your bird feeder
rose	popularity
sheep	good fortune, especially in finding sweater bargains
shell	more good news, and it sounds like the ocean
spider	reward for hard work, unless you're a fly
spoon	great generosity is coming your way
star	health and happiness. Tom Cruise is moving next door.
swallow	a pleasant journey with a happy ending
sun	happiness, success and power. With clouds, partly sunny, chance of showers.
table	social gatherings. A tea party, anyone?
tent	travel. A luxury hotel is even better.
triangle	inheritance, or something unexpected in three parts
wasp	romantic problems
waterfall	prosperity
wings	a life-changing message is coming to you

One pound of tea makes over 200 cups.

We couldn't resist adding a few interpretations of our own geared to the Pacific Northwest lifestyle:

computer	Bill and Melinda Gates are coming for tea
slug	your garden is toast. Sorry.
automobile	gridlock at rush hour on Interstate 5
umbrella	rain likely
sunglasses	rain likely
aircraft	journey or elevation of prestige in life
apple	achievement. Maybe Washington State will win the Apple Cup this year?
eagles	marvelous omen (unless you're a salmon)

Tea and Khaki for the British Raj in India

I think it was Napoleon who coined the phrase "An army marches on its stomach" and for the British army you'd better make sure that there's a cup of strong sweet tea to go with the food. It's even been said that we've put wars on hold while we "brewed up" our tea.

But in India in the 19th century one inspired army officer found another use for tea besides drinking it. Realizing that the traditional red tunics were too heavy and warm in the Indian summers most of the men wore white duck jackets and trousers. However both the red and the white tunics made excellent targets for the eagle-eyed, enemy riflemen. So the officer had his men brew up vats of tea and use it to dye their uniforms to a dull brown or tan, almost matching the dusty brown landscape. This became known as karkee and later officially as khaki drab. "Khak" being the Hindustani word for dust.

OREGON TEA ROOMS, TEA PARTIES AND EVENTS

PORTLAND AREA
Birdie's Tearoom
British Tea Garden
Creative PossibiliTEAS
The Doll House Tea Room
Evangeline's
The Gate Lodge Restaurant
  at the Pittock Mansion
The Heathman Hotel
Kashin-Tei Tea House
Lady Di's British Store
The Tao of Tea
The Tea Zone
Time and Again
Time for Tea - Tedde's Teas

NORTH WILLAMETTE VALLEY
Afternoon Teas by Stephanie
Angelina's French Tea
Historic Deepwood Estate
The Hope Chest
Lavender Tea House
Nauna's Tea Room
The Primrose Tea Room
Sundrops Gifts & Tea Room
Tudor Rose Tea Room
Your House or Mine

SOUTH WILLAMETTE VALLEY
The Campbell House
Mrs. B's Special Teas
Ruthie B's
Savouré

OREGON COAST
Gearhart Gallery
Tea & Tomes
Lovejoy's at Pier Point
Mon Ami

ROGUE VALLEY
Edens Gate Farm
Tea Cottage

CENTRAL OREGON
Sunriver Resort
Tea Events
Wild Rose Tea Room

SOUTHERN OREGON
Ashland Springs Hotel

COLUMBIA GORGE
Candy Castle

AFTERNOON TEA BY STEPHANIE

508 S.E. 9th Avenue
Canby, OR 97013
503-266-7612

The two eleven year old boys studied the floor self-consciously beneath their polished Sunday shoes as though it might contain an escape hatch. With their hands pushed deeply into their pockets, they wore an air of detachment and discomfort. That they did not want to be at a tea party was evident, let alone with a gaggle of young girls floating comfortably in their party finery engaging in politely animated conversation. This was apparent immediately to the trained eye of tea caterer and etiquette consultant Stephanie Allen. To the assemblage she announced, "We are lucky today to have two real men here. By 'real men' I mean those who are not intimidated by a new venture, those who are interested in learning something new and wonderful." The shift was palpable. The manners lesson had begun quietly with learning to show respect. During the 2-3 hour five course tea it progressed through tea table etiquette, tea history, fun facts and even a craft project. The girls' rapt faces peered out from under ladies' hats supplied by Stephanie, eager for the knowledge that seems missing from many fast paced family lives reliant on drive-through windows and take out pizza.

In 1988 Stephanie Allen began catering and/or presenting tea culture to groups of all ages. Among her most popular formats are her "Purple Party Friendship Tea" based on the poem that begins, "When I am an old woman I shall wear purple..." with each course enlivened by a touch of purple; or her "Nursery Tea for the Mother-To-Be", or her "Back to Basics" workshops intertwining the grace of tea with a refresher course on good manners.

Oh, those two eleven year old boys at the tea? They folded their napkins, pulled out the chairs of their table mates, thanked the hostess, and exited through a door they held open for several departing young ladies. And guess what.... they did it with a smile!

ANGELINA'S FRENCH TEA

P.O. Box 254
Aurora, OR 97002
503-221-3794

"We need to revisit the long forgotten lace of our lives."
Marilyn of Angelina's French Tea

Some women seem to be born of an earlier, gentler age; an era steeped in grace, elegance, and social polish. These ladies evoke, with their magically perfumed aura, long lace gowns and soft velvet cloaks. You picture them sipping champagne at some elegant 19th century European candlelit soiree, even when they're out running errands in their minivans. You know who they are when they enter a room, they simply cannot hide it. Through some unfathomable cosmic flight plan, just a handful of these ladies have been plunked down in our clumsy midst. It might be to remind us that we too could make style and grace the centerpiece of our own lives. That we should in their own words "revisit the long forgotten lace of our lives." I vote we think about it over tea. Lucky for us some of these remarkable ladies, in their quest for loveliness, make their living providing the rest of us with elegant havens of afternoon tea.

Marilyn and her daughter Angela, of Angelina's French Tea are such ladies. You name any aspect of tea, and they're involved and happy to share it with you. Importers and purveyors of absolutely luscious French teas and the toast of numerous national publications, (including the holy grail of tea lovers, *Victoria* magazine and books), this is the talent behind those glorious tea events for the oldest and grandest luxury hotel in Portland, The Benson Hotel. They have catered events for Sak's 5th Avenue, and in 2001 with the reincarnation of the old Mark Anthony Hotel in Ashland into the luxury Ashland Springs Hotel, you'll find Angelina's elegant touches on their tea program as well. They are delightful (and funny) speakers on the subject of tea as well as available to consult on a variety of tea topics: making your event memorable with tea, guiding you with your tea or lifestyle product development, marketing and promotion, consulting for restaurants and hotels just beginning with tea, or maybe tearooms who simply need to "freshen the pot." These are, after all, the very same ladies who brought us that nationally-acclaimed tea room, Angelina's in Aurora, (yes, I miss it too) which served as an elegant portal to the next step- introducing a broader audience to the joys of tea and the beauty it can bring.

ASHLAND SPRINGS HOTEL

212 East Main Street
Ashland, OR 97520
541-488-1700
www.ashlandspringshotel.net

In 1854 the first wagon load of timber creaked and rattled out of the Bear Creek Valley sawmill to eager pioneer builders. The driver tipped his hat to his counterpart on a dusty wagon just arriving in the little settlement with merchandise destined for Robert Hargadine's new general store. Among the crates of hardware and gunpowder, cast iron pots and bolts of fabric, rested the first shipment of tea sets and dishes. Civility had arrived in Ashland. It isn't really hard to imagine the longing these symbols of gentility caused in the female residents here; many of them had been forced to jettison family heirlooms enroute to lighten the load along the hard trail to Oregon. Simply basking in the glow of fine imported china in front of Mr.Hargadine's store window revived the memory of gentler, more refined times in the lives of these hardy ladies and brought them hope and joy.

Joy, once again in the guise of tea, resides today at the luxurious Ashland Springs Hotel. Originally opened in 1925 as the Lithia Hotel, this lovely 70 room, nine-story edifice, listed on the National Registry of Historic Places, has been extravagantly restored and renovated to surpass its earlier glory. Tea in the finest English tradition is now served with European flair on the mezzanine level of the grand two-story lobby. Warmed by the elegant glow of rich hardwoods and marble, afternoon tea here is surely destined to become another Northwest tradition.

Situated just a block from the Oregon Shakespeare Festival and the peacefulness of Lithia Park, the Ashland Springs Hotel once again beams as the city's beacon of civility. Help yourself to those gentler aspects of life for which the early pioneers longed, and if you choose to toast pioneer Robert Hargadine and his following, it would be especially appropriate.

Tea is planned for service between 3p.m.-5p.m. most days. Please call for information and reservations.

BIRDIE'S TEAROOM

530 First Street
Lake Oswego, OR 97034
503-636-0179

I'm not a big follower of sports, but I just read in the paper that they are considering including Ballroom Dancing and Bowling in the next Olympics! It wasn't until the end of the article that I realized they wouldn't be combining them, so it made a little more sense. Those feathery dresses and four-inch stiletto heels aren't conducive to strikes, too many gutter balls or something. But anyway, that got me to thinking how Tea Drinking should get on the Olympic event roster. "Yes, that's right, Bob, it looks like she's going to have another scone, and can it be? Yes! She's spreading it with Devonshire Cream! There's style points there!" I can just hear those NBC commentators gushing, can't you? Oh what's the use, I suppose they'd just hand the gold to Great Britain anyway, but I just bet we could get someone from our tea team on some tier of the medal podium even if they were playing "God Save the Queen."

Big points for style go daily to Birdie's Tearoom in Lake Oswego. Veteran tea catering maven Annette Suchy has found a home for her business in a room filled with light, friendliness, and elegance without primness. Rich mahoghany furnishings gleam from sunlit windows swathed in sheer white and burgundy, that on a clear day frame the majestic vision of Mount Hood. Six roomy linen covered tables are lit with a gleaming crystal chandelier hung whimsically with china teacups. Five elegant tea sets fit every appetite and are graciously presented on silver servers, the same high quality fare on which Annette's tea reputation was built. Frequent special events are enumerated in her cheery quarterly newsletter, and theme teas like her "Thank Goodness They're Back to School Tea" and "Friendship Day Tea" provide a fun forum for relaxing get-togethers.

Annette would be a star on our Olympic Tea Drinking Team, her face could grace Wheaties boxes. With her energy, style and enthusiasm we're shoo-ins for the silver at least.

Open Tuesday through Saturday, 10 a.m. to 4 p.m. with reservations suggested.

BRITISH TEA GARDEN

725 S.W. Tenth Avenue
Portland, OR 97205
503-221-7817

The twelve-foot long banner high on the whitewashed wall of the British Tea Garden proclaims "There will always be an England." Standing at the threshhold, letting my eyes adjust, it seems I have just walked into the heart of it.

Owners Judith Bennett and Carmel Ross have spent years gaily replicating the corner stores and tea rooms of their homeland. Comfortable and unpretentious, just like the owners themselves, the British Tea Garden has been serving up pots of tea and fresh authentic British fare since 1992. With origins as an imported gourmet and gift shop, the tea room evolved from customers expectations and requests. "Cuppa tea, luv?" That classic offer of exuberant British hospitality echoes through the long, high-ceilinged room where 15 tables dressed in floral chintz with bright toppers await and tea kettles whistle.

Special events planned throughout the year are growing in renown, so it's always best to call ahead. The food will remind you of a half-forgotten holiday along leafy English country lanes, with Shepherd's Pie, Bangers and Mash, and bubbling Welsh Rarebit evoking the memory. A youthful and impeccably coiffed Queen Elizabeth smiles her approval from the wall near the large fireplace. Yes, "There will always be an England," but if time and money won't allow the trip right now, this may be the next best thing.

Open Monday 10 a.m. to 5 p.m., Tuesday through Friday 10 a.m. to 6 p.m. Saturday 10 a.m. to 5 p.m. and Sunday noon to 4 p.m.

THE CAMPBELL HOUSE

252 Pearl Street
Eugene, OR 97401
541-343-1119

The stringy stray tomcat was the color of Martha Stewart's buttercream frosting. He had a pronounced limp and suspicious eyes the same color as Paul Newman's. It was a particularly harsh Northwest winter when I first noticed him along the margins of our lives; he was the blur running under the potting shed, the eyes in the bushes evaluating our suitability for adoption. On one cold, windy night my husband (a Dog Person) noticed him curled into a small tight miserable ball on the ground where the warm air from our clothes dryer vented. "Cats...." the Dog Person muttered with insincere contempt as he propped open the backdoor to the garage and prepared a basket with cushion and heat lamp for no one in particular. It was weeks before Father MacKenzie (from the Beatle's tribute to "all the lonely people", Eleanor Rigby) trusted us enough to be petted, years before we celebrated him jumping onto what must have been his first lap. He travelled to his new Camano Island home with us where he stuck his head out of the cardboard flaps, looked all around, and curled up purring on the doormat. Home is where you make it if you have good friends.

Home for Idaho Campbell was a glorious Queen Anne style home built for her by the father John Cogswell, Eugene gold and timber baron in 1892. Now fully restored from its sturdy sandstone foundation to its cherry wood railings it has been converted into a truly lovely 18 room inn of national renown. Resting gently at the base of Skinner's Butte on over an acre of groomed gardens, rock grottos, pond and gazebo, The Campbell House, now owned by Myra and Roger Plant, recently earned a four star rating by AAA and was named 6 years in a row as one of the top 25 inns in this country. At least twice a year (Mother's Day and Christmas) the old french doors to the marble floored entry are thrown open to the public for exquisite afternoon teas by reservation only. At Christmas the house is dressed in boughs and party finery for the holiday teas which often include the popular sandwich combinations of Chicken Hazelnut, Sundried Tomato, Ham-Pineapple Cream Cheese, followed by sweets too decadent to mention.

Join some friends for tea in this homiest of settings. You'll be purring too.

CANDY CASTLE

718 W. 6th Street
The Dalles, OR 97058
541-298-8070
Website: thedalles.net/candycastle

When I was a little girl living in North Bend, Oregon, my best friend Suzy Granger had all the really neat toys. What was even better - she shared them. She had a little oven that baked (if we didn't eat all the cupcake batter before getting it into the oven, a problem I still have), she had a doll that wet (that seemed like kind of a nuisance really), and she had a board game called "Candyland". I really wanted to live in Candyland. I didn't know what state it was in, but I was pretty sure it wasn't Oregon. In Candyland, California, you could zip down a peppermint slide and land in a big vat of chocolate and maybe towel off next to a Mouseketeer like Annette. I still have big dreams of chocolate but they're not quite that messy.

Lorraine Horzynek turned her own big chocolate dreams into a business and housed it in a fairy tale stone cottage in The Dalles. Lorraine, her mother Jean Miller, daughter-in-law Dorine, and sister Kathy Nock have been up to their eyes in chocolate making gourmet candies and decorated cakes here since 1988. At the urging of candy customers aglow with a sugar rush and besotted with the 1916 elegance of the Candy Cottage, the ladies are now also turning their attention and talents to Afternoon Tea.

Up to eight guests at a time are treated to Victorian elegance at two tables awash in fine china, roses and lace. As a homage to the era, black attired servers in white cutwork aprons serve a four course, full fare tea in the finest Old World tradition. Scones or crumpets, dainty finger sandwiches, tarts or flakey puff pastries filled with cream, the list goes on and on, but do remember where you are, and save room for the handmade candy, truffles or special cake finale.

Now that I'm an adult, I should invent a game called Tea Land. In this game you climb a mountain of puff pastry, paddle across the Earl Grey lake and slide down the cucumber sandwiches into a vat of Devonshire cream. In Lorraine's own words, "A little escape from the real world. It never hurts."

Tea by reservation Tuesday through Saturday. Call for candy shop hours.

CREATIVE POSSIBILITEAS

1411 S.W. DeWitt #3
Portland, OR 97201
503-263-5229

When Jane Blackman blew in like a fresh breeze from Florida after choosing the Northwest as her home in 1996 she wanted two things. She wanted a simpler life for herself and daughter Holly and she wanted to be involved in spreading the word about how tea fits into a simpler lifestyle.

Fast forward four years and 3,000 cups of tea, all served with smiles, and you find a lady who really finds joy with the life she's created. Tea planner, tea lecturer, tea importer and blender; no business card could possibly contain it all. Still ready, willing and able to assist in every aspect of your tea event planning, large or small. Jane also conducts tea tastings the first Friday of each month in historic Multnomah Village. In conjunction with A Closer Look art studio Jane brings her signature line of teas, BeLeaf Tea, to a growing throng.

When asked about her own favorite tea experience her eyes shine as she remembers Harrods in London, a special Jasmine tea on a wind swept veranda in Hawaii, holiday teas in the Chicago chill, then settles on all the simple times when she has simply connected with friends over a pot of tea. As she says in her brochure, the work she does comes "from a belief that tea speaks to a kinder purpose." Good work, Jane.

HISTORIC DEEPWOOD ESTATE

1116 Mission St. S.E.
Salem, OR 97302
503-363-1825
Website: www.oregonlink.com/deepwood/.

In the summer of 1998 caterer Janice Palmquist heard a voice that sounded like her own chirp, "I could do that," when the City of Salem began ruminating on how teas could enhance the public's experience in the living history setting at Historic Deepwood Estate. Immediately given the green light for the awesome task by Ross Sutherland, the executive director of the non-profit group that manages the property, Janice calmed herself down with a big pot of tea and a pile of books on the Victorian era. What emerged from that whirlwind summer of research is a tea experience steeped in history and rich in tradition unlike any other in Oregon.

This gloriously ornate, multi-gabled, grand dowager of 1894 Queen Anne styling sits regally on 5.5 acres of English-style gardens and nature trails. Throughout the year, intimate formal afternoon teas for 16 are presented, as well as a quarterly dessert buffet tea for 60 with speakers of cultural note. Tea in the Garden in summer draws hundreds to sip tea and stroll the grounds where regional artisans are at work.

Attired in the traditional black and white of the Victorian server, Janice treats the 16 tea guests to a tour of the residence which ends in the candlelit oak panelled dining room. The life of the Victorians is unveiled in stories of their dress, manners and customs as well as interesting tea history. The four course formal tea is all served on vintage china and crystal. Poetry and historical insights entertain and enlighten throughout the tea. Each of the courses is presented artfully and with a historic perspective. Dainty sweets and tea desserts herald the finish of the meal from elegant three tiered silver trays. Each guest departs with a little gift and a life-enhancing appreciation for the rich history of both tea and this beautiful estate, and insights into the Victorian era in which they bloomed so graciously together.

Special thanks to the City of Salem and The Friends of Deepwood for making this historic property available for seasonal teas, weddings and cultural events. Call for a schedule.

THE DOLL HOUSE TEA ROOM

3223 S.E. Risley
Milwaukie, OR 97267
503-653-6809 or 503-631-7751

"A little princess...it's always time for tea."
Lewis Carroll

Miss Barbie Doll and I came about this close to meeting. When Barbie minced onto center stage of the doll world in her high heels, fancy duds and billowing blonde mane more than 40 years ago, I was just at the age to be retiring my battered vinyl doll babies (or at least communing with them in private.) To have asked for a Barbie would have been inviting ridicule from my big brother Greg. Although come to think of it, the girls he later dated possessed many of Barbie's attributes. I have to confess to being just plain envious of the array of paraphernalia this doll towed in her wake: RV's, ski boats, airplanes, a furnished studio apartment bigger than my first one.

Jeanine Nordling has an entire cozy cottage devoted to dolls and tea parties. Beautiful porcelain dolls promenade in ladylike Victorian attire on shelves and tables, idle hours away on swings, and warm their little tootsies on the fireplace mantle. It's in this storybook setting of a pink shuttered bungalow that she provides fantasy dress-up tea parties for no more than 12 little girls aged 4 and up. The party is every girl's dream. One room is devoted to more than 100 gowns in all sizes, feathered hats, fairy halos, Ivana Trump-ish jewelry and even shoes. A fantasy beauty shop awaits each guest where nail polish is applied. A touch of color to lips and cheeks precedes the giggly fashion show and the memories are captured in a photo shoot in front of the doll and flower adorned fireplace. The tea table glows with light from a crystal beaded chandelier adorned with white flowers and each chair is a unique handpainted creation, with a "throne" chair for the guest of honor. A happy wallpaper border shows dolls and teddies sharing tea while the girls enjoy finger foods with their lemonade served in teapots. Each guest gets a party favor and the guest of honor gets a very special keepsake. Mothers of all attendees can come watch, and the guest of honor can even bring Grandmother to share the day too.

Jeanine's flyer admonishes, "Whatever you do, come with a young heart and be prepared to have an enchanting time." Barbie would have loved it.

EDEN'S GATE FARM & GIFT

15090 Highway 238
Applegate, OR 97530
541-846-9019

Covered wagons creaked and rattled through this Applegate Valley more than 150 years ago with dusty, thirsty pioneer families seeking their fortunes along the southern migration route into Oregon. A log cabin general store sprang up, crafted from the abundant forest to serve the needs of the pioneers and the miners that followed. While we can't be absolutely certain that they sold tea there then, we do know that their next door neighbors do today. Cute little Eden's Gate Farm & Gift, right next door to that original store now the Applegate Historical Museum, is serving tea amid pioneer charm in great big doses.

In an unpretentious vintage cottage full of antiques and gifts, owner Cathy Dunlap, in conjunction with her friends at Duck Duck Mousse Catering ('love that name!) are offering tea parties for your gathering. In one sunny 1890s tea room that seats eight, white wicker tables are covered with charming quilts and French doors invite you out into a river rock edged cutting garden with meandering paths. Tea can be served to you on rustic twig furniture in this peaceful setting during the summer. One of the paths leads to the pavillion where large group events can be accommodated, or the tea party can come to your own location. The five course tea features such imaginative menu choices as Mediterranean Chicken Wrap along with the traditional tea sandwiches, quiche, homemade soup, scones and trifle made with local fresh berries.

While a simple and refreshing pot of tea is always available when the shop is open, these elaborate 2+ hour special occasion teas require advance reservations and deposit. The rich history and pioneer flavor of the Applegate Valley make this a unique and hospitable spot for tea.

EVANGELINE'S

1304 E. Powell Blvd.
Gresham, OR 97030
503-669-3750

'Home.' The word must have invoked both memories and promise to the ears of the weary pioneer families who cut a swath through the forests that cloak the lower slopes of Mount Hood. Most were enroute to the heralded fertility of Oregon's Willamette Valley. Others just plain liked what they saw in the shadow of the majestic mountain and stayed, forming Gresham. One of those families claimed a 272 acre parcel outside of town and built a comfortable home in the dignified Queen Anne style from the native fir forest they cleared from their land.

Time and progress have blurred the line between that property's boundaries and the town itself. The family farmhouse, now listed on the Register of National Historic Houses, today encloses an intimate old world restaurant and gift shop, Evangeline's. Redolent with the aroma of baking scones, owner Sandra Bolin has dressed the friendly old house in its best ivory lace curtains, vintage finery and gentle music for your prearranged tea. Attentive service and tasty choices prevail is this homey setting. Sandra's special love is desserts and baked goods, and a special cake or torte can be personalized to make your special event here memorable.

It seems especially fitting to celebrate life's big occasions in this pioneer house - bridal showers, baby showers, engagement parties and anniversaries; all are celebrations of the milestones of home life, and hasn't this house seen a lot of living?

Open for all meals, Wednesday through Friday 11 a.m. to 9 p.m., Saturday and Sunday 9 a.m. to 9 p.m. Tea is served by reservation only between 2 p.m. and 4:30 p.m. on those days.

THE GATE LODGE RESTAURANT
at the Pittock Mansion

3229 N.W. Pittock Drive
Portland, OR 97210
503-823-3627

Like tenacious ivy that embraces the trunks of ever-greens, the history of Portland and of the Pittock family are tightly intertwined. Back when the city was little more than a clearing in the forest, English-born Henry Lewis Pittock arrived as a teen by wagon train. Eight years later, starting with a well-developed work ethic and the hand of an American bride Georgiana Burton, he was invested in railroads, pulp and paper, *The Oregonian*, and various real estate holdings.

It was on one of these 46 acre holdings that late in life Mr. Pittock built his family a grand manor house of the European tradition. From there Georgiana could oversee her numerous charities and focus on creating a royal celebration of her favorite flower in what came to be known as the Rose Festival.

Today the lovely manor is owned by the City of Portland who extensively restored it from the ravages of time and the 1962 Columbus Day storm. Tour information can be acquired by calling 503-823-3624. Mr. Pittock was a member of the first party to climb Mount Hood, and is quoted as saying, "The man who sits down never reaches the top." It's obvious that there's very little sitting done by the ambitious caterers, Yours Truly, who offer a tea most of the year in the four story Gate House to the estate. A most magical time is during the winter holidays when the estate is transformed with lavish decorations. Being English by birth, Mr. Pittock would have enjoyed a pot of tea, if only they could get him to sit down and relax for a few minutes.

Hours are 11:30 a.m. to 3 p.m. Monday through Saturday by reservation with four mid-day seatings. The hours are extended during December with six seatings. The Gate House is closed January 1 through 23. Call for reservations and times.

GEARHART GALLERY AND GIFTS

Highway 101 North at Pacific Way
P.O. Box 2839
Gearhart, OR 97138
888-353-8976 or 503-717-8976

"Great joy in camp." The Lewis and Clark journal entry begins.
"We are in view of the ocean, this great Pacific Ocean
which we have been so long anxious to see."

That same sense of wonder and awe has been expressed daily by visitors to the area ever since. Great joy, in the form of Afternoon Tea has now come to Gearhart, just north of Seaside, arriving in the guise of retired engineers Archie and Carol Cook from Texas. This artist couple chose this beautiful area to "relax and enjoy life," and enjoy life they surely have. Forget about the 'relax' part though, for in addition to opening and then expanding their little art gallery and gift shop, they have also opened a second gift and home decor location. In addition to that, they now offer tea and refreshments throughout the day in a cozy little eight table tea room festooned with lace.

Gearhart is a casual town, so over your sensible beach-walking wear you're invited to borrow one of their feather boas and whimsical hats to capture the tea party spirit. (They even offer $1 off your tea if you happen to be travelling the Oregon coast with your own boa or tea party hat.) The Classic Tea begins with sorbet and progresses you through pretty finger sandwiches and mini quiches; fresh scones with Devon cream, lemon curds and preserves, with a sweet treat ending. Three lighter fare teas are also available as well as one created to delight the under 12 set. There are also traditional British foods like Scotch Pie, mini Beef Wellingtons, and a daily special.

So grab your sunblock, sunglasses and camera, your boa and frilly hat and head to the beach. There will be great joy in your camp too.

Open daily 8 a.m. to 5:30 p.m. please call for tea party reservations. Ask about their Fall Fantasy celebration in October and other special events.

THE HEATHMAN HOTEL

1001 S.W. Broadway
Portland, OR 97201
503-790-7752

There is a cute little house on the island where we live. I keep hoping that someone will be out laboring in the garden when I pass by so I can roll down my window and thank them for the beauty of their yard. Let's be honest here, to pass this house I need to drive about five miles out of my way and then turn onto a dead end road, but it's worth it for the lift it gives my spirits. What distinguishes this little yard from countless others is that there is always a show going on regardless of the time of year. Season to season a glorious, everchanging montage of foliage and flowers greet passersby. Orchestrated by the hand of some anonymous garden maestro, the glow of the spring bulbs fade as the summer flowers burst into an extravagant crescendo, joined by the deep burgundy autumnal tones, accompanied by a rising chorale of thoughtfully placed winter shapes and a counterpoint of evergreen textures.

To assume it's effortless since I never see human life there when I pass may be an illusion. Perhaps they struggle with determined weeds and nibbling rabbits, short hoses and long slugs, and snacking deer families like we do. I've thought about just ringing their doorbell and thanking them for their yard, this symphony of the seasons. But I never will. Much of the beauty to me is the magic of its effortlessness.

The Heathman Hotel in downtown Portland is to Northwest teatime what our island garden maestro is to landscape. There is always something fresh and seasonal happening in the richly appointed Tea Court. Under the opulent crystal chandelier and embraced by the original wood panelling that bespeaks its 1920's heritage the stage is set for a relaxing tea. The servers, attired in period lace aprons, offer a wide variety of teas in English bone china to complement an equally elegant seasonal menu. Their mission, printed on the menu, is to "transport you elegantly to another place in time, and deliver you back refreshed." That they make it all appear effortless is part of the magic.

Tea is served 2 p.m. to 4 p.m. daily by reservation.

THE HOPE CHEST

135 N.W. Washington St.
Sherwood, OR 97140
503-925-9222
E-Mail: echristensen@worldnet.att.net

"Hope is a thing with feathers - that perches in the soul..."
Emily Dickinson

In 1892 the city leaders of little Smockville, Oregon concurred the name lacked worldliness. Apparently one of the founding fathers who enjoyed a good read, looked over the top of his book about Robin Hood and suggested Sherwood to that merry band of founding fathers. After all, Smockville had a forest too, didn't it? So it was that Sherwood began and remains today a charming little town of brick sidewalks, Victorian lamp posts, and lovingly restored old homes.

It's in one 1918 cottage here that a mother and daughter team, retired banker Yvonne Christensen and full-time nurse Lynne Gelfand, allowed their hope to perch. With Lynne's four daughters involved, they converted the house into a colorful antique, gift and collectible shop and tea room, which since its opening in 1999 has attracted a happy and loyal following.

Come for the sweet small town atmosphere of Sherwood that ranges from men in tights at the Robin Hood Festival in July to a celebration of the pungent onion at The Great Onion Fest in October. Then stay for the tea and antiques. A lavish five course traditional tea is served with style by reservation the first Saturday of each month at 1 p.m. Your own special tea on a timetable to suit you can be cheerfully accommodated, with a little advance planning, in the same warm six table dining room bedecked with vintage flourishes, antiques, lace and porcelain. Lunches are offered daily.

At The Hope Chest you are assured of finding treasures, vintage and new. You may even be lucky enough to feel a little fluttering of the feathered thing perched in your own soul with the renewing warmth of their afternoon tea.

Open Tuesday through Saturday 10 a.m. to 5 p.m. Lunch available each day. Five course teas are the first Saturday of the month at 1 p.m. by reservation. Private parties too.

KASHIN-TEI TEA HOUSE
at Washington Park

Japanese Garden Society of Oregon
611 S.W. Kingston Avenue
Portland, OR 97201
503-223-1321
E-Mail: jgso@transport.com
Website: www.japanesegarden.com

Kashin-tei translates from Japanese to the lyrical Flower Heart House. Resting peacefully on 5 acres of precisely nurtured gardens in the rolling west hills of Portland's Washington Park, this traditional Japanese tea house warms and honors the spiritual center of this tranquil setting.

The tea garden tradition is centuries old, the essence of a spirituality that celebrates the kinship of human being to nature. Subtle symbolism encourages meditation, and invites you to lift your mind beyond just what is visible. The balance of vertical and horizontal, dark with light, seen and unseen, stone with plant, blending all these elements of nature to achieve a tranquil air are the essence of Japanese garden design.

There is much to learn too about the Japanese Tea Ceremony. It is an occasion steeped in centuries of tradition and spirituality; eloquent in its simplicity and rich symbolism. The Japanese Garden Society welcomes you to understand the simple purity of it with demonstrations, private teas, and special events throughout the year.

Kashin-tei, Flower Heart House, may cause a stirring of new growth at your core, or if you're lucky, even a brilliant burst of bloom.

Daily one hour guided garden tours with reasonable admission price, April 15 through October 31 at 10:45 a.m. and 2:30 p.m. Call for information on the tea demonstrations and special events.

LADY DI'S BRITISH STORE

420 Second Street
Lake Oswego, OR 97034
503-635-7298 or 800-357-7839

Once there was a time, not so long ago, when Lake Oswego was a week-end retreat for weary urbane Portlanders seeking a haven for peace and quiet. Modest shingled cottages hugged the shoreline or peeked out from the pristine evergreen forest. Residents sipped their tea while gazing at the tranquil lake and counted their blessings.

Today Lake Oswego is a bustling bedroom community for Portland. The modest little cottages have been enlarged and remodelled to the point that now it's the lake that peeks out at you, glimmering between carefully landscaped upscale homes. The list of blessings has been expanded, however, to include Lady Di's British Store.

Under new ownership since 1999 in the form of British-born Moya Stephens, the tea and light lunch offerings have been enhanced and expanded like those little shingle cottages of yesterday. Today the shelves of the cozy gift shop bulge with a wide variety of hard to find British foods, English bone china, books, and choices of teas.

For a taste of Britain in an equally green setting, a stop for shopping and tea at Lady Di's will give you chance to count your own blessings.

Open Tuesday through Saturday from 10 a.m. to 5 p.m. with teas and light lunches served 10:30 a.m. to 3:30 p.m.

LAVENDER TEA HOUSE

340 N.W. First St.
Sherwood, OR 97140
503-625-4479

"I don't pick colors." While he cheerfully immerses himself in any project that involves a hammer or power tools, my husband Ken intones this mantra and shakes his head when it comes to deciding paint and wallpaper for the house he built us. Still I persist in attempting to include him in a substantive dialogue at the paint chip display. I am reminded of the wonderful old classic film "Mr. Blanding Builds His Dream House" in which Myrna Loy describes the color she wants for her kitchen to the painter. She goes into rich detail, straining for him to understand...."a yellow like rich buttercream frosting, like the center of a newly opened narcissus, the freshest churned butter." Nodding with seeming sensitivity, he bellows to his crew when she leaves, "A gallon of yellow!"

"What do you think?" Hopefully I hold up a paint chip that I have painstakingly color-matched to the wallpaper border. Ken nods and says, "Right then, a gallon of yellow it is!"

Choosing the colors for the 1892 Queen Anne house in historic Sherwood was easy for Dianna Soller and her partner, daughter Toni Calabrese. It had to be the color of their favorite perennial, lavender. Experimenting with many lavender laced tea blends from their harvest, they taught numerous tea classes at a local herb nursery before opening the tea room in 1997. The snowy white cottage across from a park is trimmed in the color lavender and set amid mature trees and gardens. Two rooms are set for tea decorated with vintage finds, European antiques, everlasting wreaths, original art and candles. The menu changes regularly with fresh specials and catering is also available including romantic dinners by reservation in the evening. In the summer outdoor tables are set amidst the herb garden where the wind gently sways the tall spikes of lavender perfuming the air.

Monthly special events include local musicians, Victorian carolers and other creative events all year long.

Open 11 a.m. to 4 p.m. Tuesday through Saturday.

LOVEJOY'S AT PIER POINT

85625 Highway 101 S.
Florence, OR 97439
541-902-0502

Tea is linked so completely in our minds to England these days that an important truth is often overlooked. The Britons have the Dutch to thank for their introduction to the brew. It was

the enterprising Dutch East Indies company that pried open the doors of trade with a reluctant China in the 1600's. You're unlikely to forget that bit of tea history at Lovejoy's where Dutch East Indies born Maryann shares the kitchen duties with her distinguished British husband Martin Spicknell. That tea is served in one of our favorite Oregon coast towns makes this authentically European-rooted tea experience one to savor.

Florence's location halfway along the beautiful Oregon coast and hugging the river bank of the slow flow of the Siuslaw is only part of its appeal. Enlightened locals have restored the old riverfront buildings of Old Town with enthusiasm and charm. Local lore recalls the community naming itself after some ill-fated vessel, torn asunder on the coastline. A beachcombing merchant retrieved the the masthead bearing the name "Florence" and casually hung it over his door. When it came time to choose a post office name, the sign was the first thing in sight. The largest oceanfront dunes in the world form Florence's backporch. Nearby Honeyman Park bursts into rhododendron glory every spring and is also memorable for its 150 foot dune that ends in the cool deep waters of Cleowax Lake, a compelling invitation to generations of belly-floppers (ourselves included) to run, roll, and tumble down its face, ultimately splashing refreshingly into the lake.

Beside a charming Art Deco bridge which heralds the approach to Florence from the south is Pier Point where Lovejoy's offers another form of refreshment. There is a growing regional enthusiasm for tea here, where a comfy Victorian parlour has been replicated in a room of the 10,000 square foot restaurant overlooking Old Town. A tea experience authentically rooted in the best Old World traditions of England and the Netherlands awaits you at Lovejoy's, almost as refreshing as a dip in the lake.

Tea is offered daily. Seasonal hours vary, so a phone call may be advised.

MON AMI

490 Highway 101
Florence, OR 97439
541-997-9234
E-Mail: wobbe@presys.com

If there was a way to make a living beachcombing, Ken and I would be million-aires. Years ago we spent one of the nicest winters of our life in a rented cottage in Florence so tiny our big dog, Eric the Terrible, filled the kitchen by himself. Every day, rain or shine, we three would walk the beaches or climb the dunes. We had lived in the Rockies for five years, and hadn't fully realized how much we missed the ocean. We rediscovered Dungeness crab and caught crawfish in a stream. We went after blackberries and found black bears sharing them. Florence was a lot smaller then and slower, but here is a community that still knows how to put the brakes on. It celebrates the return of the rhododendron blooms every year with a slug race, a tribute to the pace at which we lived our lives that winter.

Two longtime friends, Cindy Brent Wobbe and Cheri Rhodes, understand the beauty of slowing your pace, if only for an afternoon. Sometimes even a roomy shop seem barely able to hold all the wonderful ideas and treasures that fill it to the brim. In the historic Tidewater Electric Building on the Pacific Coast Highway they offer Afternoon Tea in a vintage antique-laden setting. The walls of the tea area are warmed and enlivened not only by the rich plum color, but with the written sentiments and heartfelt greetings of their guests from all over the world. Collectibles, antiques, porcelain, furniture, linens fill the store stylishly. A well organized gift area provides Victorian style jewelry, old fashioned bees-wax candles, tea accessories and garden delights. To see everything they offer here, read and write on the wall, and have a delightful traditional tea you will be absolutely forced to slow your pace. Do enjoy it. It's good for the soul.

Open for breakfast pastry, lunches, afternoon tea Monday through Friday 8 a.m. to 5 p.m. Saturday 9:30 a.m. to 5 p.m. Closed on Sunday. Quarterly special event theme teas seat 26 by reservation, hats and gloves optional, and they cater private teas for up to 60. Call for details.

MRS. B's SPECIAL TEAS

55 West Grant
Lebanon, OR 97355
541-259-5100

At about the same time that the Duchess of Bedford and her gal pals in England were legitimizing a late day snack known as Afternoon Tea, wagon loads full of hardy pioneers were lumbering down the slopes of the Cascades into Lebanon in search of some refreshment as well. A supply stop for many, Lebanon offered warm hospitality and practical wares to travellers celebrating their arrival into the fertile Willamette Valley after so many months on the beaten path to their future. It had to be a joyful arrival.

Today Lebanon celebrates a touch of the Victorian era with the joyful arrival of a very special 30 seat tea parlor and gourmet bakery, the creation of longtime resident Barbara Brown, of Mrs. B's Special Teas. Mrs. B herself approaches everything joyfully and with attention to detail that extends even to grinding their own flour for fresh bread. I've watched with awe from afar as she developed the plan, found the building and then completely remodelled it, with help of supportive family, to suit her beautiful vision of a haven for tea. Beginning with four heirloom cups and saucers, a gift from her great aunt, Barbara's English bone china collection has grown to the point that it graces both her Queen's Tea and Victorian Tea services, served by reservation only, with a new color or flower theme for each month.

The exterior peak-roofed Tudor facade, complete with the lathe and plaster look, belies the fact that this is in a convenient little strip mall. Inside you are transported into a cozy English country inn, with rich burgundy wallpaper and high plate rail holding vintage treasures. Lovely wood dining tables are dressed for tea with linens, lace, fine bone china, crystal stemware, and gold flatware. The table setting sparkles from the soft glow of a crystal chandelier and candlelight in the high ceilinged room.

No doubt that other Mrs. B, Lady B actually, the Duchess of Bedford would have felt right at home in this thoroughly charming Victorian setting in Lebanon.

Tea is served Thursday through Saturday with seatings at 1 p.m. and 3 p.m. by reservation only. The gourmet bakery is open for tea and treats Monday through Friday 8 a.m. to 5:30 p.m. and Saturday 10 a.m. to 5 p.m.

NAUNA'S TEA ROOM
at Historic Mission Mill Museum

1313 S.E. Mill Street
Salem, OR 97301
503-370-8855

Three years before a demure Victoria sipped her tea on the throne of England, Jason Lee was laboring to establish the first Christian mission in the rugged Oregon Country. When his coffers ran low, Reverend Lee, an impassioned and inspiring preacher, hit the trail to the midwest to raise money for his good works. Not only did he movingly exhort the congregations to take the straight and narrow path to heaven; but he ignited a passion that led many of them to a more winding and trackless path. That route was into the Oregon Country, the year was 1838. "On to Oregon," was the cry as coins jangled into collection plates and dreams to move entire families into Oregon by covered wagon were solidified over tea.

Today Jason Lee's pioneer parsonage is part of a great cultural treasure on the National Register of Historic Places of the five acre manicured grounds of Salem's Mission Mill Museum. Home to pioneer heritage exhibits and demonstrations, settlers' homes, a serene little church still used for weddings, it also encompasses the Thomas Kay Woolen Mill of 1889. Here you can immerse yourself in the infancy of Oregon's textile history accompanied by the gentle rythym of a still functioning water-powered turbine by the old millstream. Herb gardens and plants used for enlivening the wool with colors still flourish in this tranquil and timeless setting.

In a space that once housed an old yarn shop, Lisa Viegas invites you to tea in the newly-opened Nauna's Tea Room. French doors lead into the cozy plank-floored tea room that seats 35. Handpainted boughs and birdhouses grace the walls of the sunny room, which with the seasonally skirted tables impart a rustic country garden charm to your tea break. Tea and history, they've been inseparable for centuries. Immerse yourself in both at Nauna's at the historic Mission Mill Museum. Reverend Lee would surely approve.

Open Monday through Friday 9 a.m. to 4:30 p.m., Saturday 10 a.m. to 4:30 p.m. Showers and parties are welcome, and catering off-site is also provided.

THE PRIMROSE TEA ROOM

334 Third Street
McMinnville, OR 97128
503-474-1559

How I wish The Primrose Tea Room had been in McMinnville when I was a whiney, homesick freshman at Linfield College there. Thirty five years ago my inexperienced heart got broken by a boy for the first time (and last, I'm pleased to say) in that beguiling little tree-lined town. I suspect I may not have handled the breakup in a healthy manner by today's Empowered Woman standards. The smell of popcorn to this day transports me back to the term that I lived on Jolly Time Popcorn (the irony's not lost on me) rather than take meals in the cafeteria for fear of crossing paths with my lost love, a.k.a. The Jerk.

Richard Belgard opened his cozy little five table tea alcove in the back of The Book Store on Third Street just this year. A long time tea lover with meticulous attention to detail, Richard has brought his passion for tea to growing enthusiasts of the area, serving up hearty English Shepherd's Pie, scones with cream, and soups along with three tea sets for various appetites. Charmingly mismatched china and lace cloaked tables provide an elegant and cozy backdrop in charming McMinnville for this proper English tea experience.

Do make reservations for tea in this snug setting. You'll have a Jolly Time if you do!

Open Tuesday through Saturday 10 a.m. to 4 p.m., Sunday 1p.m. to 4 p.m.
Reservations are appreciated.

RUTHIE B'S
DEPOT DISTRICT TEA ROOM

100 Main Street
Springfield, OR 97477
541-988-4791

Grab your hat and gloves, I'm taking you to Afternoon Tea! Oh, and why don't you go put on these black fishnet stockings? Have you ever tried on a Wonderbra before? No, I'm sure it's comfortable. Hold still, just a little more of this fire engine red lipstick, a little beauty mark here, more perfume, a little more powder (cough), and maybe just another teensy smear of this blue eyeshadow.....there! You look great, Mom! Did I mention I'm taking you to tea with those naughty ladies of Ruthie B's?

Ruthie B's "girls" invite you to tea in an old brothel in the lumber town of Springfield. Back in the 1930s, at least until the parked log trucks around the house blocked traffic and annoyed the local tea-sipping spinsters, Ruthie B's girls plied their wares. In memory and spirit of those 1930's gals a group of completely crazy ladies, who concede "We didn't have a clue what we were doing in the beginning, we just knew we wanted to give people a lift," have succeeded in doing exactly that. Jessica (first names only of course), one of Ruthie's "girls", wrote to tell me that Ruthie "never does anything in a small way," including tea apparently. "We've been known to carry on a bit." Ten rooms, packed with antiques for sale and the handicrafts of some twenty local normal women who describe Ruthie B's as "wonderful, even therapeutic, but definitely not ordinary," houses the tea room. Four tea sets are on the menu, with only their elaborate five course High Tea requiring any advance notice. Jessica enthuses about the "raw sugar cubes, made from sugar cane cut down by little native boys wearing nothing but a loin-cloth, or at least that's how I like to envision it." (Definitely no danger of 'ordinary' happening here.) Every year special theme teas include The Mad Hatter's Tea Party, and The 1930's Girlfriends Tea Party featuring "Big Red" and "The Girls." In Jessica's words, uttered with a wink, we're all going to have tea and "a real good...real good time."

Open 10 a.m. to 5:30 p.m. Monday through Saturday. Reservations required for the lavish five course High Tea, but drop-ins welcomed warmly for lighter fare teas.

SAVOURÉ

201 W. Broadway
Eugene, OR 97401
541-242-1010
E-Mail: savouretea.com

Savouré means "savored" in France, and the word sums up the French approach to life. Our grab-and-go, catch-you-later mindset doesn't serve us well there, where succulent meals and good conversation are relished with the intensity of a new love affair. There is a magic at work in Paris that has inspired the artist and the poet for centuries, and it's at work there in a rich tea culture as well. Sisters Candi Glazebrook and Cindi Potter weren't immune to the charms of the City of Light, and on their return they found nestled there among their beautiful memories, a plan for a fresh new business for Eugene - a tea salon steeped in the finest French tradition.

Savouré is set to introduce the French tea experience to Eugene during Winter 2000 in a roomy commercial space on Broadway. Half of the sunny space will house a simple and sleekly elegant tea shop selling more than 50 varieties of premium loose teas, elegant French porcelain pots and accoutrements for gracious socializing. Seating for twenty in the adjacent *salon de the* with its rich claret velvet drapes encourages lingering over a pot of tea and treats. During afternoons their Salon Tea will be offered, which, in the European tradition is a light elegant meal, offering a variety of savory and sweet selections, served with style on a three-tiered tray.

During the summer, small bistro tables on the street will recreate a Parisian sidewalk cafe ambience. Tea was introduced to Paris in 1636, and now 365 years later the French tea experience has come to Eugene. Plan to visit, plan to linger, plan to savor this elegant vision of two sisters.

As we go to press, the planned hours are 10 a.m. to 6 p.m. daily, with extended hours until 9 p.m. on Friday and Saturday. Best to call and check.

SUNDROPS GIFTS AND TEAROOM

305 Oak Street
Silverton, OR 97381
503-873-8883
E-Mail: patsy25@aol.com

In 1852, Polly Crandall Coon Price's wagon rattled into what is now called Silverton to reunite her with her husband who had come earlier, lured by the promise of rich land. Pared dutifully down to the few worldly goods he had carefully enumerated, Polly made the arduous trip into the lush Willamette Valley with a hidden treasure, a flowered porcelain heirloom teapot packed carefully into her yardgoods.

Today that same rich land is celebrating phase one of a horticultural showpiece, a 240 acre world class botanical garden. The Oregon Garden has been drawing enthusiastic crowds since opening last spring as Silverton's backyard. Within the 10 block historic district that is the heart of this 7,000 soul community (in which my very own mother, Edythe Helen Skeels was born in 1922 I must note), visitors stroll past a series of colorful outdoor murals to revel in the old time charm, cute shops, galleries, and since 1999, Sundrops Gifts and Tearoom.

Sundrops is a joyful mother-daughter collaboration, the vision of Pam Seppala and Gloria Questad. Housed in an old high-ceilinged building with indoor murals of its own, eight tables dressed in white with gold leaves and charmingly mis-matched chairs await visitors for lunch and tea.

It has been almost 150 years since the first teapot rattled into Silverton, but the civility and elegance that it heralded is flourishing at Sundrops Gifts and Tearoom. If you feel like raising a cup to toast Polly Crandall Coon Price, by all means do.

Open 10 a.m. to 6 p.m. Tuesday through Saturday.

SUNRIVER RESORT

One Center Drive - P.O. Box 3609
Sunriver, Oregon 97707
1-800-386-1922 or 541-593-4609
www.sunriver-resort.com

Just a few enjoyable minutes to the south of Bend, the high dry desert air yields glimpses of magic through the stately Ponderosa pines. At 4,100 feet above us fog-shrouded sea-level dwellers, a mantle of crisp blue sky, clear 300 days of the year here, rests like a halo on a world class all-season retreat.

Guests of Sunriver Resort can indulge their passion for warm weather activity with mountain biking, golf, horseback riding, tennis, flyfishing and hiking, or simply unwind by the gentle sounds and sights of the cool snow-fed Deschutes River. In winter the resort transforms under starry skies into a family wonderland with more than 150 traditional holiday events of sleigh rides, cross-country skiing, moonlit snowshoe treks, elegant dinner theater and concerts. Santa's elves can even be enlisted to read your little ones a special bedtime story and tuck them in at the end of a magical day.

Teatime has been added to the list of activities at Sunriver Resort with special Teddy Bear Teas served in the lodge every Saturday afternoon during the month of December. While tea lovers and their fuzzy companions enjoy a tea in the finest English tradition amid joyful decorations of the North Pole Room, a real live friendly adult-sized teddy bear circulates among the big round tables offering delightful photo opportunities for that special Christmas card for Grandma.

Call or check the website for this year's tea events, as teatime at Sunriver Resort is new and likely to grow from its successful launch in 2000.

THE TAO OF TEA

3430 S. E. Belmont
Portland, OR 97214
503-736-0119

Generations ago an ardent yet anonymous tea lover celebrated his passion, "And let us bless those sunny lands so far away across the seas Whose hills and vales gave fertile birth To that fair shrub of priceless worth Which yields each son of Mother Earth A fragrant cup of tea." Today those sunny lands have a special new forum in which they are celebrated daily in Portland. The flagship location of a planned network, the Tao of Tea opened in the regentrified Belmont neighborhood in the autumn of 1997, providing a uniquely international experience to the tea scene.

Home for this Asian tea adventure is a building the color of Orange Pekoe with wood tea crates for outdoor tables, the gentle rustle of bamboo and rustic open shelves displaying their own unique line of tea ceramics and pottery available for sale. Large cast bronze hands beckon you to stop, slow down, and learn something new about the world's oldest beverage.

Your host, Verinder Chawla, originally from India, prides himself on his well-trained staff. His plans include the opening of another tea room in the city's Asian gardens in the near future, and continuing to expand the tea horizons of the Northwest with an impressive roster of special events and classes. The menu carries forward the Pacific Rim theme with soups and snacks that celebrate the Asian tea experience and are, like the Tao of Tea itself, a delightful change from the usual.

Open daily, long hours beginning at 11 a.m.

TEA & TOMES

716 N.W. Beach Drive
Newport, OR 97365
541-265-2867
www.teaandtomes.com

I grew up on the Oregon coast, resigned to the local wisdom that the azure glass fishing floats from Japan, which had been a treasure for earlier ardent beachcombers, had all been found. Years later when Ken and I moved to the Oregon coast for a winter's rest he announced his intention to find some. Hoping to save him disappointment I imparted the local's party line on the subject. Patiently he began consulting tide tables, weather patterns, and maps. The first day out he found two on a busy beach right in front of a resort. The second day I went with him and we found four more, lying like unstrung beads on the shoreline. Had they always been here? Almost daily that drizzly winter the ocean would yield up a bit more treasure for us. I learned something very valuable from that season by the sea - what you expect to receive is pretty much what you will get. We prize those glass balls more than any Chihuly original.

Patience and passion have paid off for Tuppence and Bert in their four year massive renovation project to open what many tea lovers who write us feel is "the best tearoom on the west coast." Tea & Tomes is located at the turn-around of the historic Nye Beach district of Newport in a wonderful old building that once provided a theater for tap-dancing vaudevillians in the early 1900s. Enchanted on their trips to England with "the stoppage of time, the pampering, the ritual and elegance of the traditional" British tea, the Aldridges have successfully recreated a tea parlor of grace and comfort. English antiques are warmed by the glow of a cast iron fireplace from the Victorian era in the Lakes District of England. The wood floors and wainscoting are original and lovingly restored. Follow your nose to the kitchen and a peek will disclose a four oven Aga cooker, essential to all British tearooms, cooking your delicious food to perfection, which is then served with flair.

Tuppence encourages you to feed the seagulls that cluster at the end of the block, for like their cousins, the pigeons of Trafalgar Square, they always seem to be hungry. Left-over bread scraps are bagged and ready. If you too expect to find treasure on the Oregon coast you're in luck, for the gem called Tea & Tomes has most definitely arrived!

Open 11 a.m. until 5:30 p.m. (last tea served at 4:30) daily except Sunday and Wednesday.

TEA COTTAGE

235 E. California St.
Jacksonville, OR 97530
541-899-7777

In the late 1800s the unpleasant howling reverberating from the little white cottage in historic Jacksonville would have been the protests of the patrons of Dr. Will Jackson, the town dentist. Fortunately for us, Dr. Jackson hung up his pliers and dentistry has come a long way in the past 100 years. Also fortunately for us, the only high-pitched howling now is from a tea kettle. Welcome to The Tea Cottage.

Four generations of ladies from one family began the business in 1996 and still work daily in the flower filled tea room and gift shop. The dream of mother Susan Sullivan and daughter Lisa Shipley came swathed in fresh linens, the aroma of scone laden tiered servers and soon grew to encompass Susan's mother and Lisa's daughter.

Resplendent with Victorian era treasures, the tea room features gifts harking back to the era when Jacksonville was in the flush of gold fever. The property, in fact, was purchased by Dr. Will's wife Hattie for $500 in gold coin. Dr. Jackson's dedication to cavity prevention may have limited his enjoyment of the ladies' Marmalade Madness tea sandwich or the crumpet dressed with Lyle's syrup and cream, but the menu also includes healthful fresh soups, scones and salads. The contented sighs of tea lovers, peaceful conversation, and the gentile tinkle of silver on china is a vast improvement over the sounds his business created anyway.

Tea and lunch are served 11a.m. to 2 p.m. Tuesday through Saturday. Reservations are recommended. The gift shop is open 10 a.m. to 4 p.m. on those same days.

TEA EVENTS

915 N.W. Gasoline Alley
Bend, OR 97701
541-382-5515
Website: www.teaevents.com

Photo: © Brian Sasse

About once a month in the clean air of Bend, if you stroll down Gasoline Alley and peek through a window, you just might see a covy of bustled and hatted Victorian ladies chatting and taking tea. No, it's not some cosmic wrinkle in time, it's "The meeting of the Ladies Tea and Rhetoric Society now come to order." Dawnya Sasse knows how to share the fun of tea. In addition to presiding as the local chapter head for this celebration of liberated tea drinking, she also is the talented purveyor of her own special tea parties.

Once a week from 2 to 5 p.m. by reservation only, Dawnya will provide five-course tea parties for your special group event of up to 20 guests at her new Tea Events' facility. English bone china, rich floral tablecloths, three tiered servers, fresh flowers and gentle music add a grace note to your fancy tea occasion celebrated at her new English-style setting. One Saturday a month a very special theme tea is open to the public. Come with friends or make some new ones, but do make reservations as the events fill quickly. It could be a Radio Mystery Tea, Mother-Daughter Tea, Christmas Cup of Tea, Winter Wonderland or any of a number of creative and fun devices to make you slow your pace, share a giggle and be pampered with tea and traditional foods. Teas classes and tea tastings as well as special dress-up parties for little girls round out a very busy agenda at this promising new business.

You can even join her celebrated tea circle of uppity Victorian ladies by attending the tea meetings of The Ladies Tea and Rhetoric Society events, bustle and hat optional, fun guaranteed.

THE TEAZONE

510 N.W. 11th Avenue
Portland, OR 97209
503-221-2130
Website: www.the-teazone.com

One of the most talked about urban renewal programs in this country is going on as we speak in the Pearl District of northwest Portland. Once a wasteland of dilapidated warehouses and decaying buildings, regentrification has created a neighborhood of some of the Rose City's most exclusive chic addresses for living and commerce. In August of 1999 The TeaZone opened its doors here. The dreamchild of a husband and wife team, she from the Northwest and he from New Zealand, this is truly an international scene celebrating tea that is delightfully short on primness.

With what's reputed to be the largest selection of teapots in Portland and more than fifty loose teas including some rare and premium, Grant Cull and Jhanne Jasmine have created a sleek, upbeat urban tea emporium. Two distinct seating areas with eight tables contribute to the enjoyment of a pot of tea, and wood floors are warmed by a high copper ceiling and faux finish walls. A nice variety of sweet and savory treats from local bakeries augment your tea from a menu that changes frequently. A whimsical teapot fountain sets the tone for casual relaxation and fun.

Tea is delivered to your table with a sand timer and guidance from your server on removing the infuser and placing it in the nest provided at the exactly perfect moment to maximize flavor. Thin glass cups allow you to savor the visual treat of the many colors of tea. The TeaZone's capable staff takes great pride in educating any customers who seek it, and are always up to date on the latest health benefits and tea preparation procedures (which vary with your choice of tea, as you may already know).

This is a great spot to obtain a little renewal of your own. You'll be relaxed and refreshed for the rest of the day by your visit to this gem of an urban tea emporium in the Pearl District.

Open all week at 10 a.m. with closing at 6 p.m. Sunday through Wednesday, and 8 p.m. Thursday through Saturday.

TIME & AGAIN

213 S. First Street
St. Helens, OR 97051
503-366-1184
E-Mail: rjavobus@ados.com

The great Italian film actress Anna Magnani was shown some publicity photos her studio was about to release. Every line, every wrinkle, every crowsfoot had been airbrushed out, time-warping her well worn face back to the dewy softness of her twenties. Outraged, Anna's emotions burst quickly to the surface, "It has taken me 45 years to earn those lines," she shouted, "and you want to rob me of them?!"

Debra & Richard Jacobus found a creaky 75 year old lodge hall in their hometown that other investors had dismissed as "too desperate for repair." Sections of wall were missing, the roof leaked, the wiring and plumbing needed upgrading, and to top it all off the enormous 7,500 square foot structure was painted an unrelenting algae green. Where others had seen only flaws, Debra & Richard saw the well-worn and loving face of their future teahouse, ballroom and gift shop.

Inspired by a memorable tea at the Ritz in London, they set about with structural repairs and then moved into yards and yards of fabric and lace, elegant vintage wallpaper, and 63 gallons of pastel paint. What they created is a serene 10 table Victorian tea parlor, two elegant lounges with wood burning stove, a gift shop and a grand ballroom where large special event teas are presented. Debra reflects, "I don't think we'll ever be completely done, but then that's like love isn't it?" The love shows on the strong, lived-in face of this old lodge hall, where every wrinkle has been celebrated and earned.

Tea is served by reservation Tuesday through Saturday, 10 a.m. to 4 p.m. Call or email for schedule and reservations for the Grand Ballroom Teas.

TIME FOR TEA - TEDDE'S TEAS

5375 S.W. Humphrey Blvd.
Portland, OR 97221 503-297-0837
E-Mail: tedde@teddestea.com

My husband says I rant, and I think I feel one coming on now: Is it just me, or have you noticed how every major store now feels obliged to issue you a plastic identification card "in order to make sure you get the best price"? Well, I'm sorry, but if I've made the effort to go to your supermarket or giant drugstore then I should get the very best price you've got just for being there, thank you. I don't need an ID card, I know

who I am. Pretty soon we'll need a forklift just to carry our purses full of plastic cards. Maybe we could just issue one card, good at every store, to every baby born and get it over with. It's issued with their birth certificate and says "Welcome future shopper..." There, I'm done.

Not all new ideas are bad, mind you. In fact, in Portland enterprising Tedde McMillen has carved out an interesting tea niche for herself. The Time-For-Tea consultant attends a party arranged by the hostess for a few of her friends in her home. The consultant entertains the guests with fun games and tea prizes, and the guests get to sample organic estate teas and delicious gourmet desserts. A virtual tea cart of accessories, hand-painted bone china, YiXing clay pots, and the teas and gourmet goodies are available for the guests to order. The hostess earns 25% of the proceeds of the party towards her own purchases, so everybody wins. I've tried to avoid becoming a tea snob, but I've been known to buy what I thought sounded like an interesting tea or succumbed to pretty packaging, without the benefit of tasting it, got it home, sat down with the pot and gone "eeewyuck," once or twice myself. Sampling at parties or stores eliminates that problem. So a tip of the old tea bonnet to Tedde. Good idea, m'dear.

You agree with my husband, don't you? Be honest. You think I rant.

TUDOR ROSE TEAROOM

480 Liberty Street S.E.
Salem, OR 97301
503-588-2345

Salem is a town that respects neatness and order. Its tree-lined streets are home to gray squirrels that are polite enough to let traffic flow, one small paw gathered up by their chests in an inquiring pose, and then scamper across when the light changes. Manicured lawns and artfully arranged flowerbeds are the norm on Gaiety Hill, a cheery sounding historic district of Salem where you will find Tudor Rose Tearoom.

The owners of Tudor Rose, Bob and Terry Brooks, offer Salem residents a bit of British tea room atmosphere complete with proper tea service, delectable treats of both sweet and savory fare, and a delightful selection of gifts. The charming location offers the ambiance one seeks for a relaxing afternoon with friends accompanied by tasty treats and a good cuppa.

Reservations are absolutely required for tea, served between noon and 4 p.m. Monday through Saturday. The gift shop and other meal service is available 10:30 a.m. to 4:30 p.m. on those days, but do call ahead just to make sure.

WILD ROSE TEA ROOM

422 S.W. 6th St.
Redmond, OR 97756
541-923-3385

In the rarefied air of the sunny high desert of Central Oregon, dainty wild roses bloom and flourish with their more rugged companions, juniper and sagebrush. When Bessie opened her tea room in 1996 she chose the beautiful and enduring Wild Rose as her name and it has been that blend of beauty and strength that has served her well.

Inspired to tea, as many were, upon reading Emilie Barnes' delightful "If Teacups Could Talk", Bessie found the perfect expression for her keen sense of gracious hospitality and soon became a destination hostess for groups of tea lovers. In keeping with her philosophy that tea should be a retreat from a busy world, Wild Rose Tea Room soothes with gentle background music and delectable treats served at your lace topped table. Invigorating aquamarine walls form the backdrop for period antiques, vintage glass display cases, collectibles and treasures.

When your life feels a little prickly from everyday thorns, the solace you seek is under the clear skies of central Oregon. Pick yourself a Wild Rose.

Open for tea and browsing Tuesday through Saturday from 10 a.m. to 4:30 p.m. Reservations are advised for groups of 6 more more. Bessie's Special High Tea is served by reservation only.

YOUR HOUSE OR MINE

117 S. College
Newberg, OR 97132
503-538-7155 or 503-281-0001

> "Why do we love certain houses, and why do they seem to love us? It is the
> warmth of our individual hearts reflected in our surroundings."
> *T.H. Robsjohn-Gibbings*

For the past decade Cathie Rawlings and Suzanne Gilliam have delivered charm to their customers' homes. When not doing that they are charming customers in one of their own homes. Are they entertainers? Interior decorators? Yes, and more. Cathie and Suzanne offer traditional English teas at your house or one of their own (between them they have three now including one in Salem).

At their homes you are invited to select one of more than 100 hats to wear for the occasion, and the table will be dressed in fine linens and fresh flowers for your group. The menus vary with the season, but chocolate usually rounds out the sweet course. When invited to your home or office, don't be surprised if you find some of your own interesting personal belongings forming a truly distinctive decorative touch to your table. These ladies have an appreciative eye for the unique and whimsical that the Victorians would have loved.

For centuries the invitation "come for tea" has always meant more than sharing a beverage. With Your House or Mine catering the event you can share not only your home, but 100% of your attention and time to enjoying your guests at a memorable and authentic English tea.

WASHINGTON TEA ROOMS, TEA PARTIES AND EVENTS

GREATER SEATTLE
Blue Willow Teahouse
The Crumpet Shop
The Garden Court
Gingko Tea
Green Gables Guesthouse
The Library Cafe
MarketSpice
Morning Glory Chai
Pekoe Teahouse
Perennial Tea Room
Queen Mary
Seattle Art Museum
Shoseian Teahouse
Sorrento Hotel
South Seattle C. College
Teahouse Kuan Yin
The Teacup
Travelers Tea Bar
Ummelina Tea Spa
The Wellington
Wit's End Books & Tea

SEATTLE EASTSIDE
The British Pantry
Country Cottage
If Only Teacups Could Talk
Museum of Doll Art
Whiffletree Tea Room
The Woodmark Hotel

NORTH OF SEATTLE
A Shade Victorian
Althea's Tea Rooms
Attic Secrets
Elizabeth & Alexander
Kate's Tea Room
Piccadilly Circus
Rose Garden Tea Rooms
Tea, Thyme & Ivy

WASHINGTON TEA ROOMS, TEA PARTIES AND EVENTS

SOUTH PUGET SOUND
British Marketplace
Enchanted Tea Garden
Exhibitors Mall
Imperial Tea Court
Jean-Pierre's
Morning Glory Tea Room
Taste 'n Time
The Tea Lady
Thornewood Castle
Victorian Rose Tea Room
Victorian Tea Potts

SKAGIT VALLEY & BELLINGHAM
A Tea for All Seasons
Abbey Garden Tea Room
Althea's Tea Rooms
Christianson's Tea
Tea at LaConner Flats

OLYMPIC PENINSULA & WHIDBEY ISLAND
Island Tea Company
Just Pretend
Just Your Cup O' Tea
La Belle Saison
Langley Tea Room
Lupine Cottage
Petals Garden Cafe
Ye Olde Copper Kettle

SOUTHWEST WASHINGTON
Afternoon Tea
  at the Victorian
Blue Gables Tea House
The Brits
Cafe d' Vine
Carnelian Rose Tea Co.
The Cheshire Cat
Fairgate Inn B & B
Grant House Restaurant
Longfellow House
Pomeroy House
Season's Coffee & Tea
Victorian Rose Special Teas

EASTERN WASHINGTON
A Touch of Elegance
Brambleberry Cottage
Country Register
Country Tea Garden
Fotheringham House
Ivy Tea Room
Lighthouse Tea Room
Pleasant Times
Tea-An'Tiques
Wee Elegance

ABBEY GARDEN TEA ROOM
in Old Fairhaven

1308 - 11th St.
Bellingham, WA 98225
360-752-1752

"Nowhere is the English genius of domesticity more notably evident
than in the festival of afternoon tea."
George Gissing, (1857-1903)

We all have special places that
nourish our spirit and renew our
peaceful centers. For me, a small
hidden cove, where agates lie at the
base of a waterfall like unstrung
gems is one of my sanctuaries. Part
of its magic is that it can only be
reached during certain low tides on
the fog shrouded southern Oregon
coast. For Anne Graham Oliver, the
lush garden cloaking the Abbey
House in her mother's ancestral town of Winchester, England, has provided
creative inspiration and refreshment for her soul. It was in that spirit that
Anne opened Abbey Garden Tea Room in Bellingham's Old Fairhaven
historic district in 1998.

Nestled in a Victorian brick building with her daughter Chinook's
paint-your-own ceramic studio, Abbey Garden Tea Room melds creativity
and comfort to create an atmosphere that is cozy and relaxed. Comfy over-
stuffed chairs snuggle by a gas fireplace, and antique tables adorned in
chintz line a gallery overlooking the ceramic studio. Fine china, old and
new, as well as a collection of tea theme gifts and gourmet items provide an
elegant counterpoint to the old brick walls of the charming building.

Abbey Garden's popular Afternoon Cream Tea and light lunches have
been embraced by locals and tourists, many using the time to create a
unique hand painted ceramic masterpiece. The recuperative blend of creativity and refreshment will nourish your spirit in this place, and you don't
even need to wait for low tide.

*Open Tuesday through Friday 10 a.m. to 8 p.m., Saturday 10 a.m. to 6 p.m.,
Sunday noon to 5 p.m., closed on Monday.*

AFTERNOON TEA AT THE VICTORIAN

(The Wedding Place)
908 Esther Street
Vancouver, WA 98660
360-693-1798

"You say potato and I say pot-ah-to. You say tomato and I say tom-ah-to..." crooned debonair Fred Astaire before he swept a feathery Ginger Rogers away in a lively 1930s musical. That scene is played out today (without the orchestra) at the kitchen table of owner Bobbee Sapp and caterer Cindy Hammond when they discuss scones - or is it "skawns"? Regardless of the pronunciation we should all be grateful these two haven't "...called the whole thing off" and remain in complete concord on offering warm, delectable scones with their delightful new afternoon teas.

Romance is in the air at this sweet 1903 two-story Victorian house in downtown Vancouver. Since 1982 hundreds of starry-eyed couples have been married here, and when they revisit their wedding day memories the charming house peeks through as the back-drop. In 1997 Bobbee Sapp acquired The Wedding Place, as it came to be known, redecorated it romantically and then recently expanded the business to include elegant tea luncheons. Tea is served throughout the main floor, which seats 35. Gentle music, a cozy fireplace, Victorian lace frills, and the signature scent of black cherry candles all add to the restful ambiance of the setting. Rhododendrons and hydrangeas surround a covered porch where a relaxing tea can be taken in spring and summer. Throughout the year special tea events are held to celebrate the milestones of Christmas, Valentine's Day, Mother's Day and Easter, but also include a crazy Mad Hatter's Tea in March and a Teddy Bear's Picnic Tea for the little ones to honor their fluffy companions in April.

So why on earth did Fred Astaire get all the credit? After all, he wasn't the one dancing backwards in high heels, panty girdle and ostrich feathers was he? Some questions may never be resolved, but Afternoon Tea at The Victorian is unquestionably on its way to making sweetly memorable teas for you to enjoy.

Open Tuesday and Thursday, 11 a.m. to 3p.m. Reservations are required. Also available for private parties and meetings at other times and days.

ALTHEA'S TEA AND SUN ROOMS

614 South First Street
Mount Vernon, WA 98273
360-336-0602

The fog blooms softly above the regimented ranks of exuberantly hued tulips, and the horizon is blurred as deftly as a water color on this early spring morning. As a bald eagle effortlessly glides low and slowly toward his breakfast on the Skagit River I am reminded of author Denise Levertov's musings in her book Settling that "Grey is the price of neighboring with eagles, of knowing a mountain's vast presence, seen or unseen." It seems a small price this morning enroute as we are on green country lanes toward a new place for tea we've heard about in Mount Vernon.

Just when you think you know pretty much what to expect from a tea business, a fresh breeze in the form of Jennifer and Roy Howson blows in and the fog lifts. Avid Grateful Dead fans (aka "Deadheads" for those of you who missed the 70's) turned trial lawyers, the business name is a tribute to a Grateful Dead song and the unexpected and unique twists don't stop there. Two tanning booths at the back of the shop will bronze up you sun-lovers and a healthy massage is available by appointment. In addition to more than 25 teas offered by the pot, you can also purchase body care talcs, lotions and potions. Bring your laptop and dash off a letter, outlets are thoughtfully provided and the menu includes healthy soups, fresh fruit smoothies and veggie sandwiches on multigrain bread. Six tables, a comfy armchair and a bright tapestry couch beckon you to linger, but this busy couple understands if you have a sprightly pace to maintain; after all they're both due back at the courthouse soon. So in the immortal words of the Grateful Dead..."keep on truckin'" to tea.

Open Monday through Friday 8 a.m. (or earlier) to 7 p.m. or later, Saturday and Sundays 10 a.m. to 4 p.m. Teatime specials 3 p.m. to 6 p.m. daily.

A SHADE VICTORIAN

7024 - 126th St. N.W.
Marysville, WA 98271
360-652-2224

Carrie A. Basher glows with the decorating knowledge that lighting is the easiest way to change the mood of a room. As a long time tea lover, she also understands that tea is the easiest way to change the mood of a day.

Skilled in the art of making ornate Victorian lampshades, Carrie's shades were in demand by antique stores and upscale gift shops since she began in 1993. Now four children later, Carrie is passionate about sharing her romantic avocation. Since 1999 Carrie has been bringing lampshade and tea parties to private homes like yours, in the company of your unique friends, where you can enjoy a light tea in the Victorian tradition. By the end of the party, guided by Carrie's art, humor and patience, each guest will have created their very own elegant fabric lampshade. What a bright idea!

A TEA FOR ALL SEASONS

180 E. Bakerview Road
Bellingham, WA 98226
360-734-8252

Since feasting on Laura Ingalls Wilder's books and my own grandmother's prairie journal as a child, I've been besotted by log cabins. Open-hearted, handcrafted and cozy, they embody a simple modesty seemingly discounted as a virtue by today's mock-Tudors and faux-Victorians. It's in the old-fashioned embrace and rustic charm of a log cottage that Marty Sargent opened an enterprise based on that other homespun tradition, tea.

Opening in the winter of 2000, A Tea for All Seasons is the culmination of years of rave reviews for Marty as a popular tea caterer in nearby Lynden. Nestled amid a covey of shops bulging with antiques and country gifts a little north of Bellingham, the 350 square foot tea room opened in a cozy log cabin that was built for the hospitality of overnight travellers in the 1920s. The open beamed, wood planked tea room is warmed by a gas fireplace. Five lace topped tables cradle Marty's personal tableware lovingly collected from more than 30 countries. The menu features Tea & Sweets, Tea & Savories, and her grandest of teas, a combination of both. Marty's special forte is creating unique international theme teas, meticulously researched for appropriate menus and music, authentic table settings and decor for your party's interest. A small alcove of the room is devoted to tea gifts, treasures, and collectibles.

A heart-warming Tea For All Seasons awaits in the simple comfort and open heart of a log cottage.

Tea is by reservation only, Tuesday through Thursday 11 a.m. to 5 p.m. Other days and hours by special arrangement as well as catering for your own tea event at your location of choice.

A TOUCH OF ELEGANCE

508 Bell Lane
St. John, WA 99171
509-648-3466

When my grandmother, Ideala Godiva Gregory, was a young girl at the turn of the century she kept a catalog illustration carefully folded in her pinafore pocket. The drawing was of a high fashion lady dressed in a floor-length gown with a long flowing train. Although this drawing was in black and white, Granny wrote in her journal that she imagined it was of "smooth yellow silk that whispered gently when she walked," and that she would be that fine lady someday. Seventy-five years later when we were pulling weeds from her raspberries, I asked if she still longed for that yellow silk gown. Standing in muddy boots, poised over her hoe, she said thoughtfully with a chuckle, "No, I've decided I'll just ask the good Lord if I can come back next time as a big yellow butterfly!"

At Barbara Kile's elegant tea room in the Palouse area of eastern Washington, rich chocolate butterflies alight daintily as her signature touch on desserts, and flowers handcrafted from butter adorn the rolls. For the past seven years touring groups and tea devotees, no fewer than 6 and no more than 27 in number, have returned here to elegant Victorian Teas or luncheons after exploring the region's dramatic beauty and bountiful harvest of antiques. Tea is served by reservation only Monday through Saturday 11 a.m. to 3 p.m. in a sunny tea room on pretty linens and fine china in Barb's home. Flowers from her yard grace the table where tea lovers relish heart-shaped tea sandwiches, chicken puffs, scones with apricot-pineapple marmalade and Devon cream, little carrot cakes, chocolate truffles, fresh fruit tarts, cheeses and sorbet in a leisurely, sociable setting.

One recent memorable group came to A Touch of Elegance to celebrate the birthday of the youngest of their gang, who was turning 88. Accessorized by the hat that each had worn to her own wedding decades ago, the joyful tea was a fun prelude to a slumber party they were headed to that evening. These are Ideala Godiva's kind of gals!

Granny's long life was definitely short of yellow silk ballgowns, but she unquestionably did become that fine lady. Now when I'm enjoying my spring garden and a big yellow butterfly flits through, it makes me smile.

ATTIC SECRETS

4229 - 76th St.
Marysville, WA 98270
360-659-7305

Digital or cellular? VHS or DVD? Cable or satellite dish? Gas or electric? IRA or 401K? Unleaded or Super? Paper or plastic? With life so complicated these days, isn't it a balm for the weary spirit to pass a peaceful hour or two where the most pressing question is "one lump or two?"

That Happi Favro understands us in our techno-muddled state is apparent immediately at her sweet little tea room in Marysville. Attic Secrets is one of the very first tea rooms north of Seattle, and still one of the best. Unassuming from the street, a visit inside is like an afternoon sorting through a favorite auntie's attic. A rich profusion of treasures, garden accessories, dried flowers, tea gifts and Victorian papers spill unabashedly from antiques, beckoning exploration, touch, and smell; but that's only part of the charm. Three rooms are dressed smartly for tea, each distinctly unique in its decor. Gentle music soothes as you await your three-tiered server laden with indulgence and proffered by a gracious server, maybe even Happi herself.

These choices are easy. Select any from the menu items of Grand Lady Tea, Serenity Tea, Primrose Tea, Afternoon Tea, Little Darling Tea (for children especially), Light Tea, or any of their sandwiches and salads or soup du jour, and you'll be making the right choice. If only life were always this easy.

Here's the answer...when it comes to "one lump or two" always, always pick two, that's my advice. Sorry, the other stuff I can't help you with.

Tea is served 10 a.m. to 5 p.m. Monday through Friday. Saturday 10 a.m. to 4 p.m. Reservations are recommended.

BLUE GABLES TEA HOUSE

5206 N.E. 78th St.
Vancouver, WA 98665
360-694-2242

Bluebirds, forget-me-nots, blueberries, dragonflies, clear skies, delphiniums. With all the glorious blues sung by Mother Nature, why that color ever became associated with "the blahs" is beyond me. Add to that list of definitely upbeat blues a brand new place to chase them with an afternoon tea, Blue Gables Tea House, opening winter 2000.

Annie Habig, Megan Oakley & Kris Close

Long-time friends Megan Oakley, Annie Habig and Kris Close collaborated to bring new life to a charming hundred year old two story house with blue gables in which to share their love of tea. Nine tables on the first floor are set for tea with linens and lace, fresh flowers and sterling. The charming mismatch of floral china echoes the sage green and gentle butter yellow rooms, brightened by an old fireplace and time-softened hardwood floors. An old spiral staircase leads to the second floor gift shop bright with Victorian treasures and tea gifts, as well as a private party parlor that seats about 15 for your special celebration.

So let's rethink the blues. Mother Nature has provided abundant symbols of its uplifting beauty, and now three hard working ladies in Vancouver have provided one of their own.

Open for tea between 10:30 a.m. and 4 p.m., the gift shop is open from 10 a.m. to 5 p.m.

BLUE WILLOW TEAHOUSE

1024 East Pike Street
Seattle, WA 98122
206-325-5140 or 800-328-0353
website: www.bluewillowtea.com

When Frank Miller speaks to you about tea, there's a reverence in his tone. For here is a fellow who continually is inspired and fascinated by it. For the past decade that Frank's company Blue Willow Tea has been importing, he has overseen everything from the growing of the leaves to the distribution to upscale markets. Their hallmark has always been that humane and environmentally responsible conditions must prevail in doing so. It is especially appropriate then that Frank share this reverence for tea in a sanctuary of sorts, and so the idea for a traditional tea room was born.

When Blue Willow Teahouse opens in early spring of 2001, the showplace flagship location for a planned network, it will represent years of meticulous planning "to pair tea with food in an inspired environment." Housed in an 80 year old, high-ceilinged building on Capitol Hill, a long expanse of sunny windows with retractable awnings for outdoor seating will greet the busy street of this hip pedestrian-oriented neighborhood. Inside the lively green tea and crimson-hued building is 2,400 square feet devoted to tea culture. A large Burmese temple gong heralds your arrival to a poetry inlaid entry. A world map is mounted showing trade routes and origins of the wooden tea chests and metal drums of tea all about. Old Persian rugs soften the terrazzo floor, and handmade tables of old Javanese teak provide your own personal niche here. The mood, enhanced by gentle world music, Asian art and textiles, is serene and rustically elegant, but on the cutting edge enough to include an internet station you're invited to explore. More than 50 teas are paired with a fascinating and vast menu of Asian-inspired food choices as well as a traditional European Afternoon Tea (from 3:30 to 5:30 p.m. daily.)

What a blessing to be welcomed into such a special place. The world's oldest beverage has a new sanctuary in Seattle.

Open Tuesday through Thursday as well as Sunday 9 a.m. to 9:30 p.m. Friday and Saturday until 11 p.m.

BRAMBLEBERRY COTTAGE & TEA SHOPPE

122 North Argonne Road
Spokane, WA 99121
509-926-3293

When we lived in the Rockies I would spread peanut butter (extra chunky) on pine cones suspended from the bare birches by our window for the funny little mountain chickadees that wintered there. On many a blizzardy morning my husband laughed over the rim of his teacup at the sight of this fluffy squadron perched patiently on my head while I spread their breakfast. Perhaps they were warming their toes in the cable knit of my ski cap, or maybe my uncombed morning hair resembled a nest of twigs. They were so light that I wasn't even aware they roosted there, but looking at photos of it years later I was struck by how Mother Nature had bestowed a most esteemed reward for feeding that hardy flock of chilly little birds - a Crown of Chickadees!

Spreading peanut butter on pine cones is as close as I get to crafts (unless you count the time I hot-glue-gunned my fingers to a birdhouse.) At Brambleberry Cottage they have molded the artless and clumsy into talented craftspeople for years, and with the opening of their Tea Shoppe last year, at last, an art I can master. In the charming Victorian era tea room adjacent to the bright and clever gift shop and craft room, proprietors Melanie and Dawn offer tea with truly artistic flair. Faux stone and stucco wall treatments with garlands and swags line this darling six table tea room. A romantic fireplace mantle and old windows transport their guests to the era of ladies of leisure and afternoon indulgences. The gold skirted tabletops hold old photos and doilies. Five different tea sets are offered on the menu, each more delicious than the one before.

A delightful quarterly newsletter outlines the arts and crafts' classes available as well as updates on a myriad of special theme teas they present. For teatime artistry, The Brambleberry Cottage & Tea Shoppe is unique. Say, could you please help me get this birdhouse off my fingers?

Open 10(ish) to 6 p.m. Monday through Friday, Saturday closing is 5 p.m. Tea is by reservation Tuesday through Saturday 1 p.m. to 4 p.m.

BRITISH MARKETPLACE & COPPER KETTLE TEA ROOM

26 - B Street N.E.
Auburn, WA 98002
253-833-2404

Every spring the phone lines buzz with breathless messages between the bird lovers on our Camano Island hill, "They're back! 'Talk to you later, I've got to go put up my feeder." (click) Without further elaboration we know our hummingbirds have returned, towing spring like a sky writer's banner. The long, gray winter will soon be a memory.

Each spring the advance guards of a squadron of more than forty hummingbirds arrives at our homes, hovering at remembered sites where sugar water feeders have been hung every year before. In the amount of time it takes to mix up the sugary solution we call "zoom juice," as many as twenty hummingbirds alight on our deck railing, their tiny feathers glistening like Christmas ornaments. These marvelous little navigators migrate annually thousands of miles from tropical climes on wing beats of 2,200 per minute, and to do so require about 10 calories a day. That sounds easy, but it's the equivalent of you sitting down to a 200,000 calorie tea. "Another dollop of Devonshire cream, m'dear?" Despite their nectar-sipping ways, they get their protein from bugs, which they also feed to their young in nests no bigger than a baby's fist, held together with spider webbing and camouflaged with lichen in evergreens. I can almost picture the tiny lead navigator with a map spread before his squadron, like the fighter pilots in old movies, stabbing his beak into Camano Island commanding, "We'll stop here for our usual sojourn and zoom juice." I am so glad they do.

Dark wood beams, brasses, and copper lend a snug and sheltered Tudor air to Copper Kettle Tea Room at the British Marketplace on a side street in historic downtown Auburn. Sharon cooks all the traditional British fare from scratch with her family recipe box and the confidence of her birthright in England. Served on pretty floral china to Battenberg lace topped tables, with the aplomb of the ex-flight attendant she is, Afternoon Tea is offered with all the right touches to cheer your spirit. Adjoining this popular 7 table tea room is a little British market for those hard to find foods, sauces, candies and imported gifts. It's a great spot for a little "zoom juice" of your very own.

Open Tuesday through Saturday 10:30 a.m. to 4 p.m. Lunch is 11 a.m. to 2 p.m. and Afternoon Tea is 2 p.m. to 3:30 p.m.

THE BRITISH PANTRY - NEVILLE'S RESTAURANT

8125 - 161st Ave. N.E.
Redmond, WA 98052
425-883-7511

"Do you think these peas are mushier than these?" The pleasant lady stood holding two different cans marked 'Mushy Peas' directly in my face in the little corner store of the village I was visiting in England. I stared at the cans with growing confusion and then at her expectant face. My blank look must have lasted a split second too long for she realized I probably didn't work at the market, and obviously didn't even understand the language. She scurried away with the cans clutched to her bosom before I could explain my unusual reaction. My jet-lagged brain was digesting a completely new adjective for peas, a vegetable I thought I knew....but "mushy?" And to realize that you even had a 'mushier' and a 'mushiest'. Variable degrees of mushiness that the world knew about and I didn't. It made my head spin. I should have just called after her with the truth, "Wait! I'm American. I'm ignorant!" But instead I bought a can myself because the conundrum fascinated me and for decades I used it as a bookend. (Until it started to swell threateningly and I worried about an explosion of peas and botulism all over my office ceiling.) There's always a great deal to learn by visiting grocery stores on your foreign trips. It's one of my greatest travel joys, as well as the big reason I usually come back ten pounds heavier.

Since 1978 the British Pantry in Redmond has been providing a taste of Britain with wonderful baked goods, a bright grocery, and a full service restaurant offering lunch, tea, and dinners. The Redman family have worked together to perfect the family heritage of traditional British baking to the point that they were even commissioned to provide food on two different occasions when the British Royal Family popped into the Northwest for a visit. Neville's is cozy and without pretense, your servers refreshingly warm and cheery, and the food will transport you to fond vacation memories quicker than you can say Yorkshire Pudding. The afternoon tea is immensely popular and just what you'd find in England. Don't blame me if you come back ten pounds heavier too!

Open Sunday through Tuesday 10 a.m. to 5 p.m. (last seating 4:30) and Wednesday through Saturday 10 a.m. - 9 p.m. Dinners are served Wednesday through Saturday only, breakfast on Sunday only. Lunch and tea on all days. Call for directions, it's a hidden gem worth finding.

THE BRITS

1427 Commerce
Longview, WA 98632
360-575-8090

Somehow the frightened young deer found itself on busy Commerce Street in historic downtown Longview, alarmed and confused as it merged with the morning traffic and darted across the lanes of the tree lined street seeking a safe haven. Joy Harris was busy preparing for her day at The Brits, the busy British eatery, gift and imported gourmet shop she owns with her mother, Pat Sprinzl, when she and the deer locked eyes at the door. "I looked at the deer and it looked at me, and I could tell it felt safe here," Joy says. "That little deer knew where to come." The Humane Society came and provided the deer with a one way trip to nearby wooded Mount Solo, where it bounded away, no doubt with fond memories of its tea shop visit.

Wayward deer aren't the only ones who know the soothing effect of finding a safe haven. For almost three years The Brits has been offering that same respite to growing numbers of regulars. A large charming mural, painted by Joy herself, showing a romantic thatched cottage surrounded by a lovely English summer garden sets the tone. Antique mahoghany displays showcase the imported bone china and tea accessories, books and gourmet goodies. In the back of the shop, near the bright red English phone box, a cozy little eclectic tea room seats 40. You'll never be rushed at the Brits. Joy and Pat often circulate among the tables, chatting and getting to know their guests, encouraging lingering. The menu suceeds in a tough challenge, melding Joy's healthy food background with the rich traditional fare of Britain.

Here in the heart of Longview a little English oasis has been created thanks to The Brits fond hope "that tea will always bring people closer together with warm conversation and good company." The little deer sensed that too.

Open Monday through Friday 9 a.m. to 6 p.m. and Saturday 10 a.m. to 5 p.m. with tea served 11 a.m. to 4 p.m.

CAFE D'VINE

**6709 N.E. 63rd Street
Vancouver, WA 98661
360-694-6461**

I once owned a washing machine that would get off balance during spin cycle, stagger around the laundry room to the end of its hose where it would complain loudly until someone shifted the load. That washing machine was a perfect metaphor for my own crazy, hectic life at the time.

Attending to the spiritually frazzled, world weary, and just plain hungry is the mission at Cafe d'Vine, a recently opened haven adjacent to the Christian bookstore, Branches. From its impressive river rock fireplace and hardwood floor to its reliance on fresh ingredients from the area, this spacious eatery celebrates the beauty and bounty of the Northwest. There is no afternoon tea service on the menu yet, but with over two dozen premium teas of the local Carnelian Rose line on the menu, your server can suggest a great sweet treat or sandwich pairing.

Created as a fund-raising venue for the good works of the Crossroads Community Church, Cafe d'Vine offers nourishment of all kinds.

Open early until 10 p.m. Monday through Thursday, and until 11 p.m. on Friday, Saturday and Sunday.

CARNELIAN ROSE TEA COMPANY

14813 N.E. Salmon Creek Avenue
Vancouver, WA 98686-1618
360-573-0917
E-Mail: tea@etiquette42day.com
Website: www.teatime.cc

"...a man by nothing is so well betrayed, as by his manners."
Edmund Spenser

With a flourish of a pen on an official parchment document that bore the word 'whereas' no less than six times and should have been accompanied by liveried trumpeters, the mayor of Vancouver proclaimed June 2000 as the first annual "Teatime Celebration Month!" How did that happen, you ask? You get a high energy, well-mannered tea lover, like Jennifer Peterson, fuel her up with some good Carnelian Rose English Breakfast Blend, and watch her go.

This is a lady who would never dream of making Miss Manners grimace. One of the region's foremost experts on etiquette, Jennifer offers her signature "Tea & Etiquette" programs to growing groups, private and corporate, seeking the latest in social and business etiquette in the relaxed setting of a tea. Single-handedly she is taking the rough edges off of business meetings one civil tea party at a time. She also caters teas for different age groups, creating theme teas specific to the interests, ages and needs of the gathering.

Jennifer is a purveyor of an extensive line of Carnelian Rose Teas, teacake mixes and cozies through mail order and website, as well as a marketer for popular tea tours to England. The saying well known to club members "If you want something done, go to the busiest lady," might have been coined for her. In her spare time (yes, she does have some) Jennifer even does consulting work for tearooms.

THE CHESHIRE CAT

2801 Fort Vancouver Way
Vancouver, WA 98661
360-735-1141

A coffee junkie friend of mine once picked up my flowered tea cozy, examined it from all angles, put it on her head and said, "I give up. What is this?" Assuming she was kidding I told her it was a poodle jacket. This seemed to satisfy her until she remembered we had a huge, lumbering malamute that would have required a much roomier cozy, and probably not chintz.

Avril Massey introduces legions of new tea drinkers to the trappings of tea everyday in the congeniality of her own little tea room, The Cheshire Cat. Opened in 1996, the authentically British enclave has become a haven to throngs of transplanted Britons, and those of us who admire them. Any attempt to capture the spirit of all British women in one sentence is doomed from the start, but I'm going to anyway. It seems to me, that Avril Massey embodies that particular spirit of resilience, good cheer, quick wit and internal strength that I ascribe to British ladies. When confronted with widowhood in 1993 she decided she needed "a new life" and moved to Vancouver, where, encouraged by her daughter, she opened the cozy tea room and shop.

Spritely and funny, Avril is energized by being a hostess. In addition to an excellent robust pot of tea, the menu includes traditional favorites like Sherpherd's Pie and Cornish Pasties. Tea sandwiches are on the daily menu, but a reservation is required for her special High Tea which includes a creamy trifle. An astute business woman must be able to assess her own strengths and weaknesses, "My scones were so heavy you could fire them like lead shot," she laughs and set about finding the very best handmade locally and delivered fresh daily.

Settle in for tea here and keep your ears tuned for all the wonderfully comfortable banter and genuine gaiety. Cast any preconceptions of tea-time stuffiness and formality aside. The Cheshire Cat in Vancouver is not that kind of tea experience.

Open Wednesday through Sunday 10 a.m. to 6 p.m.

CHRISTIANSON'S OLD SCHOOLHOUSE TEA

15806 Best Road
Mount Vernon, WA 98273
360-466-3821 or 800-585-8200
Website: www.christiansons-nursery.com

What a magical time winter is in the Skagit Valley! If you haven't visited then, you really should. Peace reigns as tulip bulbs doze under a light blanket of frost; a little beauty rest for their big spring debut as the star of next spring's Tulip Festival. Eagles ride the thermals with elegant ease, and ice crystals like powdered sugar frost the familiar evergreen shapes. Gardeners understand these cycles of the seasons. At my favorite local nursery, Christianson's, this understanding extends well beyond horticulture. For here, backdropped by majestic 40 foot firs, a humble little century old schoolhouse has experienced a joyful rebirth. Saved from destruction, it has found a new home on the lovely grounds of Christianson's Nursery, on a rural road between Mount Vernon and LaConner.

Every year, on the Saturday following Thanksgiving, the schoolhouse is dressed with nature's finery - boughs, garlands, pine cones and seed pods for a special tea. As an annual thank you to their customers, The Christianson family offers a complimentary tea by reservation only. Hundreds come, some in boots and jeans, some in ladylike hats and gloves, to share in the warm hospitality of a homespun tea buffet in this charming, historic setting and to officially celebrate the start of the Christmas season. Tables are dressed for 40 guests, with seatings every 45 minutes, beginning at 1:00 p.m. and ending well after dark.

At twilight, as traditional music gently heralds the season, candlelight beams from the eight little windows like a smile.

COUNTRY COTTAGE TEA PARTIES

12645 N.E. 68th Place
Kirkland, WA 98033
425-827-3366

Peter Pan: "Do you want an adventure now....or would you like to have your tea first?"
Wendy: "Tea first, and quickly!"

Pam Fox makes her living creating enchantment for all ages and it started with Rachel's play-house.

When Pam's granddaughter came to live with them as an infant, Grandpa Greg created the playhouse of every little girl's dreams. Behind the pink dutch door was floral wallpaper, rose carpeting, and furniture both handpainted and wicker. It had heat and lights for year-round comfort, and looking out the paned windows over the colorful windowbox planters it even had a view, the gazebo and waterfall ponds of this backyard paradise. The sixth birthday that Rachel spent with her youthful grandparents, Pam created a teaparty so special that it catapulted her into business.

Today Pam and Greg open their property to teaparties by reservation. While she gladly and graciously provides teaparties for grownups, it's the children's parties that have become Pam's specialty and won her heart. Whimsically shaped tea sandwiches, chocolate dipped strawberries, pretty cookies and warm marmalade scones are the magical fare enjoyed in good weather outdoors. Pristine white cutwork covered tables and fresh flowers dot the garden and partygoers enjoy a spirited game of musical chairs, croquet, and even craft projects. Indoors during cooler seasons, the party takes on a warm Victorian parlor flavor with timeless games and fun. A sweetly wrapped gift for each guest provides a tangible memory of the magic.

A teaparty with all the enchantment of a little girl's playhouse awaits you as a client of Pam Fox. Book one today for a child you love or the child in you.

COUNTRY REGISTER CAFE & TEA ROOM

7935 W. Grandridge Blvd.
Kennewick, WA 99336
509-783-7553

I like lists. I make lists of everything. I even make lists of lists I want to make. Lists can't just hang around, oh no, there are certain rules they must follow. Lists must be handwritten on preferably lined or grid paper, none of this point-and-click computer stuff for me, no sir. When the item is accomplished, then it's completely obliterated with a big fat marker, no dainty little checkmark or ballpoint pen line through it will do. I've taken lists to a new artform with colored highlighters but that's a whole other topic. I'm definitely in a bi-polar marriage when it comes to lists. My husband watches my compilations with bemused tolerance, as far as I know he has never made a list in his life. During a recent frenzy for a particularly complex project I looked over my pot of tea at him as my neatly printed and bulleted agenda flourished and grew. He picked up a pad and pen and wrote a list - "Get out of bed. Breathe in-breathe out (all day). Win lottery." He just doesn't get it.

Bobbi-Jo Floyd gets it. Lists, big lists, have helped her with all of the details of reopening the popular Country Register Cafe & Tea Room in its new location in Kennewick late last year. This busy eatery, formerly owned by mother Barbara Floyd, editor and founder of the beloved Country Register Newspapers, has recaptured the devotees of Bobbi-Jo's famed bread pudding and found throngs more. The updated decor is a very current look, punctuated by lovely antiques for sale, and forms the comfortable setting for both ladies and men that Bobbi-Jo's dream envisioned.

Now licensed to perform wedding ceremonies, receptions here are the house specialty. On the very first day in the new location one hour prior to her Grand Opening, she united a glowing couple in marriage, dashed back to the kitchen, grabbed her chef's apron, seasoned the soup du jour, and greeted the first day crowds at the door with aplomb. Now tell me she could've done that without a list.

Open for lunch 11 a.m. to 3 p.m Monday - Thursday, 11 a.m. to 4 p.m. on Friday and Saturday. Teas by reservation Friday and Saturday 2 p.m. to 4 p.m.

THE COUNTRY TEA GARDEN

220 Johnson Road
Selah, WA 98942
509-697-7944

Ever since the Chinese emperor Shen Nung first discovered tea when its leaves drifted into his drinking water while gardening, tea and gardens have been inseparable. Today at The Country Tea Garden those same breezes stir the more than 200 rosebushes lovingly nurtured by owner Bev Gabbard. As many as 75 garden lovers can be seated for tea in the five gazebos that dot her verdant grounds. During summer months a traditional Afternoon Tea, overseen by manager Nel Alden, is served to lace covered tables set amid lush perennial gardens. Statuary and fish ponds complete the oasis feeling.

In winter, the garden sleeps under a veil of lights and the warmth of the indoor six table tearoom beckons. The perfumed scent of summer roses is supplanted with the comfortable aroma of fresh soups and hot scones. Christmas is a very special time here, with the tables dressed festively in red skirts with lace toppers, poinsettias and lights galore. Locally known for the complete array of angel and Santa merchandise the small shop carries, it is also home to gifts and indulgences for the tea lover.

No doubt the gardening emperor would have felt right at home at The Country Tea Garden where botany and tea combine again in the nicest way.

June through September: open Tuesday through Friday, as well as the second Saturday of the month, 10 a.m. to 4 p.m. Closed in October to reopen in mid-November to the third week of December, Tuesday through Saturday 4 p.m. to 8 p.m. Available for small weddings, receptions and group events. Call to confirm the schedule or inquire on your planning an event.

THE CRUMPET SHOP

1503 First Avenue
Seattle, WA 98101
206-682-1598

In 1907 two brothers awash in riches from the Alaska gold fields improved upon a little farmer's market operating unofficially at the foot of Pike Street in Seattle. Building shops and laying out stall space in an organized manner, the Goodwin brothers created what is today the oldest continuously operating farmer's market in the United States, the Pike Place Market. The market provides a forum where craftspeople and farmers can sell their goods directly to the public. The food is always the freshest, and the presentation often verges on theatrical. Today the market welcomes 9 million folks a year, many of them tourists.

This conviction that fresh is best is embraced at the Crumpet Shop. Simple, fresh crumpets with a light and delicate texture give the shop its moniker, but colorful wall boards at the order and go counter tell a story of crumpets as art. Crumpets toasted amd slathered with Vermont maple syrup, crumpets with hot pepper jelly and cream cheese, crumpets with local smoked salmon spread, or humble crumpets with butter and fresh preserves await you. A large colorful cat on the wall proclaims "The tea is out of the bag," and these loose teas are served in a bottomless mug to your counter seat or sidewalk bistro table.

Simple, straight forward, and decidedly non-prissy, the little retail section offers local and British preserves, sensible teapots, and private-label teas. The Crumpet Shop, while always busy, will never rush you, even as you loosen your belt and lick the last bits of jelly from your fingers. Like the Public Market's founding Goodwin brothers, the Crumpet Shop's owner Nancy knows that even a good idea can be improved upon, and welcomes you to enjoy it fully.

Open 8 a.m. to 5 p.m. all week long, but the hours may vary a little in winter so it might be best to call. Closed major holidays.

ELIZABETH & ALEXANDER ENGLISH TEA ROOM

23808 Bothell-Everett Highway
Bothell, WA 98021
425-489-9210

"Imagine yourself and an intimate friend slipping away to a quiet tranquil place where gentle music drifts in upon your ear while you sip a cup of fine English style tea, as the sweet discourse of your friendship lifts your heart. Imagine the atmosphere around you warming your soul like the glow of a familiar fire. Here is where you unburden your cares and let time slip sideways. Such a simple idea in such a complex world, but if it were a real place, would you come?"

I think we'll go right now. Care to join us? This lovely invitation graces the menu jacket of Elizabeth & Alexander English Tea Room and completely captures the spirit of their remarkable achievement. Since opening in the summer of 1998 this 1,200 square foot tea room has also captured the hearts and loyalty of many tea lovers. Located at the entry to the fun rural retail area Country Village, and heralded by its proximity to a bright red double-decker London bus, Elizabeth & Alexander provides a genuinely warm, intimate setting for tea in three lovely English country style rooms. The main Tea Parlor is decorated in rich jewel tones, opulent window treatments, and the warmth of a cozy gas fire. The Churchill Room is a cozy alcove with wing back chairs and bookcases, low tables and old war medals rendering a masculine patina. The Alexander Room affords your group privacy at one large round table, perfect for showers and parties. Wherever you are seated in the 14 table tea room, the attentive service, fine food and gentle grace here will make your visit a delight. Offering more than a dozen teas and five tea set menu choices all made on site from family recipes, the owners and their daughters Sarah Mould and Amy Whelham, have succeeded in creating that illusive ambience, tranquility. You will never feel rushed here. So "if it were a real place, would you come?" Yes, it's very real, and you really should come.

Open 8 a.m. to 4 p.m. Tuesday through Saturday. Closed Sunday. Open Monday at 11 a.m. for lunch and tea until 3 p.m. Reservations are advised for groups of 5 or more. Breakfast to 11 a.m., lunch 11 a.m. to 4 p.m. and Afternoon Tea noon to 4 p.m.

ENCHANTED TEA GARDEN

3208 - 6th Avenue
Tacoma, WA 98406
253-756-6603
or toll free 1-877-286-8408

> "We'll see if tea and buns can make the world a better place."
> *Kenneth Grahame*
> The Wind in the Willows

In the shade of a gnarled old Russian Olive tree in a century-old bungalow, a mother and daughter team share their enchantment with tea. A garden arbor beckons you down a winding path protected by hidden garden deities and mirrors to a time-warped terrace. Flowering vines climb to the sun as the garden fairy offers a cool drink  basin to the fluffy birds who join you for sandwich crumbs at teatime.

Inside, cloaked in the tantalizing aromas of baking scones, four tables are set for tea. The scones are becoming legendary in their creative variety: cranberry eggnog, cream currant with orange glaze, maple glazed walnut, almond poppyseed; and even savory scones of Gruyere with thyme, rosemary and sun-dried tomato, and jalapeno and cheddar. More than sixty different teas round out the menu of delicious sandwiches, curried chicken bisque, and imaginative salads.

If "tea and buns can make the world a better place", then Allison and Bridget are doing their part in this enchanted little tea garden and cottage in Tacoma.

Open Monday through Friday 10 a.m. to 5 p.m., Saturdays 11 a.m. to 5 p.m. with lunches or afternoon teas offered on each of those days between 11:30 a.m. and 4 p.m.

THE EXHIBITORS MALL

10312 - 120th Street East #4
Puyallup, WA 98374
253-841-0769
Website: www.exhibitorsmall.com

If you've lived around western Washington for long, it's almost impossible to think about Puyallup (home of the fair) without hearing that little advertising ditty in your head, "You can do it at a trot, you can do it at a gallop....do the Puyallup!" The curse of a really good memory is that I can even picture the farm animals dancing to it. Help me!

Good old country living is celebrated at a 4,000 square foot, year round country market on Puyallup's south hill, one block off Meridian at Exhibitors Mall. Here each booth is individually owned and decorated to display arts, handcrafts, antiques, and gifts in a welcoming, down home way. Since 1998 Kimarie Johnson has been offering visitors another kind of welcome, in the form of a homestyle Afternoon Tea. It is served on a tiered rack in a dining room reminiscent of a friend's country cottage. Local artisans have painted faux rugs and a whimsical chair rail, and all the chairs date back to a men's library from the 40s. These popular teas include finger sandwiches, fresh scones, confections, rock candy and tea cookies along with an endless pot of tea.

So whether you "do it at a trot, or do it at a gallop" tea in a craft mall is a fun way to spend the day. I can't help myself. "Do the Puyallup" (for tea.)

Shops are open Monday through Saturday 10 a.m. to 5 p.m., the lunchroom is open 11-3:30 p.m. with a large menu plus tea. Advance notice is greatly appreciated for tea. Diabetic requests are welcome. Also available for fun children's tea parties too.

FAIRGATE INN
BED & BREAKFAST

2213 N.W. 23rd Avenue
Camas, WA 98607
360-834-0861
Website: www.FairgateInn.com

You might expect to hear a chorus of "Hail to the Chief" (does it even have lyrics?) as you pull into the circular drive of Chris and Jack Foyt's grand new Fairgate Inn. "Presidential" is a description that leaps to mind, and please adjust your thinking if your idea of presidential runs to Hillary throwing armloads of Bill's clothes and pizza boxes off the Truman Balcony. Make no mistake - it is dignity and grace that reside in this house, with a good dash of romance to boot. In fact, the only similarity to that dwelling in that other Washington is the elegance of the Georgian Colonial styling and its color.

On almost three acres of Prune Hill, Chris's visionary and efficient husband Jack commanded the construction of a 12,000 square foot dream. Conceived as a luxury bed and breakfast inn with eight elegant suites for guests, (each with fireplace, whirlpool tub, and a sweep of territorial views); it is also drawing groups for business meetings, artistic events, fairytale Ballroom weddings or garden courtyard ones, and now, (more ruffles and flourishes here, please) Afternoon Teas.

Four formal teas will be held in the Georgian Ballroom throughout the year with its high ceiling, five chandeliers, and grand piano. Served on crisp starched linen and fine china, these teas mark major milestones of the calendar, Valentine's Day, Mother's Day, Autumn, a grand Victorian Christmas Tea with entertainment, as well as a Children's Christmas Tea. All are open to the public only by reservation. Additionally, the inn will host festive open house Plum Pudding and Tea at various times between Thanksgiving and Christmas. The Fairgate Inn will be gloriously draped in holiday finery and lights each year from early November through year end. For parties of 30 or more seeking a private tea celebration or shower at any time of the year, Chris will be delighted to welcome you with advance consultation and reservations.

The people who live in the West Wing of this house will get my vote for tea any day.

FOTHERINGHAM HOUSE BED & BREAKFAST

2128 W. 2nd Avenue
Spokane, WA 99204
509-838-1891
E-Mail:innkeeper@fotheringham.net

There's a neighborly air at the Fotheringham House as guests gather around tables murmuring contentedly over their tea. The aromas of good baking and the tinkle of silver on china meld into a comfortable, sociable feel. From the very first day in 1891 when the storybook Queen Anne's doors opened for the first mayor of Spokane, David B. Fotheringham, it has been a center for pleasant discourse and gatherings.

Jackie and Graham Johnson have restored the home to exceed its former beauty and opened the doors for guests as a gracious bed & breakfast inn. Surrounded by a cutting garden that supplies fresh blooms for the tables, broad swaths of color and texture extend indoors where vintage wallpaper and rag-rolled walls warm the setting. Hand rubbed wood mouldings, a carved fireplace and ball and spindle fretwork lead the eye to a remarkable tin ceiling. This same celebration of history extends to the furnishings, where guests luxuriate in a four poster feather bed under down comforters.

A player piano tinkles unobtrusively at teas for groups of 16 to 20. Served at tables dressed with lace and fresh flowers, delicate porcelain and an antique samovar, the traditional finger sandwiches and rich scones are followed by three sweets, one of which is always chocolate. In keeping with the historic perspective of this lovely setting, Jackie presents a program or speaker celebrating the Age of Elegance as part of the tea. Please plan your event for 16 to 20 guests here at least three weeks in advance, and experience the neighborliness of this charming home for yourself.

THE GARDEN COURT
FOUR SEASONS OLYMPIC HOTEL

411 University St.
Seattle, WA 98101
206-621-1700

Local historian and journalist Nard Jones described early Seattle as "a sea of mud punctuated by stumpage," and early photographs don't do much to dispute his dismal viewpoint. The Great Fire of 1889 erased, perhaps fortuitously, most of the early rudimentary attempts to achieve grace and beauty in the buildings of Seattle. It wasn't for another 35 years that this clean canvas was used to create the materpiece Olympic Hotel, today the Four Seasons Olympic Hotel.

As you would expect, comfort, service and good taste abound. An enlightened renovation project in the 80s has heightened the glamour and majesty of the setting, which in turn attracts glamorous and majestic people. Almost from the beginning the hotel became the epicenter for Seattle tea culture. In the peaceful elegance of the high-ceilinged, naturally-lighted Garden Court, four or five generations have relaxed over tea. Unobtrusive, yet impeccably attentive service is the standard here. Excellent cream scones, imaginative tea sandwiches, dainty petit fours, and tea breads presented on fine china fulfill both your appetite and your high expectations.

Seattle has come a long way from "mud and stumpage", and nowhere is that evolution more evident than over a pot of good tea in the Garden Court of the Four Seasons.

Tea is served daily 3 to 5 p.m. Reservations, especially during the holidays, are strongly recommended.

GINGKO TEA

4343 N.E. University Way
Seattle, WA 98105
206-632-7298
Website: www.gingkot.com

Stress levels run high at espresso stands, and I think it's more than the caffeine content causing that restlessness. There's a harsh edge to the language of coffee as opposed to tea. Where you gently "steep" your tea, they grind and drip; we serve our beverage in a "china teacup" and cover our pot with a "cozy", they serve theirs in styrofoam and cover it with a to-go lid; while tea celebrates "leaves", theirs is dependent on the lowly bean; we enjoy ours by the "sip" and they get theirs by the shot. "Gimme a double tall skinny with a whip!" I've heard them shout shamelessly over the roar of the passing monorail. A sign at a coffeecart in Oregon threatened me with "A Slap Alongside the Head" for which they wanted me to pay them $2.50. (I was relieved to learn it was only their special high-octane java jolt du jour.) Tea is simple. Tea is civilized. Tea is never, ever harsh.

Genial Gingko Tea owner Jerry Liu understands this desire for relief from harshness and stress. In the clean simplicity of his ten table tea emporium on high energy University Way, he deftly dispenses good tea and good cheer daily. Choose from a large offering of loose teas sold by weight, or order a pot to enjoy with the ever-changing montage of pastries and Asian nibblies he offers as you watch the colorful foot-traffic of "The Ave". Gingko Tea is one of only a handful of places offering the new iced "pearl tea" with marble sized chewy, sweet tapioca balls. No kidding.

Gracious and knowledgable, Jerry and his staff would never offer you a slap anyplace.

Open 11 a.m. to 8 p.m. Monday through Friday, noon to 8 p.m. weekends.

GRANT HOUSE RESTAURANT

1101 Officer's Row (off Evergreen Blvd.)
Vancouver, WA 98661
360-696-1727

Having just emerged from an election year rife with dangling chads and bellicose rhetoric, one is struck by the simplicity of Ulysses S. Grant's 1868 acceptance speech for the Presidency. "Let us have peace," he said. A good order that still prevails at the Grant House Restaurant where special "tea and scones hours" have been decreed by owner Bill Hayden.

Built from logs in 1849 on a slope above the Hudson's Bay Company's stockade, the historic building that houses Grant House Restaurant was frequented by U.S. Grant during his term of army duty here in 1852-53 when it housed the regimental headquarters. Grant was so fond of Vancouver that he spent his year here trying out various "get-rich-quick" schemes that would have allowed him to purchase land and bring his young family west. He saw the dream melt like the blocks of Alaskan ice he tried to transport to San Francisco. He watched as the dream blackened with his potato crop on Sauvie Island when hit with flooding that year. Grant even began a used farm animal business in which he purchased exhausted and emaciated animals of the Oregon Trail pioneers. After fattening them and caring for them for two months to sell in San Francisco the bottom fell out of the market, and Grant and his hapless partners netted only enough to pay for the pampered herd's vacation trip to sunny California.

Camaraderie and good food brought people together in this old building during Grant's tour of duty 150 years ago, as it does today during tea and scones hours of the Grant House Restaurant. A changing menu of scones are offered with Devonshire cream and apricot-red onion marmalade as well as several tea choices, served at fifteen covered tables in a setting rich in history. Grant was no doubt cooking up some new scheme that would have allowed him to stay in Vancouver when he received a promotion to Captain which transferred him to a northern California army regiment of which he later said, "All I did was push a pen, look wise and draw my pay."

Tea and Scone Hours: 2-4 p.m. weekdays. Also serving lunch and dinners.

GREEN GABLES GUESTHOUSE

1503 Second Avenue West
Seattle, WA 98119
206-282-6863 Toll free 800-400-1503

In 1851 one of Seattle's proud founding fathers, David Denny, gave a quick shove to Northwest tourism. He pushed the fledgling city into the national spotlight center stage declaring,"There is plenty of room for one thousand travelers - come at once!"

Near the heart of the city is Green Gables Guesthouse. Transcending the stark simplicity of earlier Craftsman style homes, the 1904 inn embodies the best of Seattle hospitality with seven tastefully appointed period rooms on Queen Anne Hill. Inside the mood is snug and sheltered. Softly rounded hand-rubbed woods give off a warm glow as delicate patterns of color dance off the leaded glass.

Since 1991, during the inn's more peaceful months of November through May, the house has been made available by reservation for intimate groups (minimum of 12, maximum of 15) to experience the magic of a three course Afternoon Tea for your special celebration. The menu choices are lavish, and worked out with you well ahead of time. These choices can include cashew chicken tea sandwiches, Washington pears steamed in brandy, stuffed sauteed mushrooms, oven crepe with compote, open faced smoked salmon finger sandwiches, lemon tarts and souffles with a full complement of teas.

Green Gables Guest House can be an elegant backdrop for your special celebration with a little advance planning.

IF ONLY TEACUPS COULD TALK

4729 - 225th Ave. N.E.
Redmond, WA 98053
425-868-3137 or 425-844-9300
E-Mail: shawnvanh@aol.com

For centuries the simple phrase "Come for tea!" has meant so much more than simply slaking thirst. All of the letters needed to spell the word 'comfort' are nestled in that simple invitation. It conveys a message of care and connection, and says to your guest that she is valued enough that you want to slow down your busy pace and really listen and learn from her. Tea is simple, tea is civilized, and with any luck at all we will never, ever be subjected to 'drive-thru tea rooms'.

Sandy Stauffer understands tea. Sandy grew up on a dairy farm in Pennsylvania. While her memories include the 365 day a year effort of farming, frozen puddles and rising before the sun; what she remembers the most is that her mother, Phyllis Wasson Evey, would carve out a special time with her daughter everyday for tea. "Our tea times weren't fancy by any means," Sandy reminisces today, "but they were soul soothing quiet moments we cherished."

Today Sandy and tea friend, business partner, and aspiring innkeeper Shawn Van Houten offer this chance for calm and connection. Tea parties, customized for you in their charming homes are available on Fridays and Saturdays by reservation. Your circle of eight to twelve companions will be treated to traditional tea served from elegant three-tiered trays, in your choice of their private homes in Redmond or Woodinville.

With Shawn and Sandy as your hostesses, you can carve out a little time for care, comfort, and connection yourself. Come for tea!

IMPERIAL TEA COURT

18230 E. Valley Highway #135
Kent, WA 98032
425-251-8191 or 800-567-5898
Website: www.imperialtea.com

> *"Tea is a work of art and needs a master hand to bring out*
> *its noblest qualities."*
> *Okakura Kakuzo*

In a point-and-click, grab-and-go world, it's nice to know some ancient traditions and ceremonies are alive and well and living in Kent.

The Imperial Tea Court was the very first traditional Chinese tea house in the United States when it opened its rosewood doors in San Francisco in 1993. Roy Fong, celebrated tea expert, consultant and Daoist priest founded the endeavor to "reestablish the ancient and sacred rite of tea which dates back to the time of Lu Yu." That same authenticity prevails at the second Imperial Tea Court opened a couple years ago in the Great Wall Shopping Mall of Kent, a shopping area that is a virtual celebration of Chinese foods, Oriental arts and herbalists.

Jason Burke is so dedicated to tea that rumor has it that he carries his own personal teapot in a padded briefcase when he travels. As director of the International Tea Masters Association and manager in this location he brings both passion and knowledge about tea to the public. At ten tables in this serene setting you are encouraged to participate in tea tastings that not only engage all your senses, but require that you slow your pace.

Tea paraphernalia from CDs of tea music to Yixing pottery and other unique and handcrafted teapots line the shelves, but there is no question that tea is center stage here. More than 50 types of tea, some of them extremely rare and special, are offered for sale by the ounce in the retail area.

The Imperial Tea Court's trademarked byline is "Experience the Tradition." The ceremony and tastings here honor those traditions in the best possible way.

Open 10:30 a.m. to 8 p.m. seven days a week. A private room, the Lu Yu Room, is available for groups of up to 6.

ISLAND TEA COMPANY

1664 East Main - D
Freeland, WA 98249
360-331-6080
E-Mail: hallberg@whidbey.com

> "I can see the future and it's so bright it hurts my eyes."
> *Oprah Winfrey*

A few years ago two crafty young ladies stood huddled with their art under a dripping awning at yet another street fair. The gray skies and drizzle had slowed even the Goretex-cloaked Northwest art fair strollers, but the lull in business gave these friends a welcome chance to chat about their dreams. In their talks they created tea rooms in the air, brimming with their crafts and charm, lacey and comfortable, hospitable and unpretentious, havens for friendships to be renewed. Bright dreams for a gray day.

Island
Tea
Company

Fast forward to the late 90s and you will find both ladies joyfully entrenched in the dreams they envisioned. Each now owns a popular tearoom, for those two damp ladies were Happi Favro, now owner of Attic Secrets in Marysville; and Dori Hallberg founder of Island Tea Company on Main Street in Freeland.

Snug and unpretentious, this joyful little shop has the casual feel of gathering around your friend's (the artistic one) kitchen table for tea. Tea is sold by the pot or by the cup to be savored with biscotti or fresh locally made cookies at small tables indoors or outside in a little garden. Shelves display the 50 or so loose teas Dori offers for sale by weight, including her very own signature blend Island Breeze, embued with the richness of ripe Northwest blackberry. All sorts of tea accoutrements, carefully selected gifts, crafts and Northwest gourmet goodies make this a popular spot for gift shoppers.

From my Camano Island home I can see the lights of Freeland on the next island over, Whidbey, and like dreams and friendships, they glow particularly brightly at Island Tea Company.

Open Tuesday through Saturday 10 a.m. to 4 p.m. with extended hours during the Christmas season.

IVY TEA ROOM
at BJ's Corner Cottage

30 S.E. 12th
College Place, WA 99324
509-525-4752 or 877-326-2661

I can't lay claim to a family tree with boughs laden with tea drinkers, or any kind of beverage connoisseurs for that matter. It skipped like a stone over three or four generations of my gene pool I guess. To this day my Mother still considers "Taster's Choice" a gourmet coffee, "freeze-dried, Sweetie, like the astronauts drink!" Don't get me wrong, Mom likes a good cup of tea when presented to her, but anything lukewarm and brownish resembling either strong tea or weak coffee served in a mug, is "good enough." (We're going to have the teabags in her cupboard carbon-dated by a lab someday.)

The Ivy Tea Room's owner Pat Choisser's mother, on the other hand, passed on the genetic encryption for a natural born tea lover. With roots in England and enchanting childhood tea parties on porcelain, Pat grew up with a lovingly steeped cup of tea in her hand. In homage to family tradition, today ten tables are dressed in their vintage finery for tea in a quiet corner of her gift shop near the college. Old rose patterned wallpaper and soft pink lighting recall the gentility of a Victorian parlor, enhanced by the ambience of a small fireplace and bubbling fountain. A gentle piano plays. Tea is delivered, snuggled in its floral cozy, along with a timer so it can steep just perfectly before pouring into the charmingly mismatched antique English china cups.

Pat's food emphasis is on low fat and heart-healthy vegetarian fare, and recently she added lunch options and romantic candlelit dinners to her menu. While drop-ins are welcome for an Afternoon Tea of scones, finger sandwiches and desserts anytime, Pat's elegant four-course High Tea with personalized service and remarkable attention to detail takes longer for her to prepare, so she requires one day advance reservations for it. Allow up to 2 hours to truly savor this graceful meal where absolutely nothing could ever be classified as just "good enough."

Monday through Thursday 9:30 a.m. to 6 p.m., Friday 9:30 a.m. until sunset, and Sunday noon to 5 p.m.

JEAN-PIERRE'S GARDEN ROOM

316 Schmidt Place
Tumwater, WA 98501
360-754-3702

"Bring bread to the table and your friends will bring their joy to share."
Old French Proverb

I'm sure the French won't mind if I change the shopping list for their old proverb. I'd like it to be tea brought to the table *s'il vous plait*. I'm trying out a low carbo diet lately and miss my old pal bread dearly, and isn't tea just more joyful than bread anyway? There, *fini*. I am absolutely certain that French born Jean-Pierre and his American wife Kerri understand this. A raconteur in the finest European tradition, Jean-Pierre's business philosophy has been since the beginning in 1997 that "tea is a good taste to be shared with good friends."

And share they do with *savoir faire* in a charming old building that once was home to *les gendarmes*, the Tumwater Police. You're invited to take tea by the fireplace, in a comfortable old armchair, or at the table of their renovated home, and during summer months, several tables dot the garden. High Tea is served with one day's advance reservation and includes traditional finger sandwiches, pastries, scones with fruited butters, and fresh seasonal fruits all served with penache. There is plenty of joy to share, bring your friends.

Tea is offered with 24 hour advance reservation from 11 a.m. to 2 p.m. Tuesday through Friday.

JUST PRETEND

612 Lawrence Street
Port Townsend, WA 98368
360-385-0159

Be very still for a moment and close your eyes. Got them closed? Just pretend you are a little girl again and you're invited to a magical teaparty in a wonderful old storybook Victorian house in Port Townsend. There's a beautiful table set in a sunny room with pink and white china and your very own personal hand-lettered placecard.

There are pretty foods that even taste good. There's a beautiful cake and party favors for you to keep. There are games full of make-believe and a dress-up fashion show with a photo for grandma. There's music and friendship and laughter. Sound good?

Snap out of it! You don't have to pretend anymore, because children's art teacher and tasteful lady Patricia Minnish is in the business of making fantasy into fanciful reality with her charming teaparties for children. Patricia coordinates delightfully lavish theme parties (you can create the theme or use one from her collection) such as her popular Fairy Princess Party, which begins with an imaginative and original story about a little fairy who has lost her wings. There on the wall is a beautiful picture of the hapless fairy, and a game begins of 'Pin the Wings on the Fairy'. The fairy's reward to the players? Magic fairy dust, of course.

Patricia welcomes parties of four or more, any age, any occasion or maybe no occasion at all, for the young, or the young at heart. Just pretend.....

JUST YOUR CUP O' TEA

305 Pacific Avenue
Bremerton, WA 98337
360-377-9457

It's not easy being a Morning Person. Night Owls sneer at us if we chirp 'good morning'. Parties start with the Night Owls' body clocks in mind. I even uncovered that the vast government conspiracy to rob Morning People of early sunlight has a secret code name - Daylight Savings Time. Who are they saving it for, you ask? Night Owls, that's who. My British husband rhapsodizes about the European penchant for dinner at 9 p.m. I could get into that, so long as it was served to me in my pajamas. My late grandmother, Ideala Godiva Gregory Foster, was a Morning Person too, and for years we had the most precious phone conversations before the rest of the world awoke. Over our respective cups of Irish Breakfast Tea, we sorted out the state of her rosebushes and then moved on to the state of the world.

Pat and Susan Wright are Morning People too, rising early and cheerfully to open their popular purple tea shop in Bremerton every day of the week. This sunny shop is spacious and friendly, with simple seating for 45 in an uncluttered setting. Almost 50 teas are stocked here, sold by weight to take home and enjoy, or by the cup or pot to your table. Linger with your tea to savor the good company and a highly recommended variety of fresh bagel sandwiches, (their customers wrote to me about the glories of their chicken salad.) Tea accoutrements and books line the shelves, much is for sale. Retired from the Navy, Pat and Susan based Just Your Cup o' Tea on the many neighborhood tea shops they visited during their travels in Japan, where gracious service is an art with which the Wrights returned. Special events include a monthly forum for local writers and poets to give readings in the evening, and even an open mike if you'd like to share your talents. Since I have no talents at all in the evening, you'll have to join me earlier in the day at this welcoming and bright tea shop in Bremerton.

Open seven days a week. Hours vary with the season. Open early weekdays with closing about 6 p.m. but it may be best to call.

KATE'S TEA ROOM & CURIOS

301 West Main Street
Monroe, WA 98272
360-794-5199

I used to think that you reached middle-age when your age was a higher number than your bra size. I realized, however, this thinking was seriously flawed. It arrived too quickly for one thing and it only worked for women and cross-dressers. Later in life I decided middle-age arrives when you start buying sensible shoes and elastic waistband pants; clothing whose sole criteria for selection is comfort, with a sneer of disdain for fashion. When those events occured, in some distant future, the portents of middle-age would loom.

My sturdy brown lace-up oxfords (with wiggle room for the toes) make a happy scrunching sound on the walkway to Kate's Tea Room & Curios. Housed in a sweet Victorian gingerbread cottage in downtown Monroe since moving her popular tea room in March of 1999, the cottage is also home to her expanded ventures in antiques, collectibles and even a busy limosine service.

Kate's tea menu spans the globe and features an extensive variety of high quality black, herbal, oolongs, greens and flavoreds. Four different Afternoon Tea meals are featured, with or without her good scones, as well as soups, sandwiches, a salad bar and yummy desserts rounding out the comfort food fare and stretching my eleastic waistband just a little.

Everyone deserves a bit of comfort in their day. It may be as simple as stretchy waistbands and sensible shoes, or it can be a relaxing as a homey tea at Kate's in Monroe, perhaps both. Either way, welcome to middle age!

Open Monday through Saturday 10 or 11 a.m. to 5 p.m. Now offering dinner on Friday and Saturday, call for details.

LA BELLE SAISON

278 Winslow Way East
Bainbridge Island, WA 98110
206-780-4064

In May of 1792, Captain Vancouver's three masted sloop *Discovery* rode anchor at the very edge of the known world. The crew of 100 had set sail from England a year earlier, and had followed the rocky coastline of the Pacific Northwest through weather so perilous that they had even missed discovering the gaping mouth of the Columbia River when they passed it on their voyage north. Anchoring off the shore of Bainbridge Island, battered spars were refitted to the ship while the aroma of "spruce tea", a preventative brew to ward off scurvy, filled the air from the large vat in which it steeped. It is noted in Vancouver's journal they were visited by a canoe bearing local natives who greeted them with a ceremonial song, accompanied by the percussive thumps of their paddles against the sides of the canoe as they circumnavigated the 100 foot British vessel. The diary bemoans that no food accompanied the song to the ship that day, because "our sportsmen and fishermen had little success in either pursuit."

A meal the young Captain would have certainly enjoyed is offered just a quick paddle away in Winslow today at Jeannie Alexis Wood's patisserie La Belle Saison. Opened in 1999 to celebrate the local bounty of the island, this cozy little 10 table bistro offers something else the good Englishman would have savored - an Afternoon Tea, and one not made from spruce trees. Tea is offered in country Victorian charm in a sunny cream colored room refreshed with white wainscotting. An antique hutch displays pretty tea supplies, and tables topped with floral fabric echo the romantic art and floral plates decorating the walls. Chef John Hewus oversees tea sets for four levels of appetite and time, from the glories of his three-tiered High Tea, a two-tiered Afternoon Tea, to a plated Cream Tea and Children's Tea. Marvelous baked goods are the signature touch here, and while you may not be welcomed with a serenade, gentle music and warm hospitality are assured. Vancouver would have been so refreshed by his tea he probably would have taken a nice big bag of scones for the crew to have with their cups of spruce.

Open for breakfast, lunch and teas, 8 a.m. to 5 p.m. Tuesday through Saturday, and for brunch 9 a.m. to 2 p.m. on Sunday. Tea is offered between the hours of 2:30 p.m. and 5 p.m. Tuesday through Saturday.

TEA AT LACONNER FLATS

15920 Best Road
Mount Vernon, WA 98273
360-466-3190

The unpainted old building with a weathered hand-painted sign, "The Granary," intrigued us. We would peek in at it through a tall hedge as we drove through the tulip fields that carpet the flat land between LaConner and Mount Vernon on our way to Christianson's Nursery next door. The agrarian origin of the building was enhanced by a riotous rainbow of tulip fields on one side and the large well-tended grounds it shielded from view on the other. Formerly a big sturdy farm structure built in 1913 for grain storage, owner Mrs. Hart now offers Afternoon Teas here by reservation only. Rough hewn planks form the floor and walls of the rustic open-beamed room, where tea is served with grace notes of white linen, antique china and depression glassware.

Like the most intriguing person, the 11 acre gardens do not immediately unveil themselves to you. An old apple tree allee leads to a formal rose garden which in turn opens onto a grassy rhododendron walkway that leads to a large pond rimmed with lily pads. Giant poplar trees shield the entire garden from wind and impart an intimate, secure feeling. In spring the gardens come alive with both bloom and songbirds.

Teas are served year-round by reservation only, with no party size requirements at all. Several times a year good neighbor John Christianson of Christianson's Nursery leads guided walks through the Hart's gardens culminating in tea here. (Schedule information on those guided garden events can best be obtained through Christianson's "Garden Gazette," a charming newletter for which you can sign up on your next visit to the nursery.)

A rustic old granary, gnarled apple trees leading to a mature garden, heirloom roses, vintage china - tea has a timeless feel in this verdant Skagit Valley setting.

LANGLEY TEA ROOM

112 Anthes Avenue
Langley, WA 98260
360-221-6292

When Captain Vancouver explored the shoreline of the Pacific Northwest more than 200 years ago, a glimpse of nostalgia accompanies his journal entry after viewing Whidbey Island, "A picture so pleasing could not fail to call to our remembrance certain delightful and beloved situations in Old England." he rhapsodized. After two years of rugged coastal exploration who could blame the 32 year old captain for leaning on the deck rail, longing for a good cup of tea?

Today in the charming village of Langley, Pat and John Powell have created a tea room Captain Vancouver (and the more refined of his crew members) would have enjoyed. Simple and snug like a berth in a ship, two traditions meet here in tea. East meets West on their menu, with housemade scones, crumpets, finger sandwiches and savory luncheon pastries sharing the table with sushi, Japanese salads, vegetarian dishes and noodle soups. At the heart of it all, of course, is tea; more than 30 different teas are offered here.

Travel to Whidbey is scenic from both directions, either through historic LaConner and dramatic Deception Pass bridge or on the Washington State Ferry out of Mukilteo. Now when you find yourself leaning on that deck railing, relishing Captain Vancouver's view and longing for tea, you know where to go.

Open everyday except Wednesday 11 a.m. to 5 p.m. Open for Japanese dinners on Friday, Saturday, and Monday nights.

THE LIBRARY CAFE

850 N.W. 85th St.
Seattle, WA 98117
206-789-5682

"Shall we retire to the library for tea, my dear?" Dapper leading man Ronald Colman proffered his arm to some chiffon-swathed blonde actress in almost every 1930 film ever made. I've always been swept away by old movies. The people were so civil to each other, even when they fought, "Take that, old chap!" Ladies drifted through large high ceilinged rooms in chiffon floor-length gowns all day, and they even had libraries right there in their houses.

On busy 85th Street in Ballard, a 70-year-old house has seen several incarnations. At times a fireplace shop and a bookstore, it has recently been reborn into a happy amalgamation using the remnants of both, The Library Cafe. With three fireplaces and books galore, owner Mary Cleveland now invites you to Afternoon Tea, Wednesday through Saturday by reservation. The Library Cafe is a homestyle cafe-antique-bookstore housed in a white clapboard building with jewel tone trim. Reminiscent inside of the village pubs of the English countryside right down to the exposed brick walls, tea is served in a spacious and continually changing setting, because almost everything - treasures, books and furniture is for sale.

The traditional finger sandwiches, scones, cakes and pastries are made on site and served with a selection of twenty teas. You're even invited to have a glass or bottle of champagne served with your tea, (something Ronald Colman and the blonde in chiffon would have ordered certainly.)

Tea is served Wednesday through Saturday 2 p.m. to 4 p.m. by reservation only. Breakfast and lunch are offered Tuesday through Sunday 8 a.m. to 3 p.m.

THE LIGHTHOUSE TEA ROOM AND GIFT SHOP

S. 519 Scott Avenue
Newport, WA 99156
509-447-3008
E-Mail: jbwwm@povn.com

The lights of the old boarding house must have looked inviting to travellers in this most northeastern margin of Washington. Built in 1905, the three-story crisp white Craftsman style home was a comforting beacon of hospitality for those moving to and through this mining and supply area 50 miles north of Spokane. Sternwheelers plied the waters of the Pend Oreille River, docking on the west bank at Newport laden with the travel-worn and world-weary who found their way to the inviting boarding house for tea and hospitality.

Lona and John Bockmuehl bought the old boarding house in 1998 and set about creating a homey family tea room and gift shop. Sunlight filters through lace in the old dining room, dappling the battenberg cutwork covering the four tables set with vintage bone china for tea. With fresh flowers from the garden and soothing music accompaniment, more than a dozen tea blends are offered with a light treat of cookies, fresh fruit and a truffle. With advance notice, Lona will prepare her signature scones hot from the oven with Devonshire cream and apricot jelly, certainly worthy of a call ahead. A crackling wood fire warms the parlor on crisp days, and the baby grand piano shares the setting with a festively decorated tree crafted from local hops. Unique gifts and art fill two floors of the old house.

Travellers are passing through Newport in greater numbers than ever before thanks to Sunset Magazine's recent feature on The International Selkirk Loop. This is the 280 mile loop that wanders rural roads circling the scenic Selkirk Mountains, connecting the Pend Oreille River Valley with the Canadian Kootenay Valley, the website (www.selkirkloop.org) is invaluable in planning your trip. In addition to frequent sightings of moose, bear and caribou this tranquil drive encompasses two free ferry rides and towns rich with Northwest history. A new generation of travellers are welcome once again to refresh with tea in the dining room of this charming home in Newport. The glow of heartfelt hospitality still lights the path to its door.

Open 10 a.m. to 5 p.m. Tuesday through Saturday. Call for information on extended hours and days during the holiday season.

LONGFELLOW HOUSE

203 Williams-Finney Road
Kelso, WA 98626
360-423-4545
E-Mail: lngfelhs@pacifier.com

There is a note of family prophecy in beloved American poet Henry Wadsworth Longfellow's *Tales of a Wayside Inn* when he wrote: "We should be lonely here, were it not for friends that in passing sometimes tarry o'ernight, and make us glad by their coming."

In rural Kelso on a secluded lane a century later, hosts Richard and Sally Longfellow attend to business at their cozy little Bed & Breakfast Cottage. So cozy in fact, that booking a room means that the main floor of this snug shelter becomes yours, all yours, during your stay, and you will be the only guests. You can even enjoy the Longfellows' hospitality without overnighting if you prefer, with a tea.

Sally's local reputation as an excellent cook and gracious hostess led her down the tea path, and she now offers tea parties of six people or more at Longfellow House. Sally will customize the tea menu for your special occasion. Numerous birthdays, church socials and special friendship celebrations are enjoyed here regularly where the sound of a Victorian player piano can accompany your scones and local blackberry jam, tea breads, muffins and other homemade treats served on pretty china. An English visitor wrote Sally a note of tribute when she said, "...I have to say that your love of tea provided us with quite simply the best cuppa we've had this side of the pond. It's as good as anything you could be offered in the quaintest of tea rooms in any village in England. I hope you can spread the appreciation of this delight far and wide in your country."

So have your group of six or more tarry for tea at Longfellow House Bed & Breakfast Cottage. Sally will be made glad by your coming.

LUPINE COTTAGE

4830 Lupine Lane N.W.
Silverdale, WA 98383
360-692-8619
E-Mail: lupinecottage@hotmail

My Aunt Marwayne, through twist of fate and abundance of love, has raised her two youngest granddaughters, 13 year old twins Monica and Maria-lynn, since they were toddlers. Not only has this kept my dear aunt remarkably youthful at 83, but it has created two delightful young ladies with good manners and social graces whose company I enjoy. I promise I won't preach because I skipped motherhood entirely, and I swear I'm not talking about your children, but (you knew there would be a 'but' didn't you) aren't there just a few too many kids these days who, let's see - how can I put this nicely, seem to have been raised by wolves?

On more than two acres of storybook forest in Silverdale, Sandy Sinclair has been introducing the gentle art of manners one happy teaparty at a time since 1995. Owner of Lupine Cottage Gift Shop, Sandy was inspired to create theme tea parties celebrating the popular American Girl doll series, and classic literature, *Anne of Green Gables* and *Alice in Wonderland*. These successful events even led to performances of *Little House on the Prairie* drama and a Christmas play. With seating for 30, the child-pleasing menu (using her own secret recipe for tea sandwiches that draws rave reviews), miniature quiche, fruit scones, cookies and fruit is all served on fine china as Sandy deftly blends an equally palatable etiquette lesson into the tea.

Crafts, including the old time arts of quilting, flower pressing, spinning wool, and making paper round out the event. "We're trying to show children there are some graceful things to learn. I think it's important that these things be kept alive," says Sandy. I think we need a few more Aunt Marwaynes and Sandy Sinclairs in this busy world.

Advance reservations are necessary for the tea parties. Call to discuss yours, and keep in mind boys are equally welcome here!

MARKETSPICE
AT THE PIKE PLACE MARKET

85-A Pike Street
Seattle, WA 98101
1-800-735-7198
425-883-1220 office and mail order
E-Mail: mktsps@juno.com
Website: www.marketspice.com

The same year Madame Curie learned those long lab hours had snagged her a Nobel Prize for chemistry, an unheralded band of tea and spice enthusiasts were mixing and measuring and concocting in a humble little shop at the Pike Place Market. It was 1911, and alas, while there may never be a Nobel Prize for teas and spices, 90 flavorful years of happy MarketSpice customers has got to be its own reward.

This tea and spice bazaar, a fixture of the teeming public market, houses their signature tea blend, redolent with citrus oils and rich spices. It's that lively aroma that scents this little plank-floored marketplace full of hundreds of other teas, spices and accoutrements for the kitchen. The helpful staff keep a tasting pot on hand for you to sample as you browse this cozy corner of the public market. (Ducking in here is also a good way to avoid being hit with a flying chinook salmon hurled with glee by the famed zealot fishmongers.)

Do pay a visit to MarketSpice next time you're at the market, where for 90 years they have made tons of teas and spice blends, one small batch at a time by hand, with the conviction that "Spice is the Variety of Life."

9 a.m. to 6 p.m. Monday through Saturday, closing at 5 p.m. on Sunday. Call 425-883-1220 for a catalog or visit their website.

MORNING GLORY CHAI

2213 N.W. Market St.
Seattle, WA 98107
206-297-2424
E-Mail: jessica@speakeasy.org

> "Each human being must keep alight within him the sacred flame
> of madness. And he must behave like a normal person."
> *Paulo Coehlo*

Now here's a different kind of tea place that doesn't so much march to the beat of a different drummer as much as it reggaes, belly dances, salsas and tarantellas to it.

Morning Glory Chai is housed on staid Market Street in the Ballard district of Seattle, and youthful proprietor Jessica Vidican blithely describes her establishment as a "homey, hava-cuppa and stay awhile destination cafe, with Middle Eastern and Greek foods served with Latino-Asian flair and gypsy style informality."

Upbeat live music in the evenings is as spicy as the house recipe for chai, and a mini world bazaar of gifts are for sale. In case I haven't conveyed it, this is not your traditional afternoon tea spot, but shouldn't we all fan that "sacred flame of madness" every now and then?

Open 8 a.m. to whenever, and open as late as 10 or 11 p.m. on weekends.

MORNING GLORY TEA ROOM
at New Woman Books

315 W. Meeker
Kent, WA 98032
253-854-3487

In her memoir *A House with Four Rooms*, British author Rumer Godden espoused the Indian wisdom that to be human is to be "a house with four rooms - a physical, a mental, an emotional and a spiritual....unless we go into every room every day, even if only to keep it aired, we are not a complete person."

On Meeker Street in a storefront of historic downtown Kent, Judith Bakkensen has provided a sanctuary of sorts for women. As owner of King County's first bookstore to specialize in "books by, for, and about women" she has augmented that niche with seven tables thoughout the shop for a pot of good tea using triple-filtered water and light meals. Wherever possible, the use of locally grown and organic ingredients is emphasized.

This is a forget-the-hat-and-gloves, come as you are kind of haven for relaxation over tea and light meals. You'll find yourself in the best of company, books and other women on the path to wisdom. Replenishment and renewal for all aspects of your life await you on the bookshelves and in the teapots of this little bookstore/tea room.

Open Tuesday through Saturday 8:30 a.m. to 5 p.m.

ROSALIE WHYEL'S MUSEUM OF DOLL ART

1116 - 108th Avenue N.E.
Bellevue, WA 98004
425-455-1116

In 1992 doll enthusiasts of all ages celebrated the opening of a museum full of artistry, fantasy and whimsy. Rosalie Whyel's Museum of Doll Art, housed in a neo-Victorian structure in down-town Bellevue, became a great big dollhouse to a happy doll family numbering more than 1,200. Beloved companions of children of every era are celebrated here, from ancient wood effigies through Kewpie and thoroughly modern Barbie; this is a world of small wonders. The museum was created "for the preservation and exhibition of dolls as an artform." Just two years after opening, it was awarded the most coveted international prize of "Best Private Doll Museum in the World" in a ceremony in Paris.

Tea parties can now be held in the doll museum, where you may rent a sweet sunlit room adjoining the English Garden. Work with Jennifer Manatt to choose from two children's party packages - Birthday or English Tea Party. A self-guided tour of the fanciful museum and a delightful scavenger hunt is included in each two-hour event, with access to the garden as well. Either a birthday cake, balloons and party favors for the Birthday party; or traditional finger sandwiches in heart shapes with fresh fruit for the English Tea are provided. Seating for your party of up to 30 is at four round linen covered tables, and both party packages even include the invitations. A third option, for the 'do-it-yourselfer' is to simply rent the room for your own catered party plans. No matter which party plan you choose, with Jennifer's assistance this unique and special setting will assure a party that will linger in your children's memories for years and years, like the memory of a favorite doll.

PEKOE, A GLOBAL TEAHOUSE
at *World Spice Merchants*

1509 Western Avenue
Seattle, WA 98101
206-682-7274
E-Mail: hill@worldspice.com

Asking Tony Hill to name his favorite tea is like asking a father which child he loves best. Here is a tea lover with a palate so sophisticated to flavor nuances that "Guess the Tea" is a favorite pastime in his exciting spice and tea emporium perched at the top of the Pike Street Hillclimb in the shadow of the Public Market.

With comfortable plush couch and armchairs, tea chests, world maps, and a century old leather topped English table that's seen a bit of tea in its day, the shop is furnished in a color range from pekoe to jasmine. You are invited to sample any of the hundreds of the pure estate teas on hand, and a few baked goods if you're "peckish" (as the original owner of that leather topped table would say.)

Even more exciting may be to have your very own signature blend created just for you. It's a house specialty at Pekoe, and a fascinating, educational experience.

Incidentally, at least on this day, Tony's favorite was a rich, malty Assam from the Manjushree Estate. (It's Assam that gives the malty richness to many Irish Breakfast Teas.) Tony's business motto, "Authentic flavors from everywhere" sums up the ever-changing and unlimited world of tea.

Open Monday through Saturday 10 a.m. to 6 p.m. and Sunday noon to 5 p.m.

THE PERENNIAL TEA ROOM

1910 Post Alley
Seattle, WA 98101
206-448-4054
Tollfree 888-448-4054
website: perennialtearoom.com

I have a hunch that if there was a mountain of tea knowledge and you labored to the top of it to meet the resident tea guru to ask, "What is the meaning of tea?", you'd find Julee Rosanoff and Sue Zuege, and in unison they'd exclaim as they jumped up to pour you a cup, "Tea is for fun!"

Julee and Sue have been imparting knowledge and sharing the fun of tea for over ten years now in The Perennial Tea Room, a high energy little shopfront heralded from the Post Alley promenade by the traditional suspended iron tea kettle. Getting newcomers to be comfortable with the world of tea has been a quest of these two retired social workers, "There is no right or wrong with tea. It's just important that you enjoy the drinking of tea and that you enjoy your teapot. Whatever we can do toward that end, is what makes it fun for us."

With more than 70 loose teas in sniff jars and high quality prepackaged teas from England and Ireland, the sample pot is always hot. The tea advice or opinion is always free if you ask for it, and every possible functional accouterment known to the tea-drinking world rests on these simple shelves. Whether your taste runs to ceremonious Japanese cast iron pots, American-made Masa Fujii's new dripless teapots, delicate floral bone china from England, rich Russian cobalt blues, or the ever popular workhorse of teapots the comfy Brown Betty, you'll find them all here, hundreds of them. The level of service even extends to a test pour to make sure your new pot feels right in your hand. A little imported gourmet section beckons with McVities HobNobs and Cadbury Flakes, lemon curds, shortbread and Irish linen towels and cozies.

Two small tables by the window offer a nice respite in this warm, unpretentious environment, where you can have a cup or a pot of tea and a choice of four buttery shortbread. "An oasis of tea in latteland," they joke, and have discovered that some of their best new customers are those who appreciate the good coffee the Northwest offers. "Their palates are tuned for subtle tastes, much like wine buffs, and the huge flavor options tea provides can just be a whole new adventure for them to explore."

So spare yourself the effort of climbing the mountain of tea knowledge, just head to the Pike Place Market where hot tea and warm hospitality await. This is a place for fun and exploration and sociability, the meaning of tea.

Open everyday 10 a.m. to 5:30 p.m. except Sunday when they close at 5 p.m. Mail order and website shopping too.

PETALS GARDEN CAFE

1345 S. Sequim Avenue
Sequim, WA 98382
360-683-4541
E-Mail: petals@tenforward.com

"No worries, mate!" Optimistic Australians are often heard to say, and it's exactly that sunny "G'day!" spirit that's served transplanted Aussies Jim and Bronwyn Salmon well in the opening of Petals Garden Cafe in 1999. Promptly honored with 'Best Gourmet Dining Experience' title in Sequim, the Salmons' easy manner belies the three year effort that manifested the dream.

The Salmons have brought new life to an old greenhouse at the oldest herb farm in the state, lovely Cedarbrook Herb Farm. With a dramatic backdrop of the Straits of Juan de Fuca, the farm commands 12 perfumed acres. The old farmhouse, Historic Bell House, is now home to a lovely gift shop. As a gentle breeze wafts the scents of culinary herbs, elephant garlic and lavender from the gardens, diners now stroll to a converted greenhouse and patio to savor Afternoon Teas, prepared in a state of the art kitchen created from a humble tractor garage.

With a flair for a cuisine inspired by the freshness of Australian Farmer's Markets, the chefs prepare a fresh fruit sorbet with shortbread for starters, and an elegant 3-tiered stand overflows with treats handmade on site. Rich warm scones, flakey sausage rolls, toasted crumpet, lemon tart, chocolate cake, finger sandwiches, petit fours, and fruits are served on fine china, the repast augmented, of course, with good tea served from silver pots.

Sequim is a great destination for tea, with surrounding beauty to explore, 306 days of sunshine a year, shoreline and seabirds, and now a touch of Down Under for tea at Petals at Cedarbrook Herb Farm. It's all "fair dinkum, mate!"

Tea is offered from 2 p.m. - 5 p.m. daily. The cafe is open from 9 a.m. to 5 p.m. for breakfast and lunch, dinners on Friday and Saturday 'til 9 p.m.

PICCADILLY CIRCUS

1104 First Street
Snohomish, WA 98290
360-568-8212

"No little lily-handed baronet he,
a great broad-shoulder'd genial Englishman..."
Alfred, Lord Tennyson

How could the great bard Tennyson know he was describing Geoff Wall, owner with his lovely American-born wife Marion, of Piccadilly Circus in historic old town Snohomish? Apart from a few creaky middle-aged joints from sport injuries, he looks like he should be leading his beloved Manchester United Football Team (that's soccer to folks like me) onto the field, and you'd want to clear the path for him. Instead, the couple has created a little bit of Geoff's homeland right here.

Entering Piccadilly Circus transports you into a perfectly recreated British corner store, replete with the variety of foodstuffs and teas that make an anglophile or transplanted Brit stop in their sensible shoes and sigh. A large gift and collectible area sparkles with imported crystal and bone china backdropped with Irish linens and soft Scottish woolens. The Walls make frequent buying trips to the U.K. to keep the wonders flowing into this high-ceilinged and high quality gift section, and Marion's flair for display has the perfect forum in this turn of the century storefront.

Hand painted murals of the bucolic Yorkshire Dales lend enchantment to the walls of the indoor tea garden at the back of the shop. As the lights are dimmed for late afternoon teas served elegantly to your table, one by one stars appear overhead in the domed ceiling, a magical little wonderland for a tasty and authentic British tea.

Genial hosts Geoff and Marion Wall ponder "Why go to London when Jolly Old England is right here in Snohomish?"

Open seven days a week for lunch and teas, 8 a.m. to 5 p.m. Dinner is served Thursday through Saturday with the last seating at 8 p.m.

Pleasant Times

307 Third Street
Endicott, WA 99125
509-657-3727

Eastern Washington tea lovers are celebrating the rebirth, (after a two year pregnancy), of a popular European style tea room housed happily in a 1907 birthing house. Pleasant Times has returned to little Endicott, population 350. Not a moment too soon if you ask their avid fans, some who cheerfully drive five hours for their teas. Re-opened in a charmingly restored pink house that sparkles with gingerbread trim and rich period detail, this labor of love is a collaboration of the mother-daughter tea team Jean Cisneros and Marce Clements (and their hammer-wielding, ultra-supportive spouses).

Heralded from the street by lavender shutters painted with happy red Bavarian cabbage roses and a white picket fence; inside, the European flair continues with German lace sheers and cabbage rose draperies. Vintage floral carpet bespeaks a hushed Old World charm. An ever-changing mon-tage of items are available to grace your own home in the gift shop: Euro-pean new and vintage linens; antiques, collectibles, primitives and handmade folk art; books and tea party accessories.

Remarkable two hour, five-course High Teas are offered at least once a month, usually the first Saturday, many with special fanciful themes. Call to get on the mailing list for an event schedule. Each guest gets a little gift, marvelous food, and a wonderful, not just pleasant time. If you have a group of 8 or more, you can call to schedule a High Tea to suit your own schedule, and the ladies can advise you of local bed & breakfast places should you extend your stay. Little girl dressup tea parties are another popular specialty.

Blessed events are still happening in the old birthing house, and the really nice thing is, there's no labor for you at all!

Call for an event schedule for High Tea, or stop by for desserts, scones, and prix fixe luncheons Tuesday through Saturday 11 a.m. to 5 p.m.

POMEROY HOUSE
The Carriage House Tea Room

20902 N.E. Lucia Falls Road
Yacolt, WA 98675
360-686-3537
E-Mail: pomeroy@pacifier.com

The blossoms are bright on the fruit trees of the old orchards we pass on the country lane enroute to Pomeroy House. For the last three miles the road has hugged the bank of the Lewis River cascading through a lush, narrow valley, and we are reminded of Wales. With the open car windows we eavesdrop on the domestic disputes of nesting robins while carousing crows belt out a song to which only they can appreciate the melody. All the sounds of the countryside seem amplified in this peaceful setting. It seems timeless here, probably part of the original appeal it held for Mr. E.C. Pomeroy, the son of English immigrants, when he brought his wife and five children to make the valley their home in 1910.

The Pomeroy House is the oldest house in the Lucia Falls area, crafted into a formidable two story, six bedroom dwelling from logs felled by Mr. Pomeroy and his son Tom right on the property. Still owned by the same family and recognized in the National Register of Historic Places, the estate is now a nonprofit Living History Farm. Included on the grounds are an incredibly extensive British theme gift shop (with a special section for us hedgehog lovers) and tea room. Lil Freese is the granddaughter of the pioneer Pomeroys. In bringing her personal dedication, sense of order, and gracious hospitality to the daily operation Lil must indeed personify the strongest traits of that hard-working family.

The essence of 1920s Pacific Northwest rural life is captured at this functioning museum. Under the guidance of educator Bob Brink, visiting student groups are invited to share in a typical day on the farm. From grinding corn and using a scrub board, to sawing logs and pressing cider from the orchard, the farm is a hands-on learning experience. Each student leaves with appreciation for all the back-breaking, hand-powered effort that preceded electricity as well as a sense of joy in petting a baby calf or planting an onion. School groups should call 360-686-3537 to schedule a fun and enlightening visit.

The public is welcome at the farm the first full weekend of each month, June through October, Saturday 11 a.m. to 4 p.m. and Sunday 1 p.m. to 4 p.m. but the temptations of an upscale British gift shop beckon year round Monday through Saturday 10 a.m. to 5 p.m., Sunday 1 p.m. to 5 p.m. A calendar of special events is literally brimming with activities for all interests: an annual Herb Festival; craft workshops of old time arts like candle-dipping, spinning, weaving, quilt making; a real old fashioned Fourth of July with hot dogs and a softball game in "the back 40" (bring your mitt); barn theater puppet shows and plays; educational forestry walks and horse-logging demonstrations; a functioning smithy and horse-drawn hay-rides; the list goes on an on. To get a terrific little quarterly newsletter that provides the schedule as well as recipes and insights into life "Down on the Farm", sign up on the mailing list when you come for tea, or drop a note to Lil. As a non-profit group staffed with many volunteers, a modest donation is appreciated if you are able.

Follow the aroma of good baking and English tea up the creaky stairs of the Carriage House, and you'll find one of my favorite tea rooms. The fresh farm grown produce, flowers and herbs are employed to create a delightful and delicious Afternoon Tea in this truly vintage setting. Attention to all the traditional touches and presentation with flair make this a treat. Once a month special themes tea are great fun, and their Easter, Mother's Day and Alice in Wonderland Tea attract a joyful following of tea lovers every year.

The organization's motto is "When you appreciate and preserve the ordinary as well as the exceptional, you fill in the full spectrum of History." At the Pomeroy House in the countryside of southern Washington, the ordinary is indeed celebrated in a very special way.

You are invited for tea in The Carriage House year-round, Wednesday through Saturday 11:30 a.m. to 3 p.m. and special teas throughout the year. The gift shop is open Monday through Saturday 10 a.m. to 5 p.m. and Sunday 1 p.m. to 5 p.m. The farm is open for viewing the first full weekend of the months June through October, 11 a.m. to 4 p.m. Saturday and 1 p.m. to 4 p.m. Sunday. School groups call 360-686-3537 for a special tour.

QUEEN MARY

2912 N.E. 55th
Seattle, WA 98105
206-527-2770

It's been more than 12 years now since Mary C. Gringo's family hoped, in the way caring families always will, "that she knew what she was doing" when she leased the little brick building and joyfully draped and swathed it in bolts and bolts of luxurious Laura Ashley prints. An eyebrow or two was raised and a little gasp audible when she explained to her loved ones that it would be tea that would star in her cozy bistro. They were concerned after all, because there was nothing at all like that in Seattle at the time. Mary just smiled. That was exactly the reason she knew her vision would quickly become something of an institution here. Today Mary's family relaxes over a pot of tea in the comfort and English style of one of the most talked about, publicized and popular tea rooms of the Northwest, Queen Mary.

Mary has always been at the forefront, not just of style, but of afternoon tea before it became a trend in this area. Some even credit her with the proliferation of tea rooms in the Northwest, a "tea maven" they call her. It's Mary's eye for detail and penchant for perfection that were instrumental in the naming of her haven when a friend rolled her eyes and asked "So who do you think you are? Queen Mary?!" Situated in a charming single story brick building with climbing ivy and coach lights, the curb appeal of the colorful flower boxes and bright banners have lured many a curious diner to her door. The attentive service, exceptional presentation on 3 tiered servers, and tranquil and traditional nature of the Formal Afternoon Teas always brings them back as fans. Chintz, lace, rich wood paneling and comfortable vintage wicker chairs set the tone for romantic luxury, so do take your time.

Celebrate fine food and attention to detail as an artform. Queen Mary - long may she reign!

Afternoon Tea is served 2 p.m. to 5 p.m. daily, with reservations required for parties of 6 or more. An extensive menu of many heirloom family recipes and British fare is offered from 9 a.m. with closing Sunday through Wednesday at 5 p.m., closing Thursday, Friday and Saturday about 9 p.m.

Rose Garden Tea Rooms

4127 - 172nd N.E.
Arlington, WA 98223
360-659-4393

With the exception of a landslide victory of the deer over the rose bushes and the defeat of the nasturtiums by the slugs, it's been a pretty good season for the Home Team. The hummingbirds outmaneuvered the cats, the pond fish eluded the heron, the cats outwitted the owls, and the raccoons tied with the neighbor's dog for domination in the garbage can event. Six swallows returned in March and twelve left in August gorged on a bumper crop of mosquitoes and happy with the birdhouses Ken built and the feathers we provided for their nests. All in all it's been a good year on our Camano Island hill.

It's been an especially good year for nearby Arlington's Smokey Point neighborhood too. This is the year that Sharon Breon opened her charming Victorian tea rooms to the delight of all, and it has quickly become a favorite destination for many. Housed in, well let's face it, an ordinary-looking converted rambler on a busy street with charms too subtle for me to notice, crossing Sharon's magical threshold places you in one of two enchanted Victorian parlors with eight lace covered tables dressed for tea.

Gentle music and a tangible peace attend the meal, all beautifully presented with Sharon's signature rose touches. It's this kind attention to grace and artistry that is a hallmark of Rose Garden Tea Rooms' presentation. Seven different utterly indulgent tea sets are offered on lovely tiered servers, as well as salads, soups, and teacakes. She has combed antique markets and gift marts to create the balance of treasures that both decorate the rooms and are offered for your consideration as gifts or self-indulgences.

Yes indeed, I'd say it's been a very good year.

Open 10 a.m. to 4 p.m. Wednesday through Saturday.

SEASONS COFFEE, TEA & REMEDIES

113 N. Main Avenue
Ridgefield, WA 98642
360-887-7260

On a gray November day in 1805, the Lewis & Clark Expedition paddled their canoes into the Ridgefield area to make camp. The next morning with cold hands and puffy bloodshot eyes, William Clark huddled by the fire and wrote, "...I slept very little last night for the noise. Kept up during the whole of the night by the swans, geese, white and grey Brant ducks, etc....they were immensely numerous, and their noise horrid." Well, one person's horrid noise is another person's joyful music, (those of you with teenagers don't need to be told that) and to live in Ridgefield today is to be serenaded by the music of multitudes of wintering birds that call the Ridgefield National Wildlife Refuge home.

In the heart of this lovely rural community in the former lobby of a 1940's movie house turned live theater, Don and Earleen Griswold offer exactly the remedy cranky William Clark could have used, a good pot of tea. Since 1997 local artists, craftspeople, and performers have made Seasons' good pastries and teas their muse, and the fruits of their labors often adorn the walls of this simple, eclectic setting. Special seasonal and theme tea parties are regular events here with reservations required, and can serve as a delightful reward at the finish of a nature trail walk or kayak trip through the Refuge or browsing the old town shops.

For a teatime infused in history and nature, a visit to Seasons in Ridgefield will make your day brighter no matter how much sleep you had the night before.

Open Monday through Thursday 6 a.m. to 4 p.m., Friday until 7 p.m.; Saturday 7 a.m. to 4.p.m. and Sunday 7 a.m. until 1 p.m.

SEATTLE ART MUSEUM

Teahouse Gallery
100 University Street
Seattle, WA 98122
206-654-3121
Website: www.seattleartmuseum.org

It's his life's work and he does it without complaint, standing in all weather rhythmically pummeling an unseen tea kettle into shape, and whether you're a fan of the big lug or not, you certainly can't ignore The Hammering Man outside the Seattle Art Museum in downtown Seattle. He makes the entry to SAM easy to find, towering over it by three or four stories, a kinetic art tribute to life's hard work. Inside, the life works of worldwide artists and artisans created over thousands of years fill Seattle's beautiful shrine to creativity.

Traveling tea-related displays have included Porcelain Teapots, "Calligraphy, Tea and Me" in the public art studio, and a surprising and gratifying number of these quality exhibits and demonstrations pass regularly through these halls. To learn about unlimited access membership, which will also get you a big quarterly magazine outlining events, call 206-654-3180 or the general recorded info line 206-654-3100. General Admission is very reasonable for non-members too, and two days early each month admission is absolutely free, and it's on the busline.

In the third floor Teahouse Gallery, a narrated presentation of chanoyu, the Japanese Tea Ceremony, is presented three or four times each quarter. While free with your admission, you must order tickets in advance through the Box Office. In the tranquil setting of the Teahouse, you will experience the green tea beverage of the sages, a bowl of matcha, as the story of the ceremony unfolds.

Seattle Art Museum provides a wonderful escape into a world celebrating beauty, creativity and a forum for artful tea events.

SHOSEIAN TEAHOUSE
at the Seattle Japanese Garden

1501 Lake Washington Blvd. E.
Seattle, WA 98122
206-324-1483

A notable Tea Master, Soshitsu Sen, when asked to explain Chado, the Way of Tea, made a statement eloquent in its simplicity. He said "Chado is based upon the simple act of boiling water, making tea, offering it to others, and drinking it ourselves. Served with a respectful heart and received with gratitude, a bowl of tea satisfies both physical and spiritual thirst."

In 1959 the people of Tokyo gave Seattle a treasure which was received with continuing gratitude. A teahouse, exquisitely handcrafted in Japan, was carefully reassembled on a site selected within Seattle's Japanese Garden. What Western culture knows as the Japanese Tea Ceremony, Chado, has been codified and carefully nurtured for 400 years by 15 generations of descendants of Sen Rikyu, founder of the Urasenke tradition of tea. The past two generations have lifted the silk veil of privacy surrounding this living tradition, and presented it to benefit the entire world.

One part of Chado is Chanoyu, literally translated it means simply "hot water for tea". Translated spiritually it is a ritual of transformation derived from Zen Buddhism that embraces the four principles of harmony, respect, purity and tranquility. The student of tea learns to arrange things, to understand the relationship between action and interlude, to respect social grace, and then carry these principles with them from the tea experience into daily life.

Suggesting the atmosphere of a secluded mountain retreat, this tranquil teahouse is central to the activities and education services of the Urasenke Foundation. Membership is $40 for individuals, $60 for families and the benefits include special tea gatherings honoring nature such as Moon Viewing and Cherry Blossom Viewing. Another benefit, eloquent simplicity.

The public is invited to tea presentations April through October, the third Saturday of the month at 1:30 p.m. Free with admission to the Garden which costs $2.50 for adults and $1.50 for students and seniors. The Japanese Garden is open everyday, March through November, 10 a.m. til dusk.

SORRENTO HOTEL
The Fireside Room

900 Madison Street
Seattle, WA 98104
206-622-6400

Four or five generations ago, cable cars wobbled up steep Madison Street enroute to the forested shoreline of Lake Washington on the far side of First Hill. One of the first stops it creaked to was the Sorrento Hotel. Here elegant ladies and gentlemen in hats would disembark and drift through the iron-gated courtyard to take tea. In 1908, when the Sorrento was built, it immediately became the most prestigious destination for spending an afternoon by the fire with friends.

The cable cars are gone now, early victims to debatable progress in the city's transportation. The stately mansions of the neighborhood, winter residences for many of Seattle's early upper crust and nouveau-riche gold prospectors, have gradually been replaced with a battalion of physician's offices, clinics, and full-care multi-story hospitals that have earned the the area its medicinal nickname "Pill Hill". Time has been kind to the Sorrento though. Inspired by structures of the Italian Renaissance, the warmth and character of this old hotel have aged and mellowed like a late-harvest Tuscan wine. Elegant without pretense, the Sorrento achieves that easy balance between relaxing comfort and traditional formality.

Especially nice on a blustery winter day in Seattle, teatime here by the fire will be a pleasant tradition for you to begin. It's a shame arriving by cable car is no longer an option.

Tea is served daily 3 p.m. to 5 p.m. in the mahogany panelled Fireside Room in the lobby.

SOUTH SEATTLE COMMUNITY COLLEGE
Rainier Dining Room

6000-16th Ave. S.W.
Seattle, WA 98106-1499
206-764-5344 or 206-764-5300
Website: www.chefschool.com

In 1860, the Earl of Lytton in England proclaimed (probably while his stomach was growling) "We may live without friends, we may live without books, but civilized man cannot live without cooks."

Thanks to the prestigious Culinary Arts and Pastry program of the Food Sciences Department of South Seattle Community College, we may never be forced to test the epicurean Earl's theory. For the past few years this center of learning has been producing world class chefs in growing numbers, and offering popular High Teas under the tutelage of Chef/Instructor Stephen Sparks. Offered on Fridays during the spring and summer quarters, the teas are available to the public only with advanced ticket sales, and well worth the planning. Various premium teas are offered with a fine array of accompaniments served in multiple courses in the formal setting of the Rainier Dining Room. All of the food and pastry creations are produced on the premises by the program's instructors and students.

The menu changes for each tea in order to offer the greatest variety for those smart folks that purchase tickets for multiple tea events. Various jams, jellies, relishes, chutneys, curds and spreads are created to complement the freshly baked scones and muffins. A delightful presentation of sandwiches and savory spreads are served along with a bowl of fresh soup. A final sweet of petitfours, French pastries and hand-made chocolates are served to each guest.

To arrange for a schedule of this year's teas for spring and summer, call, write or email for a copy of the Food Sciences great newsletter "Bill of Fare." The Culinary Arts Program website is listed above for those of you with internet access. No matter how you get in touch with this creative program, you will be glad you did, year after year.

TASTE 'N TIME TEA ROOM
in Clock Tower Square

3617 Bridgeport Way W.
University Place, WA 98466
253-564-6373

In our married life we have owned, or been owned by depending on your viewpoint, two equally wonderful but completely different Alaskan Malamutes. Eric the Terrible was a lofty thinker, gazing into fireplaces and off at distant vistas absorbed in thought. He only had one shortcoming. He hated cats. Perhaps that was what he thought about. We spent the better part of eight years keeping him away from cats and vice versa. It was natural then that we would enforce strict dog/cat apartheid with our last malamute, Cody Coyotey. As an adult at 140 poinds with paws the size of Marie Callender pie pans, he cut an imposing figure, but being a simple fellow he never once had a lofty thought unless it related to sausages. One chilly morning we looked out to greet him and found he was curled up on his bed with a small stray tomcat. Sensing imminent peril we crept out just as they both stirred, yawned, stretched and rubbed up against each other. That was the beginning of his five year friendship with Father MacKenzie, the stray tomcat who adopted him.

Actuarial tables and tea tables may seem strange bedfellows as well, but at Taste 'n Time Tearoom they've gotten along just fine since 1996, thank you. Housed with their full service insurance agency these civic minded tea ladies also provide a free community room frequented by a myriad of local clubs. Debra Melleby and Dixie Harris dispense a big dollop of community goodwill along with tea, insurance, (and a bit of coffee voted the best in a recent Tacoma newspaper poll.)

A bright little tea room with four tables and rattan chairs is a delightful spot for lingering. The sunlit room embodies the relaxing essence of afternoon tea, a good place to review your insurance coverage or renew a friendship. Your hostesses Dixie and Debra genuinely enjoy meeting people and sharing teatime hospitality of the nicest kind.

Teas are served daily Monday through Friday 7 a.m. to 5 p.m. Saturday 8 a.m. to 5 p.m. with teas that day served by appointment only.

TEA-AN'TIQUES

618 N. Monroe
Spokane, WA 99201
509-324-8472

Where we live, a crow settled into life with a broken wing. He is still remembered on our Camano Island hill as "The Walking Crow" and had apparently adjusted well to his pedestrian lifestyle over a period of a few earthbound months. The neighbors, even those known to be less than chari- table when awakened at dawn by their unruly gangs, left goodies for him ranging from stale raisin bread to smoked oysters, and he strolled amiably up and down the road selecting his favorites from among the offerings with a proprietary air. Convalescence was one big buffet for The Walking Crow, and at sunset each evening he would jump into the branches of a large forsythia bush with his belly full to dream about his days of flight or whatever it is that crows dream about. I watched from my window as he practiced with his mending wing a deter- mined downhill run on the pavement that would launch him briefly into the air. Each day the run would be a little shorter, the flight a little longer and then one day after four months of canvassing the neighborhood on foot he was gone. Now when a crow lingers in our yard we ponder briefly whether it's The Walking Crow or just a crow walking.

Jackie Hayes understands hospitality and how dreams can come true. With a spirit of joy in hard work, she has envisioned and created Tea An'Tiques in 1994 in Spokane's earliest commerical district. Now experi- encing a regentrification as something of an antique row, Jackie's business unifies her two passions, antiques and tea. Jackie scours antique markets around the country to keep a fresh mix of old treasures flowing through her shop. Almost everything is for sale.

A variety of options are available to you for Afternoon Tea as well as a fresh soup of the day. This is a one-woman operation, a tribute to dreams in flight.

Open Tuesday through Saturday. Tea is offered with reservations, 11 a.m. to 4 p.m.

THE TEACUP

2207 Queen Anne Avenue North
Seattle, WA 98109
206-283-5931, Fax 206-284-6754
E-Mail: tearanch.com

Queen Anne Hill holds court 450 feet over Seattle and from Kerry Park you can look the Space Needle straight in the eye. On this lofty perch Seattle's founding fathers built grand homes in the Queen Anne style for their families in the mid 1800s, and sighed contentedly, "Paradise". While Seattle at that time was boisterous and rough-hewn, Queen Anne City, as it came to be called, was refined and gentile. And in this rarefied air a comfortable community could take tea on their porches and look down upon Seattle, literally and figuratively.

Today that comfortable sense of community thrives and Queen Anne has become a bustling close knit neighborhood of ethnic restaurants, salons, boutiques and bistros. Brian Keating, national tea trend tracker, makes sure you can still find good tea on Queen Anne Hill seven days a week at The Teacup. The Teacup is primarily a tea retailer, with hundreds of varieties of bulk teas dispensed by a knowledgeable staff in a bright, urbane storefront setting. With the launch of their new website this year, The Teacup has positioned itself on the world stage.

You're invited to have a pot of tea and a baked treat at their standup bar or at one of four simple wood tables inside, two on the sidewalk. One entire wall is devoted to teapots and accessories from around the world. A mail order catalog assures your favorite blends delivered, and a quarterly newletter will keep you up to date on the world's oldest beverage. Like the neighborhood founding families who considered the place paradise, Brian's company byline is "Tea Lover's Paradise." Many agree.

Open Monday through Saturday 9 a.m. to 6 p.m., Sunday 10 a.m. to 5 p.m.

TEAHOUSE KUAN YIN

1911 N. 45th St.
Seattle, WA 98103
206-632-2055

A gentleman named Kuan Yin lived in the 6th century B.C. in China. As a disciple of the tea philosopher Lao Tse, it was Kuan Yin who instituted the ritual mark of hospitality of offering a bowl of tea to a travel-weary guest. Whether this teahouse is named for him, the owner is mum, but at Teahouse Kuan Yin the tea is offered in a unique multi-ethnic atmosphere redolent of broadened horizons through travel.

This veritable world bazaar of a tea house in the eclectic neighborhood of Wallingford has been around for years. With more than 40 teas and tisanes from around the world and international food treats like spring rolls and green tea ice cream, you can almost hear the bells of the trade caravan jingling. Linger and enjoy, relax and reflect. Kuan Yin is glad you're here.

Open everyday, long hours for weary travellers.

THE TEA LADY

430 Washington Street S.E.
Olympia, WA 98501
360-786-0350 or 877-330-7521
Website: www.olywa.net/picard/tea_lady.htm

One of the new buzz words for business in this new millennium is "multi-tasking". Apparently that's what the business world calls it now when you're involved in several projects simultaneously. Well, I'm sorry to burst corporate America's bubble, but that term had to have been coined by a man, and he probably didn't have a mother. Every last woman I know has been "multi-tasking" for years, we just called it something different - "life." Don't get me wrong, I make no personal claims to be proficient at multi-tasking. In fact, in a rush to get ready for a date in 60s while ironing a blouse and teasing my hair at the same time and I once confused Vano Liquid Spray Starch with AquaNet Hairspray.

Now take The Tea Lady, there's a good example of proficient multi-tasking as an art form. About 1996 Carol Welch, a long time tea lover, Doctorate of Demography, and fulltime high level state employee decided to open a tea emporium in Olympia. Being a nice person as well as an astute businessperson, Carol was able to attract and delegate authority to sociable and knowledgeable employees like Cari and Christina, who run the day to day operation. Tea lovers have beat a path to her door ever since.

Teas from Pacific Northwest blenders find a forum here as well as hundreds of high quality, premium and even rare teas from all over the world. Sold by weight and offered in-store for tasting at simple tables, they now offer soups, desserts and light fare in the tea bar area. Kettles, teapots, books, a few imported foodstuffs round out the tea lover's larder here. On her days off from the state, you may find Carol in the store stocking shelves, making tea, filling orders, and running the register, but you're more likely to find her relaxing at a table with her loyal customers, enjoying a cup of special tea, and unwinding from a hard day herself. Now that's my idea of proficient multi-tasking.

Open Monday through Saturday, 10 a.m. to 6 p.m. Sunday noon to 5 p.m.

TEA THYME & IVY
at Country Village

23710-1/2 Bothell-Everett Highway
Bothell, WA 98021
425-482-1668

Day begins when the self-important rooster proclaims it so at Country Village. Negotiating the parking area I find myself in the middle of a flock of darting chickens, geese and peacocks and as my van gently parts this parade of poultry I find myself humming "ducks and geese and chicks better scurry..." I can easily picture steering that surrey with the fringe on top instead of a Chevy with Firestones on the bottom.

Old time boardwalks connect many of the little awning-fronted shops, and curving pathways meander past ponds on which duck families glide contentedly. A redwing blackbird whistles with a proprietary air from a cattail as a chuckling mother hen leads her fluffy yellow brood toward the comforts of shade and corn. Long a haven for suburban wildlife as much as for unique gifts, Country Village is a destination for the breed of shopper that seeks a change from the standard mall experience. Songbird nests cling to willow branches where mother robins zip in and out with fruit, and an amusing vending machine dispenses bird seed and crumbs, reminding you that a pot of tea and a baked goodie would hit the spot. Your own creature comforts will be attended to in the nicest way at Tea Thyme & Ivy.

Debi Kraft, confronted with an empty nest of her own when her fledglings spread their wings, considered only briefly a return to teaching. Instead, with the blessing of a supportive husband, she followed her dream of being a tea shop owner and bought Tea Thyme & Ivy in 1998 (from the previous Debbi who started it). She delights in the opportunity to "meet wonderful people everyday, and work surrounded by pretty tea things, serving friends old and new." The charming little two room shop features more than 80 premium loose teas, a vast assortment of china teapots, teacups, decorated sugar cubes, serving accessories and joyful gifts. In the back of the shop a snug little two table tearoom provides an enchantingly sunny spot to relax and linger with a pot of tea and scones or dessert (save a crumb or two for the birds).

The shop is open Tuesday through Saturday 10 a.m. to 6 p.m., Sundays 11 a.m. to 5 p.m., serving good tea and baked goodies until 4 p.m.

Ken and Dick Thomas at the Teapot Dome landmark near Zillah, WA.

Roadside Tea Follies

Like you, I'd rather they not happen at all, but isn't there a perverse sort of comfort in knowing that political scandals are nothing new at least? The big political debacle of 80 years ago revolved around secret oil leases for profit in an area of the west called Teapot Dome. No White House interns were tiptoeing around with midnight pizzas back in those days. In Zillah, Washington, Dick Thomas's family has owned a gas station that commemorates the earlier scandal, appropriately in the whimsical shape of a teapot. Built in 1922, the teapot gas station survived a move in the 1970s to accommodate the construction of the I-82 freeway, and still serves motorists today at 14691 Yakima Valley Highway. The spout was the chimney for a wood-burning stove, the handle pure decoration. Today the gas station is listed on the National Register of Historic Places as a landmark of roadside follies. Stop in on your way to visit the tearooms east of the mountains for a photo with genial owner Dick Thomas and a tankful of tea, oops, I mean unleaded.

THORNEWOOD CASTLE

8601 N. Thorne Lane S.W.
Lakewood - Tacoma, WA 98498
253-584-4393
www.thornewoodcastle.com

That most quintessentially British of polite customs, Afternoon Tea, has found the perfect setting at the lovely old Thornewood Castle. After all, even the bricks from which this grand Gothic home was built were imported from Wales, and some 15th century manor house in England yielded its massive oak doors and grand staircase. When Deanna and Wayne Robinson purchased the house on four manicured acres of American Lake shoreline last year the only missing grace note was tea.

Chester Thorne, founding father of the Port of Tacoma, commissioned the construction of his 27,000 square foot family residence in 1909. Tons of soil from the Nisqually River delta were transported by horse and wagon to enrich his half-acre sunken garden which has been celebrated as one of five grand American gardens recently honored by the Smithsonian.

Afternoon Tea here is a gratifying, four-course affair for which guests are encouraged to dress for the elegance of the setting. The fare of the day may include chicken salad crepes, savory tartlets, mushroom turnovers, cucumber sandwiches, steamed English pudding, Russian tea cakes, hot currant scones and other delightful, traditional dishes. An enlightening presentation by Deanna of Victorian tea history and lore enlivens this elegant event, which is followed by an escorted tour of the historic house and its award-winning gardens.

It is the Robinson's hospitable hope that your time spent here at tea "will temporarily interupt your rush-a-day life and cause you to reflect, dream, and forget about your stresses."

Tea is served by reservation only as this is a gated community. Tea is served more frequently during holiday seasons and generally the first Thursday of each month. Please call or check the website for details.

TRAVELERS TEA BAR

501 East Pine Street
Seattle, WA 98122
206-329-6260
E-Mail: akorn@concentric.net

A journal that I kept from more than 20 years ago chronicled a trek Ken and I took on trails through the foothills of the Himalayas in Nepal. While this journal is in no danger of ever being confused with a literary master work, revisiting the battered spiral notebook still invokes the memory of simple grace and kindness. After one particularly arduous day, (straight up and straight down for 15 miles to my recollection, but probably not true) our Sherpa guide Sonam passed on an invitation for tea at the home of a family with whom we had shared smiles and greetings,"Namaste", as the trail passed their door. The benefit of a common language was unnecessary as we sat on the rustic bench by an open fire built on the floor of their home. Tea, laced with yak butter and served in a treasured English bone china cup, formed the cultural bridge over which friendship and grace passed freely.

Allen Kornmesser is, in his own words "a refugee from Academia." With a doctorate in Indian politics, he has lived and traveled in that part of Asia extensively so it was natural that he would share his love for it through tea. In 1998 he opened a very special place, Travelers. Travelers sells a large variety of bulk teas and provides an on-site tea bar and three simple tables where you are invited to read Indian newspapers, enjoy the monthly art exhibits and browse handcrafted Indian and Nepalese wares that warm the shop, while the 'chai' (Hindi for tea in general) warms your body. Their Masala or spiced chai here has a large, enthusiastic following. With an herbalist on duty most days, you can become educated on the therapeutic benefits of the numerous herbal simples (single ingredient), their signature custom blends, and herbal elixirs like ginseng. All are brewed to order using pure mountain spring water.

An excellent newsletter presages seminars, Sanskrit lessons, meditations, and Tibetan chanting demonstrations. There is always something interesting going on at Travelers, where tea once again forms a bridge between cultures.

Open everyday at noon, closing at 8 p.m. Sunday through Thursday and at 10 p.m. on Saturday and Sunday. Served by the #7 and #10 city bus.

UMMELINA TEA SPA

1525 Fourth Avenue
Seattle, WA 98101
206-748-9116
E-Mail: ummelina@aol.com
Website: www.ummelina.com

Just steps away from the bustle of down-town Seattle, at treetop level, you'll find a soothing retreat. Gentle music plays as the door closes softly behind you, shutting out the outside world. You have crossed a threshold at which you shed tension and stresses amid a setting rich with Indonesian salvaged teak accents, soft white draperies, cool glowing glass and polished stone.

In this urban oasis, natural healing treatments and herbal products from every corner of the world are presented. With a spa nutritionist, naturopathic physician, massage therapists, licensed acupuncturist and host of trained herbalists on staff, Ummelina's is an international day spa designed to soothe and pamper.

Ummelina's also has its own Tea Ceremony, a mini class in herbalism just for you. Everything harmonizes with artful simplicity in this tea spa, and they suggest that you enter their world "on village time," lingering as long as you can in the serene surroundings. An herbalist will guide you through the menu of botanical teas, helping you to select a tisane suited to you. She will bring the different herbs to your table and teach you their traditional applications. Organic fruits and nuts are the only foods available.

Unique treasures from Bali are for sale, and a roster of classes encompasses all aspects of healing body and spirit in this global marketplace of peace and healing through herbs.

Open Monday through Friday 9 a.m. to 9 p.m., Saturday 9 a.m. to 5 p.m. and Sunday 10:30 a.m. to 7 p.m.

VICTORIAN ROSE SPECIALTEAS

514 S.W. Newaukum Avenue
Chehalis, WA 98532
360-740-8952

"They saw a Dream of Loveliness descending from the train."
Brand New Ballads - *Charles G. Leland*

Two venerable symbols of an era of gentility meet every summer weekend when the old Victorian era steam engine of the Chehalis-Centralia Railroad puffs and wheezes past the scone scented doorway and lace curtains of the Victorian Rose SpecialTeas.

Tea Proprietor, Kathi Mann, is an avid fan of Victoriana. For years she has been creating lovely, hand-sewn and embellished Victorian lampshades, and within the past year, she has turned a spotlight onto another passion of that era, Afternoon Tea. Victorian Rose SpecialTeas offers afternoon teas almost daily by reservation in the little three table shop. Growing numbers of antique and factory outlet shoppers make Victorian SpecialTeas their afternoon treat, and in the summer, to immerse yourself completely in the era, you can ride the steam train on a little 12 mile roundtrip journey before or after your tea.

Kathi Mann has her own Victorian "dream of loveliness" to share with you in the form of five different tea sets on the menu, and the ability to cater your tea party or business meeting to meet your own need for a touch of nostalgia.

Afternoon Tea, tea parties for adults or children, and catering by reservation please.

VICTORIAN ROSE TEA ROOM

1130 Bethel Avenue
Port Orchard, WA 98366
360-876-5695

Somehow my childhood zoomed by before I got around to whining about wanting a dollhouse. I doubt my common sense parents would have trusted me anyway with the upkeep of a small residence with frilly curtains. I have never been able to keep lace on anything and they knew it from seeing my underwear. While my playmate (and still best friend) Suzy Granger played with pristine girlie dolls in pastel finery, I had Rusty. He came with a daytime-into-evening ensemble of denim overalls and a plaid shirt. I think he may have even had a hat the first day, come to think of it. Rusty had a bad habit of losing his head (literally) which was held on with a bandana like Roy Rogers. If I had a dollhouse for Rusty it should have been a mobile home or even a tent. So you see I simply cannot help my adult fascination for pretty doll houses with lace curtains.

The building that is home to Victorian Rose Tea Room in Port Orchard looks like a great big dollhouse with its charming gables and big round turret painted a soft rosey hue. Old fashioned charm permeates the tea service at Victorian Rose Tea Room. Servers in traditional black and white offer sweet, light scones, hot from the oven with flavored butters and cream to slather, lovely tea sandwiches, mini quiche and an assortment of sweets are all garnished with fresh flowers and fruit. A light Cream Tea is available daily with hot scones and flavored butters and preserves, and the desserts here are the stuff of legends. Special theme teas herald the annual holidays and should be booked well in advance at this popular spot.

After tea a little stroll through the newly expanded shopping village will yield such treasures as Precious Moments, Cherished Teddies, Department 56 Villages, Thomas Kincade Gallery, plush bears and a very special doll gallery, many of them collectible, every single one of them with their heads on, in lace-filled luxury.

Breakfast 9-11, lunch 11-2:30, Cream Tea and desserts 2:30 - 4:30. High Tea is the fourth Sunday of the month, 3 p.m. with prepaid reservations required. High Tea can be served for your group of 15 or more any time with advance notice.

VICTORIAN TEA POTTS
At the Pacific Run Antique Mall

10228 Pacific Avenue
Tacoma, WA 98444
253-537-5371

The idea for the very first tea room in England was cooked up by a bakery worker at ABC Baking Company in London who put a few tables into some unused space, put the kettle on, and the rest is tea history. Tea rooms, in fact, were the only place "a lady of good breeding" could go in public during early Victorian times without the presence of a chaperone.

After 30 years as a professional baker, you'd think Mrs. Potts might just want to dust off the flour and take a little break. Instead, she and other supportive family members have opened a little haven for tea in the back of the Pacific Run Antique Mall. With seating for 36 guests at mock lace-topped tables, tea is served with advance notice in their little soup and sandwich establishment. Tiered servers hold an assortment of tea sandwiches, fresh scones with cream, fresh fruit, and a sweet treat that varies with the season. The scenery changes all the time because everything is for sale here, including the old teapots, framed art and mismatched china.

Some of the best ideas are given time to rise and seasoned 'just so' by bakers, and this is certainly one of them. Lose your chaperone and go.

Open 10 a.m. to 5:30 p.m. everyday except Sunday 11 a.m. to 5 p.m. Please make reservations for Afternoon Tea.

WEE ELEGANCE TEA TIME

330 Lampe Road
Selah, WA 98942
509-697-8874

Shakespeare said "Those that do teach young babes do it with gentle means and easy tasks." With more than 35 years' experience as an Early Childhood Educator, Judy Popp practiced this philosophy daily in the classroom, and today brings it to her memory-making dress-up teaparties.

These special occasion tea celebrations, designed for girls aged 3-10 or so, are planned expressly for age-appropriate activities, and are generally held at the guest of honor's home on which Judy performs a touch of magic. From curved-top trunks the guests are encouraged to transform themselves with costumes and accessories, flowery floppy hats, tiaras and gloves that free the imagination and set the fun tone for the party. The table is set in the fine Victorian tradition with lace, fresh flowers, hand-decorated sugar cubes, and a bone china cup and saucer sized to fit the small hands perfectly. Judy knows even the best mannered little girl doesn't want to sit for long, so music and a costume fashion show engage the girls in movement that transports them to "far away places and high society ballrooms" in front of a full length mirror in which curtsies are perfected. Games and a story read by the "tea lady" (who is often attended by her tuxedo-attired "butler" for the day and husband for life, Harry) delight the girls.

Tea is presented elegantly on be-ribboned silver three-tiered trays and include traditional tea sandwiches, flower topped petit fours, dainty cookies and luscious sweets. Embroidered napkins provide the precious opportunity to learn and practice social etiquette, or the "Proper Thing to Do" segment of the party.

At the end of the two hour party, each guest leaves with a prettily wrapped porcelain cup and saucer, an interest in social graces taught by "gentle means", and fond memories to last a lifetime.

THE WELLINGTON

4869 Rainier Avenue South
Seattle, WA 98118
206-722-8571

"Polish it 'til you can see your smile in it, sweetie!" Gwyn Baker fondly recalls her grandmother Betty guiding her as a little girl during preparations for teas on a porch during hot North Carolina summers. Time hasn't dimmed the memory of those meticulous preparations, but has instead sweetened the recollection of warm times shared in the closeness of family and friends over those teas.

In 1993 Gwyn opened her own little tea room on a maple-lined street of Seattle. Housed in a dignified 1910 brick building that was once home to a pharmacy and soda fountain, a tall old clock on the block reminds you that life moves quickly and things change. Couldn't we all benefit from slowing down and connecting with friends and family with a gracious tea?

Gwyn has combed antique markets to create the traditional look in this bastion of southern hospitality. White skirted tables, gold bead shades soften tea lights and floor lighting imparts the elegance of an old manor house. Luxurious damask chenille swags the windows. The menu has elegant touches as well, and the High Tea is served on three-tiered servers by attendants in formal attire. Lighter teas are served plated to your table.

The ambience is a fusion of formal elegance and the warmth of southern hospitality. Grandmother Betty would be proud.

Tea, as well as lunch and dinners are served Wednesday through Friday from noon, Sunday by reservation. Closed Monday and Tuesday.

WHIFFLETREE TEA ROOM

14-102nd Avenue N.E. #3
Bellevue, WA 98004
425-451-0062

In 1945 a band of volunteer firemen pitched in and built a firehouse for "Old Bellevue" that today is home to the engaging Whiffletree Tea Room. Hopefully more adept at putting out fires than wielding hammers and levels, "The crooked walls and high ceilings remind us," says Sherrill Shamitoff, co-owner with her mother Pat Ellis, "that we have created a bright and charming atmosphere in two fire engine bays." That they have.

South facing windows with lace curtains flood the nine table tea room in brightness even on a gray Northwest day. The tables are set with linens and lace, and gift and collectibles spill from antique displays and side-boards. The ladies offer a full lunch menu with a daily soup or salad special and a variety of yummy desserts for your three alarm cravings. Near the big Downtown Park, there is still a small town feel to Old Bellevue that deserves leisurely discovery and lingering over a pot of good tea.

The fires of hospitality burn brightly at the old firehouse, and Sherrill and Pat have painted their door a cheery fire engine red to help you find your way.

Open Tuesday through Saturday 10 a.m. to 4 p.m.

WIT'S END BOOKS & TEA

770 N. 34th St.
Seattle, WA 98103
206-547-2330

> "Go, little book, and wish to all
> Flowers in the garden meat in the hall,
> A bin of wine, a spice of wit......"
> *Robert Louis Stevenson*

All right, so Stevenson should have said "a pot of tea, a spice of wit..." because that's what you'll find in this bookstore-bistro-teashop in Seattle's eclectic and quirky Fremont district. Let's think about this a moment, Wit's End has quickly become the center of Fremont, and if that sign by the bridge is true, "Welcome to Fremont - Center of the Universe"....Q.E.D. that would make Wit's End....well, to draw from the vernacular of 60's hippydom, doesn't it just boggle the mind?

Wit's End's manager Steve Herold set out with a cosmic vision. He blithely combined a liberal arts bookstore with uniquely creative fresh food, and paired it with the highest quality single variety estate teas. "Cerebral pizza and cultural cuisine," promises food director Darren Patillo, ex-Microsofty.

A cozy tea alcove in the front spills over to tables and chairs through-out the store, inviting you to browse the hand-labeled bookshelves while you nibble and sip. It's enough to make a ruler-wielding school librarian swoon. Tea in both the Pacific Rim style and the English style is served appropriately potted in its clay or porcelain vessel. Easy-going and relaxed, this is the perfect spot for those Northwest gray days when you seek suste-nance for both your brain and your tea-loving body.

Open everyday, Monday through Saturday 10 a.m. to 9 p.m. Sunday open at 11 a.m.

THE WOODMARK HOTEL
on Lake Washington

1200 Carillon Point
Kirkland, WA 98033
425-822-3700
Website: thewoodmark.com

WOODMARK HOTEL
on Lake Washington

Kirkland's hillside was once cloaked in lush, ancient forests. City dwellers from Seattle would make the weekend crossing by steamboat in the early 1900s to the verdant Kirkland shore for communion with nature. Today a fast-paced, four-lane floating bridge unites the two areas, blurring the distinction between city and retreat. Still Kirkland has managed to retain the casual appeal of a lakeside village and embroidered it with a lavish dose of urban elegance and worldliness. Nowhere is that combination more evident than at The Woodmark Hotel on Lake Washington.

The Woodmark Hotel holds the distinction of being the only hotel located on the lengthy and convoluted shoreline of metropolitan Lake Washington. Intimate, by hotel standards, with 100 beautifully appointed guest rooms, it is at the same time imposing due to its location. The four-story hotel presides with an air of businesslike authority over the 30 acre lakefront grounds that include marina, pier, gardens, waterfront promenade and salmon stream.

Afternoon Tea is served daily on fine Lenox China in a comfortable, book-lined nook known as the Library Bar. In this restful setting, as their menu suggests, you can "...continue the European custom of taking a mid-afternoon respite from rounds of shopping, business appointments, or simply treat yourself to a small whim."

The Woodmark Hotel's quiet charm and attention to creature comforts make their teatime a special treat. Once again, as in years past, Kirkland offers a soothing retreat for the jangled sensibilities of urban dwellers.

Tea is served daily between 2 and 4 p.m., reservations are appreciated.

YE OLDE COPPER KETTLE

18881 Front St.
Poulsbo, WA 98370
360-697-2999

As recently as the 1920s Norwegian was the language of choice in Poulsbo, but by 1992 you could be just as likely to overhear, "Cuppa tea, Luv?" as an "Uff-da". This was when transplanted Brits Tina and John created their cozy little English eatery in the heart of old Poulsbo. With their success, the international cuisine horizon of Poulsbo has expanded beyond lutefisk to include freshly made Shepherd's Pie, Cornish Pasties, and Victoria Sandwich Cakes of the British Isles.

With cheerful pinks and abundant copper pot accents, framed manorial prints, and heraldry, there can be no mistake that a good cup of tea can be found here. When tea rooms first opened (and literacy was just beginning to bloom) in Britain it was the custom to simply hang a kettle in front of the shop to announce the nature of your business. Using fresh local smoked salmon and delectable sweet treats in creative ways Ye Olde Copper Kettle has clearly announced that it means business too.

Open Tuesday through Thursday, 10:30 a.m. to 3:30 p.m. a little bit later on Friday and Saturday. Open Sunday from 11 a.m. to 3 p.m. Catering and private parties on site are available. Reservations are advised for parties larger than 4.

BRITISH COLUMBIA TEA ROOMS, TEA PARTIES AND EVENTS

VANCOUVER ISLAND
NEAR DOWNTOWN VICTORIA
  The Empress Hotel
  Gatsby Mansion
  James Bay Tea Room
  Olde England Inn
  Point Ellice House

OAK BAY
  Blethering Place
  Oak Bay Beach Hotel
  Windsor House

SAANICH PENINSULA
  Adrienne's Tea Garden
  Butchart Gardens
  Four Mile House

NANAIMO
  Calico Cat

MAINLAND, VANCOUVER
NEAR DOWNTOWN
VANCOUVER
  Hotel Georgia
  Hotel Vancouver
  Plaza Escada
  Secret Garden Tea Co.
  Sutton Place Hotel
  Sylvia Hotel
  Tearoom T
  Wedgewood Hotel

STEVESTON, RICHMOND
  British Home
  Cottage Tea Room

WHITE ROCK
  Clancy's Tea Cosy

NORTH OF VANCOUVER
  Britannia House
  Chateau Whistler
  Durlacher Hof

EAST OF VANCOUVER
  Clayburn Village Store

ADRIENNE'S TEA GARDEN
at Mattick's Farm

5325 Cordova Bay Road
Victoria, B.C. V842LE
250-658-1535
E-Mail: t-tyme@home.com

Farmer Bill Mattick's portrait in oil hangs in the entry to Mattick's Farm. In it Bill smiles proudly around a slim cigar, glowing with paternal pride at the two enormous cauliflowers he cradles with his one good hand and the utilitarian hook that replaces the missing one. In his wool buffalo plaid shirt he looks folksy and colorful, probably brimming with advice on natural fertilizer and good old common sense.

Today Bill's farm is a local landmark on the well-travelled scenic route from the Swartz Bay ferry terminal heading to Victoria. As vibrant and colorful as farmer Bill himself, Mattick's Farm now embraces upscale art, gift and fashion boutiques, craft and florist shops, garden center, golf shop and wine merchant. Farmer Bill may have been gone for years, but his vision of abundance on his plot of land surpasses mammoth cauliflowers, and is his legacy to the thriving merchant community here.

For more than 12 years, Adrienne's Tea Garden has been providing a cozy parlour setting for Afternoon Tea, abundant pastries, breakfasts and lunches graced by the culinary talents of owner Fay Hextall. Fay's menu item "High Tea" includes finger sandwiches, assorted dainties, a hearty raisin scone with Devonshire style cream and homemade preserves, finished by a fruit cup. Fay also offers her own "Sconwich", a fresh cheese scone sandwich with a variety of filling choices, as well as homemade soups and chowder.

Since Farmer Bill devoted the greater part of his life supplying fresh produce and flowers to Vancouver Islanders, it seems especially appropriate that good fresh food and pleasant hospitality continue to thrive on this plot of land.

Open 9:00 a.m. to 5:00 p.m. with Afternoon Tea available from 11:30 a.m.

THE BLETHERING PLACE

2250 Oak Bay Avenue
Victoria, B.C.
250-598-1413

The Blethering Place is something of an institution now, ensconced as it is in the oldest building of this enduringly charming town center of Oak Bay. Transplanted New Zealander Ken Agate created his tearoom almost twenty years ago in a 1912 building whose previous incarnations were as a grocery and post office. This veritable landmark attracts regulars with its comfortable lack of pretense, good food, and a special sense of heart.

The decor echoes the menu with its emphatic embrace of traditional British fare. Old toys, books and prints line the paneled walls and the engaging servers are attired in period costume. On many summer evenings, you will hear spontaneous songfests with hits from the 40s hammered out on an old upright piano in the corner, and an open invitation to command the microphone to share youthful memories of that era.

"Blethering," you will learn from the notes on the menu, is Scottish for "robust senseless chatter", but the spirit of good nature, community involvement, and cheerful camaraderie experienced here makes a great deal of sense to me.

Tea and other meals are served from 11 a.m. to 6:30 p.m.

BRITANNIA HOUSE

Highway 99 halfway between Vancouver and Whistler
Box 3
Britannia Beach, BC V0N3G0
604-896-2335
E-Mail: seadog@mountain-inter.net

"Come join us by the sea halfway between Vancouver and Whistler," the proprietors beckon, and how could you possibly you say no to that? It's in this breathtaking setting that Eileen and Howard Kelly offer tea to passersby on the busy road to the resort.

In the 1905 vintage historic building, tea is served in a sunny room the color of buttercream and warmed by a crackling wood stove. The tables, dressed in floral and Battenberg lace, are backdropped by the awesome beauty of Howe Sound, snowy mountain peaks, and evergreen cloaked hillsides. Served on a three-tiered bone china tray is an array of savory tea sandwiches including asparagus with cream cheese, turkey, ham and cheese and traditional English cucumber. The rich scones (declared the best they'd had in North America by numerous British tourists) are served with Eileen's own signature cream mixture with jam and are followed by a dessert treat. Breakfasts and lunches are also available.

Take a little time after tea to experience the Kelly's new gift area, Singular Sensation Gifts, which features unique hand-crafted arts, all one of a kind and created locally (some even by the Kellys). Britannia House is an ideal break on a busy route in a glorious setting and they serve tea, could you ask for more?

Open Thursday through Monday, 9 a.m. to 5 p.m. with full menu service. Tea is served from 2 p.m. to 5 p.m. Reservations are recommended on weekends year round.

BRITISH HOME

3986 Moncton at #1 Road
Steveston Village
Richmond, B.C.
604-274-2261

On a warm July morning in 1889, the 200-foot clipper ship, "Titania", pushed off from the sleepy fishing village of Steveston under full sail. With a rich history in the glory days of tea trade, the vessel was now riding the winds of its rebirth as a freighter for another type of precious cargo. This time the holds were full of Fraser River salmon bound for the dinner tables of Victorian England.

This aging dowager's cargo was so well received in England that the increased demand resulted in a dozen canneries opening in rapid succession. A "boomtown" atmosphere engulfed this once quiet tip of Lulu Island in southern British Columbia, and weekends would find the village swelling to 10,000 rough and tumble inhabitants. Enterprise that feeds on a quick flush of money followed; gambling halls, saloons, and houses full of naughty ladies thrived along these shores of the Fraser River. Optimistically the Salvation Army band would parade along Moncton Street every busy Saturday night, admonishing with the flourish of a tambourine and a spirited bugle blast that it was time for those with regard for their souls to head home for the evening. Whether the advice was heeded is not chronicled.

Today the six square block area that constitutes the hub of Historic Steveston Village's tourist district is bustling with a 21st century version of that boomtown venue. Presumably today's throngs are a better mannered group, happily partaking of the new enterprises that have emerged to meet their needs. Gift shops, nautical stores, T-shirts, seafood vendors, street musicians, and more than three dozen restaurants offer something for everyone by this busy harbor. One of the more unique businesses, delighting locals and tourists alike, is British Home.

British Home authentically replicates the friendly corner stores of Britain. Its engaging proprietors, Mary and Ray Carter, stock a complete array of British teas, groceries, and meats. They also offer some cooked food reminiscent of their homeland. Meat pies, sausage rolls, pasties, even hagis and black pudding are available at the counter as well as strong pots of English tea. Four tables by the windows, covered in blue smocked gingham rest humbly under the regal countenances of framed effigies of the Royal Family. The bonneted ghosts of the Salvation Army paraders must be smiling on this proper British business. Certainly they drank a bit of tea in their day.

Open 11 a.m. to 6 p.m. everyday except Sunday - 1 p.m. to 5 p.m.

THE BUTCHART GARDENS

800 Benvenuto Avenue
Brentwood Bay, B.C.
Tea reservations 250-652-8222
Garden information 250-652-4422
Recorded information 250-652-5256

What a playful irony that the Butcharts earned their fortune with a product that is lifeless, gray, flat and boring. Those adjectives are not descriptive of any other aspect of their life when their cement business was thriving in the early 1900s, and certainly not of their masterpiece garden legacy today.

On the 130-acre site of an abandoned quarry on the shores of a peaceful inlet 13 miles north of Victoria on Vancouver Island, the Butcharts built their home, "Benvenuto," the Italian word for "welcome." To grace the naturally verdant setting, Mrs. Butchart ventured to plant a rose bush and some sweet peas, and from this simple act a dormant love of gardening sprouted. Over the next few years of nurturing, Mrs. Butchart grew one of the most splendid gardens in North America, a garden masterpiece of world renown.

From the beginning, an almost constant flow of gardening enthusiasts were welcomed to the Butchart estate. With gracious hospitality the Butcharts saw to it that tea was always offered. In 1915 alone, it is reported that tea was served to 18,000, and it was not uncommon for strangers admiring the grounds to be invited to the family table for dinner and pleasant conversation.

Today not only is Jenny Foster Butchart's glorious garden thriving, but that same spirit of gracious hospitality flourishes as well. Afternoon Tea in the Dining Room of the old estate is lavish and presented with great style. Edible flowers are often used in creating the medley of imaginative finger sandwiches, the selection of which varies with the season but may include peppery watercress with ginger cream cheese, smoked salmon mousse roll, egg salad with fresh spinach, and Roma tomato and pesto. A plate of sweets may include an apple streudel, chocolate brandy Napoleon, and a double chocolate dipped strawberry. Their delectably light candied ginger scone with whipped vanilla Devon cream is legend. Profusions of fresh flowers grace the antique-laden room with views to the Italian Garden plaza below. A photo of Afternoon Tea in the dining room appears on our back cover.

The Butchart Residence - Summer   Courtesy of the Butchart Gardens, Ltd.

Allow plenty of time to explore. Internationally acclaimed, there is something special and unique to be discovered at every season of the year. The gardens host spirited musical revues, old time sing-alongs, and lavish fireworks displays during warm summer evenings when the garden is transformed by thousands of gently colored lights. In winter a special magic prevails with the sound of strolling carollers filling the crisp clean air. Comfortable benches invite peaceful contemplation of this changing beauty at all times of the year.

The estate was aptly named, Benvenuto. As in the days when Jenny Butchart approached guests in her garden to come for tea, the tea room is offered as a service for today's garden visitors. As such, you will need to pay the reasonable admission price to enter the grounds where the tea room is located. Once there you will, like millions of international visitors for the past 95 years, feel very welcome in this glorious setting, a tribute to all that is good about warm hospitality and superior horticulture.

Tea is served seasonally from 1 to 4 p.m. Please call for reservations. Admission fee for the garden is required for access to the tea room.

CALICO CAT TEA HOUSE

1081 Haliburton Street
Nanaimo, B.C. V9R6N6
250-754-3865

They say that the real difference between cats and dogs is that if you call a dog it will come galloping to see what you have in mind. If you call a cat it will take your number and call you back. A calico cat ignores me completely while licking her fur by the flower pots on the porch of the charming little bungalow that is home to Heather Frank's tea room.

Heather renovated the 1910 railway cottage and dressed it in soothing green and plum. The dining room features the original fireplace and vintage stained glass lights the area where tea is offered on tables set with floral toppers, or on the patio in spring and summer. Fresh cream scones, finger sandwiches and sweet treats are all made by Heather on site and served to your table on traditional tiered servers.

A seer by gift and a tealeaf reader by her grandmother's training, Heather has developed a widespread reputation for her personal readings. With advance arrangements and a modest fee, she will see what the tea leaves show for your future. While I can make no claim to be an expert, I think I see a delightful Afternoon Tea in your future in a cozy little house in lovely Nanaimo.

Save a little treat for the porch kitty, but you'll have to deliver it, she's much too busy to come when called.

Open seven days a week for meals 8:30 a.m. to 4:30 p.m. with tea served anytime after 2 p.m. Open for dinner twice a week, Wednesday and Thursday.

CHATEAU WHISTLER

4599 Chateau Blvd.
Whistler, B.C. V0N1B4
604-938-8000

Years ago I was invited to join a group of acquaintances sharing a condo at Sun Valley for a weekend of skiing. I was an accomplished snowplower at that time and had almost perfected stopping (if there was a tree nearby to grab or bump into) so I readily accepted. When we assembled for our first day on the slopes, I trudged behind them to the bus stop as they slipped into their matching-sleek-shiney-regulation airline ski-team jackets (embellished with pins that read 'first place slalom'). I knew I was in trouble. I struck out on my own, but unfortunately the easy slopes were on the wrong side of the mountain, where I boarded the wrong bus at the end of the day, in search of a rented condo of which the only thing I could tell the helpful driver was that it was just plain brown. It was a long weekend.

That never could have happened to me at Chateau Whistler. No, my skiing wouldn't have been any better, but Chateau Whistler is hard to miss. Located at the base of Blackcomb Mountain about 60 miles north of Vancouver, the imposing chateau style luxury hotel stretches its ten-plus stories into the clear mountain air. This extraordinary resort has been voted #1 ski destination by all three major ski publications, and since its birth in 1977 has attracted year round visitors for skiing, golfing, hiking, and now Afternoon Tea.

A tea like none you've yet experienced is offered in the high country elegance of the Mallard Lounge. Here you can sip your Orange Windsor while dipping your freshly baked bread into the creamy lager-laced Ontario cheddar fondue and nibbling baby bratwurst or savor warm Bavarian onion tarts and smoked salmon palmiers accompanied by a nice Earl Grey. For a sweeter approach relish the local wild berry chocolate tartlets or lemon roulade with a robust English Breakfast.

What can compare to magnificent food in unsurpassed beauty, where nothing, absolutely nothing, could be described as just plain brown.

Tea is served daily from 2 to 4 p.m. Reservations are recommended.

CLANCY'S TEA COSY

15223 Pacific Avenue
White Rock, BC V4B1P8
604-541-9010

"May the roads rise with you, and the wind be always at your back..." begins a traditional Irish blessing. As we climb the hill toward Clancy's Tea Cosy a fresh salt breeze pushes gently off Boundary Bay behind us.

Family and tea are pleasantly intertwined in proprietor Dina Clancy's life. Her affection for tea time was nurtured by her Irish grandmother until it became a passion, resulting in the opening of this award-winning tea room in 1994 with her parents.

Ken's mum, Emily Lewis, enjoys tea with Clancy's co-proprietress, Willy Clancy.

This cheerful tea room embraces you immediately with rich deep colors and an ebullient welcome by Dina's mother Willy. A well-worn Irish fiddle, Victorian garden art and wreaths adorn the walls above the hunter green wainscotting, and Battenberg lace topped tables are set with charmingly mismatched china and a simple goblet of fresh flowers.

With father Patrick concocting fresh soups and salads, and Dina crafting the tea sandwiches and baked goods, this little business is a true family jewel. Recognized with an Award of Excellence by the Tea Council of Canada, Clancy's Tea Cosy truly is an Irish blessing of its own special kind.

Open daily except holidays 11 a.m. to 4:30 p.m.

CLAYBURN VILLAGE STORE & TEA SHOP

34810 Clayburn Road
Clayburn, B.C. V2S7Y9
604-853-4020

I have a theory that it's tea drinkers who allow you to merge into rush hour traffic on Interstate 5, especially when they top it off with a little wave and a smile. It's like a secret tea drinker greeting I think. This doesn't mean that coffee drinkers are discourteous drivers, they might just be preoccupied, reloading their weapons or something. Perhaps I can get a government grant to explore this theory someday.

Clayburn doesn't have to worry about rush hours, located as it is on peaceful Clayburn Road north of Abbottsford. Clayburn is a lovingly preserved company town for the production of bricks, fired from clay hence the name.

If Clayburn has more than its share of tea drinkers, that's probably due to Clayburn Village Store. Built from the town's brick in 1912, today the establishment offers gourmet and imported foods, old fashioned candy, and Devonshire cream teas all in a turn of the last century setting. The dignified two story building, its countenance softened by clinging vines, features vintage display cases and wood plank flooring. Recipes from Britain are often served in the tea area, including Sticky Toffee Pudding and Gingerbread Cake with Maple Sauce, as well as a variety of cobblers employing local fruit. The currant scones with Devonshire cream is always available and always good.

The next time you're locked in bumper to bumper gridlock, let your thoughts drift to tea in the peaceful village of Clayburn. Oh, and while you're sitting there, let me merge into traffic in front of you. I'll smile and wave back.

Closes periodically for buying trips, so best to call ahead. Usually open Tuesday through Saturday at 9 a.m.

COTTAGE TEA ROOM

100-12220 Second Avenue
Steveston Village
Richmond, B.C. V7E3LE
604-241-1853

The south arm of the Fraser River forms a well-used harbor at historic Steveston Village. Seals spy back at tourists with reciprocal curiosity, as the day's catch is unloaded from commerical boats at Fisherman's Wharf. Sea gulls circle overhead, hoping for dinner and making greedy noises. There is something to do in Steveston at every season of the year, with much of it revolving around this maritime activity. You can book a river tour, and in April and May special sea lion tours will give you a close look at these formidable giants. In winter, the melancholy sound of a foghorn replaces the rousing street music of summer.

One block north of these nautical pursuits you can escape to the Cottage Tea Room, haven for castaways from the dockside scene. Well-lit and peaceful, this cozy and unpretentious tea room is a tribute to the owner, Margaret's fond childhood memories of the Lake District tea rooms of England. A collection of crisp linen souvenir tea towels forms a colorful montage on one wall, and a massive antique hutch commands the other. During good weather, tables outdoors fill up quickly, and inside floral fabric covers several more.

The English Tea Set includes assorted finger sandwiches, a chocolate, cookies, and a freshly made scone with Devon cream and jam. The menu also includes homemade soups, sandwiches, and pies. Margaret has a wide variety of teas to complement the food, and invests a great deal of thought to the comfort of her guests for tea. The service is gracious and attentive. Thus renewed, one can then really enjoy a dockside stroll and gift shop crawl in this quaint and little known corner of British Columbia.

Open daily 10 a.m. to 5 p.m. in the summer. Call ahead other seasons.

DURLACHER HOF
ALPINE COUNTRY INN

P.O. Box 1125
7055 Nesters Road
Whistler, B.C. V0N1B0
604-932-1924
Website: www.durlacherhof.com

If you still get a little chill like I do each time they show the zoom-in on Julie Andrews with arms outspread spinning on the mountain top trilling "The hills are alive, with the sound of music...", then you're going to feel right at home in Whistler. Innkeeper Erika Durlacher has created a bit of alpine Austria right here in her southern British Columbia home and guest inn, Durlacher Hof.

Well known to Whistler visitors as the most welcoming and gracious of the numerous inns of this resort, Erika knows that nothing says wilkommen in any language better than a European country casual Afternoon Tea.

Weather permitting, tea is served in the outdoor courtyard affording mountain and meadow vistas. Indoors, tables are set for tea in the lounge. White cotton damask and French country plaids cover tables set with colorful Villeroy & Boch whose floral motif is repeated in the centerpiece, freshly plucked from the garden. Equally fresh is the Austrian inspired menu which may feature such delights as fresh berries in tulip cups with fresh farm cheese, puff cheese sticks, savory biscuits with dill butter, warm scones with Erika's own preserves and sweet butter, an assortment of imaginative and pretty sandwiches or French onion tartlets. Top that with plum kuchen squares, meringue tarts or fruit-filled rouladen and you'll be looking for liederhosen in the next larger size.

So let "the hills fill your heart" as the tea fills your stomach at this most memorable and hospitable locations for tea.

Tea is offered from 1 p.m. to 4 p.m. daily.

THE EMPRESS HOTEL

721 Government Street
Victoria, B.C. V8W1W5
250-384-8111

In the beginning there was The Empress, and it was good.

For more than 82 years this bastion of old world dignity has kept a detached and imposing vigil over the heads of camera-toting tourists and aspiring bag-pipers on Victoria's Inner Harbour. Grand in the European chateau tradition, it is the quintessential teatime destination for those seek-ing an authentic Afternoon Tea.

There's a tangible peace to this the oldest of Victoria's afternoon teas, set as it is in the elegant Tea Lobby and spilling over in sum-mer to the Palm Court and the Empress Room. Tea is served from sterling tea pieces and bone china, meriting that you dress for the occasion and setting. The decidedly formal setting is at the same time comfortable, and the term "appropriate attire" has recently been updated in deference to travellers to include walking shorts and good casual clothes.

The assorted tea sandwiches verge on art, the honeyed crumpets and raisin scones delight, and no attention to elegant detail is overlooked in the signature elements that make this tea so special. Ample enough to replace a meal or to carry you through to a fashionably late dinner, admittedly this is one of the pricier teas in the Northwest, but it will continue to be an elegant memory you savor.

Summer sittings are 12:30, 2, 3:30 and 5 p.m. in the Tea Lobby. The Palm Court opens June 25 and has sittings at 1, 2:30 and 4 p.m. Winter sittings are 2 and 3:30 p.m.

FOUR MILE HOUSE

199 Old Island Highway
Victoria, B.C. V9B1G1
250-479-2514

In 1849 Peter Calvert left Scotland to start a new life in Canada. At that time the powerful Hudson Bay Company provided free passage around the Horn in return for a five year commitment to labor for their company. During the voyage Peter met and fell in love with another passenger, Miss Elizabeth Montgomery. They both worked hard, fulfilled their contracts, got married and saved enough money to buy six acres on a hill outside of Victoria where they built a little cottage that grew along with their family.

Cognizant of the tough four mile uphill struggle the horse-drawn coaches had on the road passing their home, Peter and Elizabeth opened a roadhouse. Here the horses could rest and the passengers quench their thirst and leave refreshed. Local lore recalls a time that the Calverts positioned a pet parrot that lived for years in a tree outside their door. The parrot had learned to whistle and call out "Whoa!" at the horses as they struggled with the incline. They would stop and turn in.

Extensive renovation has preserved the building and restored the charm to this fourth oldest structure in Victoria. Once again hospitality reins them in at Four Mile House, where Afternoon Tea is being served to the road-weary travelers steering a different type of horsepower. Served in old world charm on tables set with linens and fresh flowers in the old beamed dining room, it includes a selection of sandwiches, cream and raisin scones with jam, lemon tarts, cakes and fruits and variations on that traditional theme.

The entrepreneurial parrot and the Calvert family have been gone a long time now, but the spirit of hospitality in the form of Afternoon Tea still lingers.

Open daily with tea served from 2 p.m. to 4 p.m. Reservations during the summer months especially are advisable.

GATSBY MANSION BED & BREAKFAST

309 Belleville Street
Victoria, B.C. V8V1W3
250-388-9191

William Pendray made a promise to his new bride, Amelia. When they made their fortune, he would build her a home to rival the elaborate Queen Anne "painted ladies" she had admired on their honeymoon to San Francisco in 1877. True to his vows, hard work at his soap and paint business allowed the construction of a dream mansion overlooking the Inner Harbour of Victoria before the turn of the century.

No detail was overlooked. Layers of sweet molasses protected the Italian stained glass from harm during shipment. German fresco painters were commissioned to paint the ceiling which would be lit with the sparkle of imported crystal chandeliers. Mr. Pendray's passion for topiary resulted in a yard replete with fancifully shaped yews, holly and cedar. A huge shrub coaxed with clippers into the shape of a teddy bear held hidden Easter eggs for his enchanted children.

Tea is served in all parts of the lovingly restored mansion, owned today by Mrs. Rita Ray-Wilson. Resplendent with period antiques, original polished hardwood and old world charm, its location walking distance from the harbor makes it a favorite of visitors. The dining room seats 65 in a tone of casual elegance, and the plated fare includes all the traditional trimmings.

A glimpse into the glory of early Victoria is yours as a guest for tea in this amiable and homey setting.

Tea is offered daily from 2 to 4 p.m. Reservations are advisable.

CROWNE PLAZA HOTEL GEORGIA

801 West Georgia Street
Vancouver, B.C. V6C1P7
604-682-5566
Website: www.hotelgeorgia.bc.ca

The year was 1927. While people cheerfully foxtrotted to the strains of "My Blue Heaven," Charles Lindbergh flew through it to Paris. Stravinsky unveiled a new musical creation, and the paint was still drying on the canvasses of artists Matisse and Chagal. It was in this atmosphere charged with achievement and creativity a masterwork of another kind was created, The Hotel Georgia, today the Crowne Plaza Hotel Georgia in downtown Vancouver. A comprehensive restoration of this classical beaux-arts style hotel was completed in 1998, reviving its original warmth and dignity. Declared a Historic Site by the city that same year, the Hotel Georgia is now assured to be "protected for all time."

Elegant Afternoon Teas are currently offered in their restaurant, which will be undergoing a facelift and tummy tuck of its own shortly. Look for the reconcepted venue to be unveiled in the spring of 2001. Until then, rich baked goods, Devon cream and fresh strawberry preserves, a variety of traditional tea sandwiches and teacakes are offered with a wide tea selection. Port, sherry and sparkling wines are offered to round off the tea if you choose.

Exciting things are happening to tea here, including a partnering with those youthful dynamos of 'T' to supply a fresh and interesting variety of premium tea blends to the newly reconcepted tea area in the works. Be sure to foxtrot your way downtown for tea. I get out of breath if I sing while I'm dancing, but here goes, "you'll see a smiling face, a warm embrace, a cozy room....(something-something-something)...the roses bloom." 1927 was a good year in this blue heaven known as Vancouver.

Tea is offered 2:30 p.m. to 5 p.m. daily. Call for reservations and updates.

HOTEL VANCOUVER

900 West Georgia Street
Vancouver, B.C.
604-684-3131

The gaily wrapped boxes formed a promising little pile. My family had gathered around a cake that screamed "Good Luck, Sharon!" in day-glo frosting to celebrate my graduation from high school 35 years ago. Layers of festive giftwrap and shiney bows gave way to a slow dirge of serious-minded gifts. While I did my best to appear enthralled with each black pen set and career-minded brown leatherette calendar notebook binder, these carefully selected gifts heralded nothing but serious Responsibility. I felt weighted down with the gray cloud of looming dutiful adulthood. One last little box remained, from my favorite Aunt Marwayne. The card read "Don't forget to have fun too!" Nestled there inside layers and layers of cloudlike tissue was a satin-lined, sparkly pink crystal-beaded evening bag with adjustable gold strap. The cloud lifted.

The Hotel Vancouver is a formal and serious-minded building. The verdigris copper roof no longer dominates the skyline as it did in 1939 when the Canadian Pacific Railroad barons built it, but the dignity still remains. Tea, guaranteed to make the day's clouds lift, is offered once again in the 900 West Lobby Lounge, a recently restored room of old world charms and polished wood, and includes pastry choices, warm scones with cream, and traditional tea sandwiches presented with great style.

Tea at the Hotel Vancouver promises great fun in dignified surroundings. Try to behave like an adult.

Tea is offered daily from 2 p.m. to 4 p.m.

JAMES BAY TEA ROOM

332 Menzies Street
Victoria, B.C. V8V2G9
250-382-8282
E-Mail: jamesbaytearoom@home.com

Early on sleepy Sunday mornings in summer, the calm of the Inner Harbour of Victoria is roused by a goofy little water ballet of sorts. Seven diminutive harbor ferries, all bearing remarkable likeness to Popeye's cartoon craft, churn the waters to the strains of the Blue Danube Waltz over a loudspeaker. Their chorus line gives way to watery figure eights, fleur de lis, and starburst maneuvers as they ply through each other's wakes with a serious looking captain at the wheel and an equally intent seagull or two riding along on top. It's delightfully quirky, and part of the charm of the Inner Harbour that makes even the sleepy Sunday morning dockside crowd smile and cheer.

The day begins early at the James Bay Tea Room too. In the shadow of the dignified Parliament Building, a short walk from the harbor, Bernd and Yvonne Woerpel have risen early for the past 12 years preparing meals and teas to the delight of growing fans. Touted as "an English atmosphere in Victoria", this busy eatery operates from a charming 1900's two story clap-board house, adorned with colorful hanging baskets and striped awnings, that once housed a corner market. The comfortable and unpretentious English country decor provides the perfect setting for the hearty British fare and afternoon teas, that most civilized of British customs. It is the perfect way to keep that silly ferry boat water ballet smile on your face throughout a pleasant Victoria afternoon.

Open Monday through Saturday 7 a.m. to 8 p.m. and Sunday 8 a.m. to 8 p.m. Afternoon Tea daily all day with a special Sunday High Tea.

OAK BAY BEACH HOTEL

1175 Beach Drive
Victoria, B.C. V8S2N2
250-598-4556

I am married to an optimist who will pull me onto a bus and then find out where it's heading. With the same anticipation that Captain Vancouver must have felt turning the bow of this ship *Discovery* into the uncharted harbors of the island that bears his name, my husband is always certain there is some destination worthy of exploration on any city's community transit bus he picks at random. We have done this all over the world. Sometimes he's right. That was how we ventured out of downtown Victoria one beautiful summer day years ago and found ourselves in the enchanting little community of Oak Bay.

Oak Bay hugs the shoreline of Haro Strait, the strip of blue water that separates Vancouver Island from the U.S. San Juan Islands fifteen miles to the east. Mount Baker forms an imposing backdrop to this maritime view, and the fortunate visitor with sharp eyes may see the distinctive dorsal fin of the resident orcas cruising the chilly waters. In this neighborhood, the 75 year old Oak Bay Beach Hotel proudly rests, a dignified dowager of Tudor styling lifting her hem at the shoreline of well manicured grounds and pristine flower beds.

Welcomed into the serenity of dark wood mouldings and traditional furnishings and antiques, the hotel has a stately and tranquil air. An open menu for tea is most hospitable and well presented living up to their solid reputation for "Olde English Comforts and Fine Service."

Tea is served daily from April 15 through October 14, 2:30 p.m. to 5 p.m.

OLDE ENGLAND INN

429 Lampson Street
Victoria, B.C. V9A5Y9
250-388-4353

A deep fold of time cradles the Olde England Inn invoking the exalted period of Elizabethan England. Shielded from the 21st century by imposing Douglas firs, this stately manor built in 1910 was converted into a popular inn more than 50 years ago. The five acre grounds on which the inn rests recreate an exuberant English village, including full size replicas of Anne Hathaway's cottage, gardens, and The Ark at Tadcaster (where the Pilgrim fathers chatted over an idea of a little boat trip with their families to the New World.) Strolling down Chaucer Lane reveals leaded windows of little shopfronts displaying artifacts of cultural, historical and educational value.

A remarkable collection of period antiques look right at home in the richly panelled Baronial Hall. A 300 year old table once owned by the Bronte sisters may hold your tea service, and unique rooms dressed for the period are available to extend your stay overnight in ornate canopied beds formerly owned by European monarchs.

Old Country Teas are offered in a romantic, informal setting, and feature traditional fare redolent of the era. The timeless mystique of this tea time would no doubt cause Shakespeare to exclaim, "O England! Model to thy inward greatness..." and "Prithee, pass the scones."

Hours for tea are noon to 4:30 p.m. Monday through Saturday, and Sunday 2:00 p.m. to 4:30 p.m.

THE TEAROOM AT PLAZA ESCADA

757 West Hastings Street
Sinclair Centre
Vancouver, B.C. V6C1A1
604-688-8558

The Plaza Escada pulses with an upbeat energy. While the changing rooms are filled with smart, self-reliant, young professional women trying on the very latest fashions in the chic Euro-boutique, in the adjoining area the really smart ones are sitting, refreshing themselves with a relaxing cup of tea.

In keeping with the less-is-more influence, the setting for The Tearoom at Plaza Escada is millenium sleek and uncluttered without being sterile. More than 40 teas of the Republic of Tea's line are offered for sale or for your on-site refreshment. Shelves with modern tea accessories and stylish pots beckon.

Can't squeeze into that sleek little size 5 spandex micro mini that looked so chic on the pouty mannequin? That little cashmere number over your credit limit without a second mortgage? Who cares? Immerse yourself in something new, imaginative and creative. Have tea at the Tea Room at Plaza Escada next time you're in downtown Vancouver.

Tea is served from 10 a.m. to 6 p.m. Monday through Saturday.

POINT ELLICE HOUSE

2616 Pleasant Street
Victoria, B.C.
250-385-1518 or 250-380-6506

When the cry of "Gold!" echoed along the canyons of the upper Fraser River in 1858, Victoria was transformed almost overnight from a quiet outpost for the Hudson Bay Company to the major outfitting headquarters for the goldfields. The price of a building lot in town rose from $5 to $500 as more than 20,000 fortune hunters staked claim. Thousands more arrived from Europe flushed with the prospects of easy wealth. One of these was Peter O'Reilly of Ireland.

Upwardly mobile and socially connected quite quickly, the O'Reilly family was able to buy an Italianate house on the shore of Victoria Arm after only 9 years, and there they raised four children. One daughter, Kathleen, was so strongly attached to the property that she lived in the home for 78 years, spurning suitors. There are those who feel she may still reside there in spirit.

Today the B.C. Heritage Attractions manages the house and gardens and presents Afternoon Teas on the croquet lawn May 13 through September 8. A tape-recorded self-guided tour is the perfect preface to a leisurely tea on the lawn. All the furniture, art, wallpaper, china, and clothing are original to the house.

As it was in the late 1800s, Point Ellice House has once again become a magnet for pleasant social activities and teas. The Irish eyes of Kathleen O'Reilly must surely be smiling.

Outdoor teas are served May 13 to September 8, noon to 4 p.m.

SECRET GARDEN TEA COMPANY

5559 West Boulevard
Vancouver, BC V6M3W6
604-261-3070

Frances Hodgson Burnett was a Victorian writer embraced by readers on both sides of "the pond". During one gray part of an otherwise vivid life she became a divorcee, a scandalous state for that time in England, and consequently fell out of favor with society. It was during her emotional convalescence that she "spent nearly three weeks in soft Kentish rains kneeling on a small rubber mat on the grass edge of a heavenly old herbaceous border bed," then arose completely renewed and crafted the magical 1911 classic *The Secret Garden*.

The Secret Garden Tea Company offers that same sense of personal renewal and magic. People linger here, on a big soft sofa by a large welcoming fireplace, and at tables dotting the comfortable and popular tea room in this fashionably eclectic Kerrisdale neighborhood of Vancouver. It has been the mission of owners and friends, artists and mothers, Kathy Wyder and Andrea Wadman from the beginning to create a charming place "where the traditions of afternoon tea are delightfully intertwined with the comforts of home." The proof of that success is in the following for their traditional tea, and the desire you'll have to linger over it in gracious surroundings.

Tea is offered daily, all completely handcrafted with no mixes or artificial ingredients, served amid flowers and ivy on a three-tiered tray, with magical star-shaped scones and artistic touches. One day advance reservations are required for the preparation.

Experience your own sense of renewal and magical refreshment with The Secret Garden's special tea.

Open for breakfast, lunch and High Tea - Monday through Wednesday 7 a.m. to 6 p.m., Thursday and Friday 7 a.m. to 9 p.m., Saturday 8 a.m. to 9 p.m. and Sunday 9 a.m. to 6 p.m. with High Tea requiring 24 hour advance notice, served from noon to closing.

SUTTON PLACE HOTEL

845 Burrard Street
Vancouver, B.C. V6Z2K6
604-682-5511
E-Mail: info@vcr.suttonplace.com

In 1886, from the mountains to the east of Vancouver, the rythmic ringing of metal on metal signaled great change. The final miles of track were being laid for the transcontinental railroad. The invisible cargo being drawn in was government and commerce. Within two years of its completion, the population of Vancouver had swelled from 2,000 to 27,000 hearty souls.

Today Vancouver has blossomed into the fastest growing metropolitan area of North America. With a backdrop of mountain grandeur and pristine bays and inlets its natural setting commands that you slow your pace to appreciate it glories. The road system does the same thing. Enlightened urban planning has resulted in a municipality of 135 parks covering some 2,700 acres. No major urban freeway scars this city, forcing you to slow down, exactly what you must do to enjoy the delights of a good Afternoon Tea.

The Sutton Place Hotel offers such a tea in the heart of this vibrant city. Reminiscent of stately European manors, this luxury five star hotel is furnished with subdued elegance. A tranquil setting for tea is provided in the award-winning Fleuri Restaurant, recently selected by readers of "Where Vancouver" magazine as "Best Hotel Dining" experience. Its damask covered walls and soft chairs provide a soothing site for a memorable tea. Traditional English finger sandwiches, warm scones with rich Devonshire cream, French pastries and jams are served with a large selection of teas, most notably their signature Sutton Afternoon Blend. German born and French trained chef Kai Lermen is the inspiration for the international essence of the tea. Attentive service, tasteful touches and delicious food and tea make it a delight to accept their invitation to "indulge and escape".

Tea is served Monday through Saturday 2:30 to 5:30 p.m. Special teas in the Chinese and Japanese traditions are offered as well.

SYLVIA HOTEL

1154 Gilford Street
Vancouver, B.C. V6G2P6
604-681-9321

I know you cannot stand in the way of progress, but all of the tinted glass skyscrapers springing up in Vancouver these days makes the unassuming little Sylvia Hotel all that much more beloved to me. Eight brick stories veiled modestly in creeping vines present a face onto English Bay of simple dignity and old world charm. Located on the south edge of Stanley Park, the Sylvia was built in 1912. It was the dream of a local businessman to build a hotel as a legacy for each of his daughters. This first, for his oldest daughter Sylvia, regretably turned out to be his last, as his fortune went the way of many during the Depression.

Tea is offered daily. Fresh warm scones, finger sandwiches, and local fruit are plated and presented on attractive china.

The businessman's daughter Sylvia is 100 now and still resides in Vancouver having aged with the grace and dignity of her namesake hotel.

Tea is offered every day from 4p.m. to 6 p.m.

'T'

1568 W. Broadway
Vancouver, B.C.
604-878-3000
Website: www.tealeaves.com

In 1995 fifteen youthful tea lovers (all under the age of 30) combined their passion, financial resources and boundless energy to create 'T'. With a mission to provide the public with "education, enlightenment and enchantment" you might expect it to be called 'E', but the means to that lofty goal is through whole leaf premium teas from all over the world.

'T' is a happy celebration of cultural diversity, and an energetic and imaginative forum for tea education, cuppings (tea tastings), and tea rituals and ceremony. Last year, in fact with the consultation and blessings of three Japanese tea masters, 'T' opened an authentic Cha-si-tsu, a room in which Chado, the ceremonial tea can be conducted every third Friday at 7 p.m.

Primarily a tea retail/wholesale operation, more than 170 fine teas are stocked, 60 of which are always available to be served to you by the pot at simple wood tables in a sleek, uncluttered and modern setting. The artful simplicity extends to food refreshments in the form of modest baked goods, but there is no question that they are only the back-up singers for the star, tea.

Tea pots ranging from upscale Italian designs to England's beloved "Brown Betty" form an international fashion parade along the electric green shelves, punctuated with hundreds of tea boxes in glossy basic black. Sniff jars provide an olfactory treat, and tea tastings are conducted every third Monday at 7:30 p.m. In addition to a landslide mail order and cutting edge web business, 'T' even hosts popular afternoon tea dances reminiscent of the 1940s at many of the city's finer hotels. Details are available with a call, visit, or cyber view at their website.

You must marvel at the sense of direction and purpose that energizes this eclectic group. I wonder, could it just be possible that tea drinking imbues that wonderful vigor? "Another pot over here, please."

Open 9:30 a.m. to 7 p.m. Monday through Thursday, open until 11 p.m. on Friday and Saturday, and 11 a.m. to 6 p.m. on Sunday.

WEDGEWOOD HOTEL
Bacchus Restaurant

845 Hornby Street
Vancouver, B.C. V6Z1V1
604-689-7777

An almost constant flow of trendy and interesting people flood Robson Street daily, drifting in and out of the intimate chic shops, eddying in the sidewalk cafes and ethnic eateries that define the area as Vancouver's premier shopping district. Less than a block away, the serenity and charm of an elegant boutique-style luxury hotel offers a cool, refreshing respite from this flow of humanity with a delightful Afternoon Tea in the finest European tradition.

The Wedgewood Hotel, owned and operated by Greek-born Mrs. Eleni Skalbania, was created as a hospitality haven for discerning guests seeking luxurious surroundings in an intimate European atmosphere. Small by North American hotel standards with 89 rooms on 14 floors, each with a balcony, the manageable size allows a refinement of detail and personal service. This extends to the tea service in the Four Diamond Award-winning Bacchus Lounge, overseen by Canada's National Chef for 1999 Robert Sulatycky.

The Greek god of revelry, Bacchus, smiles down from the canvas on which he frolics, perhaps amused by your choice of tea over wine. Polished cherry wood gleams under Venetian glass lighting, and rich tones cover the plush banquettes by the stone fireplace. Opulent floral displays and antiques dress the high ceilinged room. Tea is served on three-tiered trays, beautifully and traditionally presented. Your choice of tea is complemented by a fresh fruit compote, finger sandwiches that celebrate the region's bounty with their fillings, pastries, a chocolate square, and fresh hot scones with Devonshire cream and preserves.

As it has since 1984, the Wedgewood Hotel offers a refreshing eddy in the flow of life in this busy and fashionable district.

Tea is offered every day 2 p.m. to 4 p.m. Reservations are appreciated.

WINDSOR HOUSE TEA ROOM

2540 Windsor Road
Victoria, B.C.
250-595-3135

Locals jest that a visit to Oak Bay is so British one crosses behind "The Tweed Curtain". It's true that this spectacular little community unabashedly revels in its authentically British roots, after all, even Rudyard Kipling felt at home here. Riding the free double-decker bus you pass Tudoresque shopping areas, tea rooms, crisp white cricket matches, and lovingly nurtured rose gardens, ("green fingers" they call it in England. In my homeland we can only lay claim to the lowly thumb.) Flakey-crusted meat pie aromas emanate from lace-curtained kitchen windows. Tweed-clad men stroll respectfully a few paces behind their swaggering Welsh Corgis and Jack Russells. This cultured civility extends even to that dying art form, courtesy behind the wheel of an automobile.

A welcoming two story Tudor style building a block from the rocky shoreline of Oak Bay has been home to the Windsor House Tea Room for the past seven years. The dignity it emanates bespeaks centuries' longer. Authentic Victorian floral wallpapers, coved ceilings, polished hardwoods, and leaded glass windows empart the essence of the era when "the sun never set on the British Empire." In this homey setting, delicious teas and critically acclaimed meals are served in several dining areas and private rooms of the old house in true Victorian style. The Timmers expressed their clear vision for this tea room they have nurtured on their menu. It reads, "A good meal....a good friend...a time treasured." If there is a British equivalent to "green fingers" for hospitality, you'll surely find it here.

Open Monday through Saturday 11 a.m. - 5 p.m. High Tea is served by reservation all day.

TEATIME IN THE NORTHWEST

"I have never tasted tea like this. It is smooth, pungent, and instantly addicting. This is from Grand Auntie, my mother explains . . . she told me if I buy cheap tea, then I am saying that my whole life has not been worth something better . . . If I buy just a little, then I am saying that my lifetime is almost over, so she bought enough tea for another lifetime."

Amy Tan
The Kitchen God's Wife

CAMILLE'S TEA SHOPPE & GIFTS

9375 N. Government Way
Hayden, ID 83835
208-762-4472
E-Mail: camille'stea@bigplanet.com

Our Camano Island home must have been written up in some gourmet guidebook for deer. They come everyday to our yard, feasting on my herbaceous border with the abandon of a Weight Watchers' convention at a well-stocked salad bar. They wash it down with water from our fish pond, and for dessert, lick up the seeds I spread on an ancient stump every sunrise for the birds (who watch them petulantly from the overhanging madrona.) We've got an agreement. If I don't complain about the missing flowers, they'll leave Ken's young apple trees alone, and they'll throw in some joyful entertainment to boot. I think I've made a good deal. We're on our fourth generation of leggy, dancing spotted fawns this spring. That's entertainment.

Entertainment of a different type is offered in Hayden, Idaho, now that Camille's Tea Shoppe & Gifts opened in 1998. In a cute little blue bungalow with 1930s charm, Johanne Haymond serves popular afternoon teas. The quirky little house provides interesting nooks and crannies for tea, lit by leaded glass windows and dressed in Canadian Victorian family heirlooms. In the main dining room, which seats 14, a fireplace casts a warm glow on a vintage teacup collection. Tea can also be in the parlor setting of the second floor reading room where seating is upon a five piece parlor set that once graced the home of Johanne's great-grandmother in Quebec. Yet another dining room seats eight more upstairs for private parties. Homemade scones, fruit, soups, finger sandwiches and a dessert appear on both tea sets, and even adorable teapot cakes can be made for your special celebration here.

The drawing of a grand lady in Camille's logo was drawn by Johanne's grandmother, Delia Chabot-LaCroix, when she was only twelve years old. Johanne used the art to honor her grandmother and named this lady (and her shop) "Camille's" to honor *Camelia sinensis* - tea! Here you will find a great little gift shop as well as a relaxing tea in the warmth of vintage charms and family heirlooms. Now that's entertainment in grand style.

Open different hours for the seasons. Teas require one day advance notice.

IN CAHOOTS FOR TEA

118 Central Avenue
Great Falls, MT 59401
406-452-2225
Website: www.in-cahoots-for-tea.com

Almost two hundred years ago when the Lewis & Clark Expedition portaged through this area, they carried in their buckskins compressed bricks of tea from which a little chunk would be broken off and plunked into a pot of boiling Missouri River water. It probably helped to wash down the roasted beaver tails and buffalo humps they ate.

Sophistication and quality in tea drinking has come to Great Falls, ushered in by lifelong resident, farm wife, mother of six and tea lover Pam Cahut in her roomy tea emporium, In Cahoots for Tea. Housed on the street level of an old three-story hotel, its high coved ceiling has the original embossed copper panels from the early 1900s. Antique fixtures hold an array of tea wares and gifts, and yards and yards of salvaged book shelves hold the 100 plus bulk teas, decorated sugar cubes and British pantry goodies she stocks. Unique teas are available here as well. Pam offers a line of Native American therapeutic herbals as well as packaged teas from England and Ireland.

Next door to a gourmet candy shop is always a good place to be. Just through a little garden gate is a new tea room called Primrose. The three businesses complement each other nicely as the line between them is blurred with shoppers nibbling their hand-dipped chocolates as they make their tea purchase and await their tea reservations.

A big celebration commemorating the upcoming 200th anniversary of the Lewis & Clark Expedition is gaining momentum in Great Falls, and if you love history like we do, it sounds exciting. Pam reports that one local outdoorsman will even guide you in rustic handmade canoes to visit the encampment sites. She ought to know. Nestled there amid her gourmet imported teas and special blends are the bricks of tea they use around the campfire. Bring your own buffalo humps and beaver tails.

The shop is open Monday through Saturday 9:30 a.m. to 5:30 p.m. Mail order and website sales as well.

THE BEST TEAROOMS OF HAWAII

Late in the 18th century winter drizzle often dampened Captain Vancouver's enthusiasm for mapping the intricate Pacific Northwest coastline. With his outdoor plans impeded by misty weather and low visibility, it's likely the good captain found his thoughts turning to sunnier climes and pineapples. Like countless Northwesterners for the next 200 years who shed their goosedown jackets and followed, Captain Vancouver pulled up anchor and headed down to the islands of Hawaii.

Honoring that fine tradition of escapism, the following section features many of the best tearooms in Hawaii. Aloha!

ASTON WAIKIKI BEACHSIDE HOTEL

2452 Kalakaua Avenue
Honolulu, Oahu, Hawaii
808-931-2100

In Hawaiian, Honolulu means "sheltered bay", a place of safety and repose. Now each weekend, and other days by special arrangement, a group of good friends and tea lovers provide that haven in the form of a peaceful afternoon tea at the Aston Waikiki Beachside Hotel. Renowned in Honolulu as the Ladies of Winterbourne, these generous caterers have pooled all their family heirlooms and pressed them into tea service. "How sad not to use beautiful things," partner Nikki Yasutake muses while re-membering her grandmother who left her the porcelain legacy used at today's tea, "I can't remember any occasion being special enough for her to bring them out of the storage chest."

Every Saturday and Sunday the Palm Court and Lobby of this cozy little hotel are transformed with traditional lace tablecloths, fresh flowers, and the ladies' antique china. The tea is a celebration of Queen Liliuokalani's personal fascination with another Queen, Victoria, and all things British in general.

The three course afternoon tea is accompanied by three different teas all prepared at your table. Classical music and a bubbling fountain strewn with rose petals attest to careful attention to a detail; and from the warm blueberry scones with clotted cream through to the ginger cream puffs and delicate sherry cake the food and presentation reinforces that art.

Nikki's grandmother must be pleased that her china and silver are being so lovingly honored at this most special of occasions, Afternoon Tea at the Aston Waikiki Beachside Hotel.

Tea is served Saturday and Sunday from 2 p.m. to 5 p.m. with one day advance booking. Weekdays tea is available for groups of 10 or more by appointment.

BANYAN VERANDA
at the Sheraton Moana Surf Rider

2365 Kalakaua Avenue
Honolulu, Oahu, Hawaii
808-922-3111

Waikiki's social history is written on the faces of the landmark hotels on the shoreline, and the "First Lady of Waikiki"- The Moana has been a social beacon for pleasant discourse and refreshment since it opened in 1901. That year rooms overlooking the blue Pacific cost $1.50 per night and Afternoon Tea was offered by attentive servers in white gloves.

Family members of the Big Five sugar agents always took tea at the Moana, perhaps sweetening their Earl Grey with the fruits of their labors, and watched as workmen planted a small banyan tree by the terrace. Today that banyan tree stands 75 feet tall with arms that spread 150 feet over the veranda where tea is served, by a new generation of white gloved attendants. Wicker furniture and fresh flowers invoke a bygone era of leisure, as three-tiered servers arrive at your table bearing traditional tea sandwiches, pastries and cream scones served with their delightful signature blend Moana Royale, (a tropical blend of mango, passion fruit, and pineapple) or any of the more traditional teas.

Life certainly is sweet in Hawaii, and not all of it is because of sugar production. To immerse yourself in the sweet, soft days of another era, the Banyan Veranda is a delightfully shady spot for tea overlooking the Pacific.

Tea is served Monday through Saturday 1 p.m. to 4:30 p.m. and on Sunday from 3 p.m. to 5 p.m.

HALEKULANI

2199 Kalia Road
Honolulu, Oahu, Hawaii
808-923-2311

With a name that translates from Hawaiian to "house befitting heaven," you already have been given a big clue as to the structure that awaits you on the two mile strip of sand that constitutes Waikiki. The original hotel was built on the beach in 1917, added onto stylishly in 1932, and then lovingly restored in 1984 to regal opulence.

Tea is served from cane tea carts to your flower adorned table on the veranda. In addition to caviar garnished smoked salmon sandwiches, camembert en brioche, this comfortable tea includes currant scones with cream, tropical fruits and light pastries. A tea truly "befitting heaven" awaits you at this famed hotel.

Tea is offered everyday from 3 to 5 p.m. with no reservations required.

HAWAII PRINCE HOTEL

100 Holomoana Street
Honolulu, Oahu, Hawaii
808-956-1111

My sailor husband never met a yacht harbor he didn't like. The sound of wind rattling, clanging and clanking the mast fittings is sweet music to his ears. Like a water spaniel following some unhearable high-pitched dog whistle, he can sniff out an enclave of sailboats at great distances and find the shortest route to their dock. His idea of heaven includes a sleek fully-equipped sailboat with self-polishing brass, self-oiling teak, and a self-filling teapot, perpetually heeling to warm, steady winds blowing us to some sandy shore where he can pick our dinner off a tree.

The Marina Front Lounge of the Hawaii Prince Hotel affords like-minded folks a glimpse of such a heaven. Not only can you monitor the activities of the Alawal Yacht Harbor, but there's tea too! The high-ceiling lobby is a mass of pink Italian marble with English slate accents. A grand piano provides a soft musical accompaniment, surrounded as it is by linen covered tables for afternoon tea. Tea includes assorted tea sandwiches that can include fresh shrimp, watercress, and cucumber. The scones are offered with rich Devonshire cream, and followed by chocolate dipped strawberries and lovely little petit fours. While touched with grandeur, the atmosphere and service is casual and comfortable, and in at least one man's opinion, overlooks heaven.

Tea is offered every day 4 p.m. to 6 p.m. with one day advance reservation and guarantee please.

LODGE AT KOELE

Kaemoku Highway
Lanai City, Lanai, Hawaii
808-565-7300

"Norfolk Pines?" Visitors often scratch their heads quizzically as they stare up at this unexpected flora on the central plateau of Lanai. It was a New Zealander and naturalist, George Munro, on his days off from managing the Lanai Ranch, who rode on horseback through the mountains casting seeds to control erosion. Since that time in 1910, the seedlings have become statuesque at this 1,600 foot elevation, and generations of visitors have relaxed in the shaded seclusion, the result of the Kiwi's labors.

In 1924 the entire island was purchased by pineapple baron Jim Dole for $1.1 million (about the cost of Bill Gate's garage.) Today more than a million pineapples a day are loaded onto barges for the sea journey to the canneries of Oahu, and the glasses of Mai Tai lovers everywhere.

The Lodge at Koele was gently developed by the corporate successor to Jim Dole's company, Castle & Cooke, to celebrate the unique natural beauty of this the "Pineapple Island." Island stone fireplace, heavy beamed ceilings and inviting verandas define the lodge, where tea is served daily. In the casual setting of the Tea Room, Music Room or the porches tea is offered buffet style. Local coconut makes melt in your mouth macaroons, local citrus curd, light freshly baked scones, and assorted tea sandwiches platters are always adorned with the fresh pineapple that played such a role in the history of this paradise island.

Tea is served at 3 p.m. everday with reservations a good idea.

PRINCEVILLE HOTEL

5520 Kahaku Road
Princeville, Kauai, Hawaii
808-826-9644 or 800-826-4400

When explorer Captain James Cook dropped anchor off the island of Kauai in 1778 he was well into his voyage of discovery. Historians agree that his landing clearly delineates the beginning of uniting European and Hawaiian influences on this paradise of sheer cliffs, dense jungles, volcanos and beaches. One can only speculate that this brave British explorer might have relished a good strong pot of the brew that unifies East and West too, tea.

The North Shore region is an area rich in sacred sites and unrivaled beauty. It is also the location of one of the world's best resorts, the Princeville Hotel. Afternoon tea at the Princeville is served on soft couches and armchairs of the great room with a clear view of Hanalei Bay, film location for the movie *South Pacific*. Tea fare varies with the season, but can include fresh fruit tarts and the elegance of strawberries in Grand Marnier and cream.

With the perfumed breezes blowing up from the bay mingling with the aroma of rich hot tea, Captain Cook must have felt that all was right with the world.

Tea is served everday from 3 to 5 p.m., reservations are a must.

RITZ-CARLTON KAPALUA

1 Ritz-Carlton Drive
Kapalua, Maui, Hawaii
808-669-6200

Like generations of us who shed our thermal underwear and followed, Captain George Vancouver was no doubt dreaming of Hawaii when winter weather impeded his mapping expeditions of the Pacific Northwest. Turning the bow of his good ship *Discovery* southward he accomplished a great deal. He solidified the British presence in the Hawaiian Islands in the 1790s, gained the friendship and trust of King Kamehameha, made his cold and miserable crew happy, and got to feel the warm sand between his toes.

Set amid the dramatic scenery of craggy cliffs and the sparkling blue Pacific, the Ritz-Carlton Kapalua nestles like a jewel in the sun. Consistent with the elegance and quality that one associates with all of the Ritz-Carlton properties, superb service is the rule. Afternoon tea here rises to those expectations as well with your choice of the indoor elegance of the darkly panelled Lobby Lounge or on the terrace under gaily colored umbrellas amid blooms of tropical plants.

Like Captain Vancouver and his crew, isn't it always nice to have a choice?

Tea is served daily from 2:30 p.m. to 4:30 p.m. with one day advance notice and guarantee please.

THE VOLCANO TEAPOT TEA ROOM

19-4041 Kilauea
P.O. Box 511
Volcano, Hawaii 96785
808-967-7112

At an elevation of 3,800 feet on the side of an active volcano in Kona coffee country lies a tea room like no other.

The Volcano Teapot is a combination tea room and bed & breakfast housed in a restored turn of the last century guest cottage in the heart of Volcano Village. Originally part of a large estate, the cottage now sits on the remaining two plus acres of pine trees, fruit trees, camellias, fern and native exotics. In an area where the winter temperatures can reach as low as 38 degrees and the lava flows as hot as 1,000 degrees, it is an area of unexpected contrasts.

Antoinette Bullough and her husband Bill chose this setting for their charming business. Special tea events and classes are set amid antiques, fresh flowers, and the soft comforters of the guest cottage, warmed by the glow of a wood stove. Less than a mile away lava flows magically at Volcanoes National Park. With Pele, the Goddess of Fire overseeing the preparation of your tea, a visit to Volcano Teapot Tea Room is likely to warm you from head to toe.

Call or write for a schedule of upcoming tea events or to schedule a tea during your next visit.

FAVORITE TEATIME RECIPES

SANDWICHES & SAVORIES

CHICKEN ALMOND TEA SANDWICHES

Time & Again – St. Helens, Oregon

*The almonds and celery provide a little welcome crunch
in this tea sandwich.*

3	cooked and finely diced chicken breasts
1	cup finely sliced celery
1	cup slivered almonds
1	tablespoon dry or fresh dill
1	8 oz. package of cream cheese, softened
1	cup mayonnaise
	Green leaf lettuce
1	tomato, thinly sliced
4	slices of bread

Beat cream cheese with mixer until fluffy, add mayonnaise and dill, beat until mixed well. Fold in rest of ingredients adjusting the amount of mayonnaise to achieve the consistency you like.

Spread on walnut wheat bread or Oregon hazelnut bread with a light coating of mayonnaise, green leaf lettuce and thinly sliced tomato. Cut into eight finger sandwiches.

CHOPPED EGG & BLACK OLIVE TEA SANDWICH

My husband thinks black olives ruin anything they're in the same room with.
I disagree. Before you pick sides, try this tea sandwich spread for yourself.

6	slices buttered whole wheat or hazelnut bread
4	hard boiled eggs, chopped
4	tablespoons chopped black olives
2	tablespoons mayonnaise
2	tablespoons sour cream
1	tablespoon Dijon mustard
1	teaspoon chopped thyme
	Salt and pepper to taste

In a large bowl combine the eggs and the remaining ingredients. Toss with two forks until well blended.

Place 3 tablespoons of the filling on each of 3 slices, spread evenly. Top with remaining bread, trim crusts and cut diagonally into triangles.

NASTURTIUM TEA SANDWICHES

1	4 oz. container softened cream cheese
8	thin slices focaccia bread or any rustic bread, with crusts removed
	Unsalted butter, softened for ease of spreading
1-1/2	cups nasturtium flowers from your own garden, pesticide free

In medium bowl beat the cream cheese with electric mixer until light and fluffy and set aside. Thinly spread each slice of bread with butter.

Top half the buttered slices with the cream cheese, spreading evenly to edges. Arrange the flowers on top of the cream cheese, making sure to extend some petals over the edge for showy color.

Cover with the remaining slices of bread and press gently into place. Cut into finger sandwiches or triangles.

CUCUMBER TEA SANDWICHES

Samuel Johnson said, "A cucumber should be well sliced, and dressed with pepper and vinegar, and then thrown out, as good for nothing." My husband agrees with him, but I most emphatically do not.

2	medium cucumbers, peeled and sliced thinly
1	cup apple cider vinegar
1	tablespoon sugar
	Salt and pepper
	Fresh mint leaves
1/4	cup mayonnaise

Marinate the sliced cucumber in the brine made from vinegar, sugar, salt, and pepper for about one hour. Drain well and pat dry with paper towels.

Remove the crusts from 6 slices of thin white bread. Spread lightly with mayonnaise. Lay four fresh mint leaves on each of 3 slices. Over the top of the mint, layer the thin cucumber slices.

Top with the other bread slice, mayonnaise side down and cut into four small finger sandwiches. Garnish with mint.

Makes 12 tea sandwiches.

CURRIED CHICKEN CROISSANT

Victorian Rose Tea Room – Port Orchard, Washington

This tasty croissant sandwich has its perfect pairing with Market Spice Tea according to Sandy O'Donnell, owner of the popular Victorian Rose Tea Room in Port Orchard.

2-1/2	cups cubed cooked chicken
1/2	cup chopped walnuts
1/3	cup grated celery
2	tablespoons grated onion
1/2	cup mayonnaise
2	tablespoons sour cream
1/2	teaspoon curry powder
1/8	teaspoon Cajun Seasoning
	Lettuce leaves and/or alfalfa sprouts
10	small croissants

In food processor process chicken until finely chopped. Transfer to a large bowl, add the walnuts, celery and onion.

In a small bowl combine the mayonnaise, sour cream, curry powder and Cajun Seasoning. Mix well.

Pour over chicken mixture and stir well to combine. Refrigerate for at least 1 hour.

Place approximately 1/4 cup on each split croissant. Garnish with green leafy lettuce and/or alfalfa sprouts.

GARDEN SANDWICH

Enchanted Tea Garden – Tacoma, Washington

This triple-decker tea sandwich is one of the most popular at mother-daughter owned Enchanted Tea Garden in Tacoma. Hearty yet healthy, just like a good pot of tea.

4	slices multi-grain bread
2	slices whole grain white bread
2	tomatoes, sliced thinly
1	cucumber, sliced thinly
1	avocado, peeled and sliced
1	cup sprouts
4	oz. cream cheese, softened
	Salt and pepper to taste

The Garden Sandwich is a triple-decker. The outside is a multi grain wheat bread and the center is one piece of whole grain white bread.

Spread cream cheese on the bread, (both sides on the center piece whole grain white).

On one layer place the tomato and avocado slices. On the second layer place the cucumber and sprouts. Cut sandwich into quarters and trim crusts.

Variations could be fresh herb cream cheese or chopped green onion.

HAZELNUT CHICKEN TEA SANDWICHES

Campbell House – Eugene, Oregon

*Owner Myra Plant's sister, Sonja Cruthers created this recipe
to take advantage of local hazelnuts and good bread.
It's always a hit at the special teas.*

4	cups shredded chicken
1/3	cup mayonnaise
1/2	teaspoon salt
1/2	teaspoon Cajun Seasoning
1/2	cup chopped hazelnuts (optional, but good crunch)
1	loaf Oregon Hazelnut Bread

In a large bowl mix all ingredients together, adjusting mayonnaise and seasoning to taste. Finely chopped hazelnuts can be added if desired.

Spread mixture on a slice of bread, top with a second slice. Trim off crust and cut into three fingers.

Makes approximately 21 finger sandwiches.

SALMON MELT SANDWICH

Time & Again – St. Helens, Oregon

16	oz. poached salmon
4	oz. cream cheese, softened
2	tablespoons capers
1	tablespoon dill, fresh or dried
1/2	teaspoon lemon pepper
1/2	cup mayonnaise
	Dijon mustard
1	tomato, sliced
2	thin slices, Swiss cheese
	Salt to taste
	Orange slices and cucumber for garnish

Beat cream cheese until fluffy, add mayonnaise, dill, and lemon pepper. Beat until well blended, then fold in the salmon and the capers. Season with salt to taste.

Broil 2 slices of sourdough bread in oven until brown on one side.

Take out and turn over. Lightly spread this side with mayonnaise and Dijon mustard, then spread salmon mixture on top of this, add two slices tomato and top with Swiss cheese.

Place both slices on broiler pan and put back in oven and broil until cheese starts to melt.

Serve open faced, cut into finger sandwiches. Garnish top with orange slice and cucumber.

PESTO CREAM AND SUN-DRIED TOMATO SANDWICHES

The mayonnaise mellows the pesto nicely in these finger sandwiches.

1/2	cup fresh basil leaves, washed and dried, plus 16 more leaves for garnish on top of sandwich
1	tablespoon pine nuts
1-1/2	tablespoons grated Parmesan cheese
1	small clove garlic, minced
3	tablespoons extra virgin olive oil
2/3	cup mayonnaise

Place the basil, nuts, cheese, and garlic in the bowl of a food processor. Pulse until finely chopped. While the motor is running, slowly add the olive oil until well blended. Transfer to a small bowl and stir in the mayonnaise.

Drain and slice 16 sun-dried tomatoes. Spread the pesto cream on 4 slices of good bread of your choice, and top with the drained tomatoes. Cover each with 4 more slices of bread, trim crusts and cut into small sandwiches.

SMOKED TURKEY SANDWICHES WITH ORANGE BUTTER

1/2	cup unsalted butter
2	teaspoon fresh orange juice
1	loaf white bread, thinly sliced
	Smoked turkey, sliced
1	bunch watercress
	Organically grown nasturtiums

In a bowl, whisk together the butter and the orange juice. Spread a thin layer of orange butter onto slices of bread. Place a slice of smoked turkey on top and top with another slice of the orange-buttered bread.

Cut sandwiches into shapes with a cookie cutter. Top with orange nasturtium and a sprig of watercress.

CLAIRE'S FAMOUS FRESH TOMATOES

*You can count on our good neighbor Claire Winget's tomatoes
to perk up a summer high tea, proving simple is best. Her husband Kim has been
known to grow some good tomatoes, but most markets all carry
the delicious on-the-vine types now too.*

2 or 3	fresh tomatoes, vine-ripened
1/4	teaspoon garlic, minced
1	teaspoon salt
1/2	cup extra virgin olive oil
2	tablespoons wine vinegar (or balsamic)
1	teaspoon fresh basil, chopped
	Fresh ground black pepper
1	teaspoon chopped fresh parsley
2	tablespoons chopped green onion

This dish is best if done immediately before serving so the tomatoes maintain their firm texture. Combine the garlic, salt, olive oil, vinegar, and pepper and blend well. Stem and slice the tomatoes and lay on a plate. Pour the dressing over the tomatoes and sprinkle the fresh parsley and green onion over the top. Serve immediately.

Variations: You can alternate slices of a good mozzarella cheese with the tomatoes, or slices of a ripe avocado alternated are equally good. For variety a yellow tomato augments the dish nicely too.

CHERRY TOMATOES WITH CRAB FILLING

These brightly colored finger foods are the perfect way to use a small amount of crab and the bounty of your late summer cherry tomato harvest.

3/4	lb. crabmeat, picked over and drained
1/2	cup light mayonnaise
2	green onions, finely chopped
2	tablespoons yellow bell pepper, finely chopped
2	tablespoons shredded carrot
2	teaspoons fresh parsley
2	teaspoons fresh lemon juice
	Salt and pepper to taste
30	cherry tomatoes

Finely chop the crabmeat in a medium bowl. Mix into it the mayonnaise, green onions, yellow pepper, shredded carrot, parsley, lemon juice, salt and pepper. Set aside.

Using a small sharp knife, cut a thin slice from the bottom of each tomato so they will stand. Cut a thin slice off the top, scoop out the seeds with a tiny spoon. Spoon about 1 teaspoon of the crab filling into each tomato and arrange on a platter.

This makes a nice companion to a finger sandwich course.

SCOTCH EGGS

I ate my very first Scotch Egg in Wales at a little pub in coastal Conwy. I remember looking at it and thinking "How'd they do that?" Conwy Castle, built in 1292, today houses Britain's first and most famous teapot museum. Home to more than 1,000 pots, there is also a gift shop called Char Bazaar for replicas.

2	teaspoon all-purpose flour
4	hard boiled eggs, shelled
1	teaspoon Worcestershire sauce
1/2	lb. bulk pork sausage
1	egg, beaten
1	cup fine dry bread crumbs
	Vegetable oil for deep-frying
	Parsley for garnish

Combine flour with salt and pepper in a small bowl, sprinkle over eggs. Add the Worcestershire sauce to sausage and mix well. Divide sausage into 4 equal portions and form each into a flat patty.

Place 1 of the hard boiled eggs into the center of each patty and shape the meat around the egg, covering the egg completely.

Coat the meat with the beaten egg, then roll in bread crumbs. Heat 3 inches of oil to 350° F. and gently add the meat-covered eggs. Cook for 7 or 8 minutes until crisp and golden.

Drain on paper towels and cool before slicing in half and serving, garnishing cut side with the fresh parsley.

Makes 8 halves. Serve with salad for high tea.

TOASTED PECAN TEA SANDWICHES

Like a little spice with your tea?
These are not your ordinary tea sandwiches.

2	teaspoons melted butter
3	tablespoons Worcestershire sauce
3	dashes of Tabasco sauce
2	cups pecan pieces
8	oz. cream cheese, softened
1/4	teaspoon garlic
	Cayenne pepper
	White bread, thin sliced

Preheat oven to 300° F. In a bowl combine the melted butter with the Worcestershire, Tabasco, and salt to taste. Add the pecans, toss to coat thoroughly and set aside to marinate for 10 minutes.

Drain the pecans, saving the marinade, and spread a single layer on a large cookie sheet and toast in preheated oven for 15 minutes, or until dry. Chop the pecans and set aside. In another mixing bowl blend the cream cheese with the reserved marinade. Stir in the chopped pecans. Taste and adjust seasonings to taste.

Trim the crusts from the bread. Spread a thin layer of the cream cheese on the bread, place a top slice of bread on it and cut the sandwich into four finger sandwiches.

TEA AN'TIQUES BAKED BRIE

Tea An'Tiques – Spokane, Washington

Charles DeGaulle said of his people, "The French will only be united under the threat of danger. Nobody can simply bring together a country that has 265 kinds of cheese." Here's a recipe for one of the most popular.

Take a wheel of brie, leaving the white skin on. Slice in half horizontally so you have two round pieces. Place chopped dried fruit (apples, apricots, dates, raisins) or a fruit chutney spread thickly on the bottom half. Replace the top half.

Place the wheel on a sheet of rolled puff pastry and wrap the Brie entirely, using a little water to seal it well, trim off the excess . Use the trimmings to make a design for the top. Baste the top and sides with an egg wash.

Place in a glass pie plate in a preheated 375° F. oven and bake for 25–30 minutes, or until browned on top. Remove from oven and let sit 10 minutes before slicing into wedges to serve.

Variations: Take any jam or jelly of your choice heat in microwave until melted, add a little sherry and pour over as a sauce. Try varying the filling using fresh mushrooms, green onion, spinach, herbs and walnuts without any sauce.

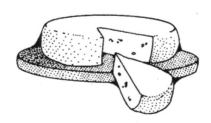

CHICKEN SALAD

Morning Glory Tea Room at New Woman Books – Kent, Washington

*You'll feel like a new woman too with Judith Bakkensen's tasty variation
on the popular chicken salad with currants and Indian flavors!*

3	cups diced, cooked chicken breast
1/2	cup mayonnaise
1/2	cup sour cream
3	tablespoons mango chutney
1	teaspoon curry powder
3	green onions, minced
1/4	cup celery, finely diced
1/2	cup chopped cashews
1/3	cup currants
	Pinch of salt and freshly ground pepper

Mix all ingredients together and serve as a tea sandwich filling or on a lettuce leaf.

CHICKEN CASHEW SALAD

Elizabeth & Alexander English Tea Room – Bothell, Washington

These fresh flavors meld well in this popular salad from a great little tea room at Country Village in Bothell, Washington.

4	cups diced chicken breast
4	cups celery, diced
4	cups pineapple chunks
4	cups grapes
3	cups sliced water chestnuts
3	cups mayonnaise
	Soy sauce to taste
	Curry power to taste
1	cup whole cashews
	Kale or any leaf lettuce for each plate

Mix the chicken, celery, pineapple, grapes, and water chestnuts in a large bowl. Make dressing of 3 cups mayonnaise seasoned to taste with a splash of soy sauce and curry powder. Fold into the ingredients in the bowl.

Place fresh kale on a salad plate. Top with 1 or 2 cups of Chicken Cashew mixture. Garnish with the cashews and a sprig of parsley.

DUNGENESS CRAB QUICHE

"Can Kenny come out and play?" Our neighbor Pat Moody queries when he wants to launch his inflatable boat for an afternoon of crabbing off Camano Island. They were so proficient at "hunting and gathering" this season that we got to try a lot of different recipes. Here's one:

1/4	lb. chopped button mushrooms
5	shallots, minced
2	tablespoons butter
1	teaspoon olive oil
1/2	teaspoon garlic
1	teaspoon dill
1	tablespoon thyme
2	tablespoons fresh lemon juice
	Red pepper flakes to taste
	Salt
2	cups Dungeness crabmeat
3	eggs
1	cup half and half
3/4	cup grated Parmesan cheese
1	9-inch pastry crust, unbaked

Preheat oven to 375° F. In a skillet, cook the mushrooms, shallots and garlic in butter and olive oil over medium-low heat to sweat for about 5 minutes. Stir in the dill, thyme, lemon, salt and hot pepper flakes. Remove from heat and add the crab.

In a medium bowl, combine the eggs and half and half and 1/2 cup of the Parmesan cheese, (reserving the other 1/4 cup for the top). Spread the crab mixture in the pie crust, pour the egg mixture over and sprinkle with the remaining Parmesan.

Bake about 40 minutes, testing the center with a toothpick after 35 minutes. Allow to stand about 10 minutes before slicing and serving. Also good served cold.

GINGER CHICKEN SALAD PUFFS

For the puffs:

1	cup water
1/2	cup butter
1	cup all-purpose flour
4	eggs

For the filling:

2	cups finely chopped, cooked chicken breast
1	cup mayonnaise
1	teaspoon fresh grated ginger
1/2	teaspoon dry mustard
1/4	cup drained canned water chestnuts, chopped fine
2	green onions, including green tops
1/4	teaspoon salt
1/4	cup Romaine lettuce, cut into very thin strips

Make the puffs: Bring the water and butter to a boil over high heat. Add the flour all at once, stirring briskly until mixture leaves the sides of pan and forms a ball (about 2 minutes), remove from heat. Add eggs, one at a time, stirring well after each addition until dough is smooth and well blended.

On greased baking sheet, drop 1 tablespoon of the dough for each puff, spacing them about 2 inches apart. Bake at 400° F. for 20 to 25 minutes or until well browned and crisp, cool thoroughly on wire rack.

Make the filling: In a medium sized bowl, blend the mayonnaise with the mustard and ginger. Add two cups finely chopped chicken, salt, the water chestnuts and the green onions. Mix lightly to coat with the mayonnaise mixture, and refrigerate for at least 2 hours.

Assemble: Split the puffs horizontally, pull out and discard moist portions of dough. Remove tops and fill each puff cavity with about 1 tablespoon of the chicken filling. Top with Romaine and replace the tops. Makes about 30 filled puffs.

FRIED WON TONS
WITH SPINACH FLORENTINE FILLING

30	won ton wrappers
1	egg, beaten
	Vegetable oil for frying

Spinach Florentine Filling

3/4	cup chopped fresh spinach
1/2	cup ricotta cheese
1	clove garlic, minced
1	scallion, finely chopped
2	tablespoons grated Parmesan

For filling: Combine spinach, ricotta cheese, garlic, scallion and parmesan. Blend together until all ingredients are incorporated.

Assembly: Place each square won ton wrapper on a flat surface with a point towards you. Place 1 teaspoon of the filling in the center of the wrapper. Brush the edges with a little of the beaten egg. Fold the top point over the filling toward you to form a triangle. Press to seal. Moisten the remaining two points and fold left and right sides toward center pressing to seal. Repeat with the remaining won tons.

Cooking: In a heavy skillet, heat 2 inches of oil to 350 medium high. Cook won tons in small batches, turning occasionally for about 1 minute, until crisp and golden. Drain on paper towels and serve hot.

You can make these in advance and reheat in 375° F. oven for 15 minutes until hot.

NORTHWEST SMOKED SALMON SPREAD

Victorian Rose Special Teas – Chehalis, Washington

4	oz. smoked salmon
2	tablespoons finely chopped dill pickle
2	tablespoons lemon juice
1/2	cup mayonnaise
8	oz. cream cheese, softened
1	teaspoon fresh dill weed

Mix all the ingredients, except the salmon, and beat until smooth. Remove skin and bones from salmon, crumble with fingers. Add to mixture and stir until smooth.

Spread on crustless bread and serve. Also good as a cracker spread.

NAUGHTY LADY
BAKED POTATO SOUP

Ruthie B's - Springfield, Oregon

Prepare to be welcomed boisterously by those crazy ladies of Ruthie B's, housed in a former brothel from the 1930s. Cinderella, who oversees the teas,. is also the harvester of the fresh garden herbs used in this delicious soup.

2	large baking potatoes
3	tablespoons green onion, plus
3	tablespoons green onion, for garnish
4	slices cooked, crisp bacon, for garnish
1/3	cup butter
1/3	cup flour
2	teaspoons fresh dill
1	teaspoon fresh thyme
3/4	cup cheddar cheese, grated
4	cups milk

Bake the potatoes and cool to room temperature. Remove the jackets and dice.

In a soup pot, saute 3 tablepoons green onion over medium heat in the butter. Add the flour stirring constantly while you pour in 2 cups of the milk. Cook just until it begins to bubble and thicken.

Add the remaining 2 cups of milk, the cooked and diced potatoes, fresh dill, fresh thyme and cheddar cheese. Stir until the cheese melts and soup just comes to a boil. Garnish with green onions and crisp bacon.

POTATO DILL SOUP

The Tea Cottage – Jacksonville, Oregon

What's better than a nice bowl of soup to start a tea?
This one is simple and good, adapted from the recipe
of a friend of owner Susan Sullivan.

4	cups chicken stock (if fresh use some salt)
4	cups cubed potatoes
1/2	cup chopped onion
2	tablespoons dill

Cook the potatoes and onion in the chicken stock on stove until soft. Puree and cook on low until smooth. Add the dill.

Stir and serve. Serves 8.

SALLY'S EASY SAUSAGE & EGG PUFF

Longfellow House Bed & Breakfast – Kelso, Washington

"Many's the long night I've dreamed of cheese – toasted, mostly."
Robert Louis Stevenson
Treasure Island

5	eggs
1/8	teaspoon salt
2	tablespoon half & half
3	Brown & Serve sausage links, thawed & cut in half
1/2	cup shredded cheddar cheese
	Dash of pepper
	Fresh or dried parsley, chopped

Preheat oven to 375° F.

Spray 6 muffin cups or small soufflé dishes of the same size with non-stick vegetable spray. Place a half sausage in each cup. Put 1 heaping spoonful of cheese on top.

In a large bowl, beat eggs with half & half, salt and pepper. Pour 1/4 cup of egg mixture in each cup and sprinkle with parsley.

Bake 20-25 minutes until it tests done. Serve with crusty toast and fresh fruit.

EASY AVOCADO SALAD

Talk about an unflappable hostess, Judy Carroll could cater a White House dinner on short notice. This easy salad is made by marinating garbanzo beans in the Italian dressing or vinaigrette of your choice.

1	can garbanzo beans
1/2	cup Italian dressing or vinaigrette
1	avocado
	Lettuce leaves for garnish
	Small shrimp (optional)
	Sliced black olives (optional)

Drain a can of garbanzo beans, put the drained beans into a lidded container and pour your favorite Italian dressing or vinaigrette over to cover. Refrigerate for as long as two weeks, the marinade permeates the beans over time, intensifying the flavor.

When ready to serve, slice a small ripe unpeeled avocado in half, remove the pit, and place on a lettuce leaf. Spoon some marinated garbanzo beans into the cavity and drizzle on the dressing.

Variations: Excellent with fresh salad shrimp and/or sliced black olives added to the avocado right before serving too.

SCONES, BREADS & MUFFINS

CHAI SCONES

*I guess if it happened more frequently the novelty would be gone,
but isn't it fun to be right? In our first book in 1996 we predicted that
chai would become the beverage of choice for many in our latte-soaked
Northwest, and now it's everywhere! I use Oregon Chai concentrate when
making these scones.*

2	cups all-purpose flour
1/4	cup well-packed light brown sugar
1	teaspoon baking powder
1/4	teaspoon ground cinnamon
1/4	teaspoon ground cardamom
1/4	teaspoon ground ginger
2	tablespoons unsalted butter
1	egg yolk
1/4	cup milk
1	oz. Masala Chai concentrate (now at most grocery stores)
	Egg wash (1 egg yolk mixed with 1 teaspoon milk)
1/8	cup granulated sugar
1/2	teaspoon ground cinnamon

Preheat oven to 425° F.

Mix together flour, brown sugar, baking powder, cinnamon, carda-mom, and ginger and add butter with an electric mixer. Mix on low speed until the mixture resembles coarse meal.

In a small bowl, combine egg yolk, milk and chai concentrate. Add wet mixture to dry and mix until just combined. Remove from bowl to a lightly floured surface and knead briefly. Shape into 4 small or 2 large rounds. Brush the rounds with egg wash and score decoratively with a fork. Mix the granulated sugar and cinnamon and sprinkle on top of rounds.

Bake for 15 minutes or until golden brown. Serve warm with jam, Devonshire cream or softly whipped sweetened cream.

GOOD NEIGHBOR SUSAN'S BANANA SCONES

The most I could wish for any new homeowner is that your own next door neighbors are as great as ours. Ones that come bearing hot scones are especially good!

1	cup all-purpose flour
1	cup whole wheat flour
1	tablespoon baking powder
1/4	teaspoon salt
1	teaspoon nutmeg
1/2	cup chopped dates
1	tablespoon vegetable oil
1	cup mashed bananas
1	egg (beaten)

Mix together flour, salt, baking powder, nutmeg, and dates. Mix together banana, oil and egg. Combine the wet and dry mixtures well, add a little milk if too dry.

On a floured surface, knead a few times. Pat into 3/4 inch thickness and cut into desired shapes.

Bake at 400° F. for 15 to 20 minutes or until lightly browned.

CANDIED FRUIT SCONES

Lupine Cottage – Silverdale, Washington

This variation of a traditional tea treat is Sandy Sinclair's signature scone at her popular children's tea parties. The candied fruit looks like jewels, adding to the magic of the day. Sandy serves a black currant tea with these.

2	cups flour
1/4	cup sugar
2	teaspoons baking powder
1/8	teaspoon salt
1/3	cup chilled butter
1/2	cup whipping cream
1	large egg
1-1/2	teaspoons vanilla
1/2	cup candied fruits (for fruit cake)
1	egg mixed with 1 teaspoon water for glaze

Preheat oven to 425° F.

Mix flour, sugar, baking powder and salt, and cut in the butter. Add whipping cream, egg and vanilla. Stir in the candied fruits.

Roll out on a floured board and cut into 8 wedges, glaze if desired. Bake 13 to 15 minutes until golden. Serve with a dollop of whipped cream.

CAMILLE'S CRANBERRY-ORANGE SCONES

Camille's Tea Shoppe and Gifts – Hayden, Idaho

These scones, instead of using fresh cranberries, get a rich, ruby color from cranberry sauce. Camille's owner, Johanne serves these with jam and crème fraiche.

2	cups flour
1/3	cup sugar
1	tablespoon baking powder
1/2	teaspoon salt
5	tablespoons butter
1/2	14-1/2 oz. can whole cranberry sauce
	Zest from half an orange
2	eggs, one separated
3/4	cup evaporated milk

Put first 5 ingredients in food processor and blend well. Remove from processor into a large mixing bowl and add cranberry sauce and orange zest, stir together well.

Slightly beat 1 egg and extra yolk with the evaporated milk and stir into the flour mixture.

Beat remaining egg white and set aside.

Grease 12-inch round pan. Turn dough into pan and, with floured hands, pat mixture to edges of pan. Brush egg white on top and sprinkle with sugar.

Bake in preheated 400° F. oven for 20 minutes.

CHERRY SCONES

*"Loveliest of trees, the cherry now
Is hung with bloom along the bough.....
And since to look at things in bloom
Fifty springs are little room,
About the woodlands I will go
To see the cherry hung with snow."*
- A.E. Housman

1/2	cup dried cherries
	Apple or grape juice (enough to cover cherries)
2	cups all purpose flour
1/2	cup sugar, divided
2	teaspoons baking powder
1/2	teaspoon baking soda
1/2	teaspoon fresh ground nutmeg
1/2	teaspoon salt
1/2	cup (1 stick) cold butter, cut into 1/2-inch cubes
1	egg
1/2	cup vanilla yogurt
1	teaspoon lemon or orange zest

Soak cherries in apple or grape juice at least 15 minutes. Drain well.

In food processor, mix flour, 1/4 cup sugar, baking powder, soda, nutmeg, and salt. Add butter and process until mixture resembles coarse crumbs. Stir in egg, yogurt and the drained cherries.

Turn dough out on lightly greased baking sheet. Lightly flour hands and pat dough into a 9-inch round. With a knife cut into 8 wedges. Sprinkle with remaining 1/4 cup sugar.

Bake in preheated 375° F. oven until golden brown, about 20 minutes. Serve warm with butter or orange marmalade.

LAVENDER SCONES

Tea and Tomes – Newport, Oregon

Where else can you hear the sound of the ocean and gulls, drink excellent tea, and have lavender scents waft from the kitchen but at this unique tea room, Tea and Tomes on the Oregon Coast.

2	cups flour
1	tablespoon baking powder
4	tablespoons butter
1/4	cup sugar
2	teaspoons fresh lavender florets or
1	teaspoon dried culinary lavender, roughly chopped
2/3	cup milk, plus extra for glazing

Preheat oven to 425° F. Grease and flour a large baking sheet.

Sift the baking powder and the flour together in a large mixing bowl. Rub in the butter until the mixture resembles fine breadcrumbs. Stir in the sugar and lavender, reserving a pinch to sprinkle over top of scones before baking.

Add enough milk to make a soft, sticky dough, knead briefly on a well floured surface. Shape the dough into a round about 1" thick. Using a pastry cutter, stamp out about 12 scones.

Place scones onto the prepared baking sheet, brush tops with a little milk and sprinkle on the reserved chopped lavender.

Bake for 10 to12 minutes until golden. Serve warm with cream and jam.

DATE NUT ORANGE QUICK BREAD

Woodmark Hotel on Lake Washington – Kirkland, Washington

1	cup fresh orange juice
1	cup dates, chopped
1/4	cup unsalted butter
1/4	cup brown sugar, packed
1/4	cup granulated sugar
1	egg
1/2	teaspoon orange zest, minced
1-3/4	cups flour
1/2	teaspoon salt
1/2	teaspoon baking powder
1/2	teaspoon baking soda
3/4	cup walnuts, chopped to 1/4"

Bring orange juice to a boil, pour over dates and set aside.

Cream the butter with the two sugars, beat well. On low speed add the egg and the orange zest. Without draining, stir in the date and orange juice mixture.

Sift together the flour, salt, baking powder and baking soda. Add to the butter and sugar mixture and stir until well combined. Stir in the chopped nuts.

Grease and flour one 8 x 4-inch loaf pan. Pour in the mixture, spreading to even. Bake at 325° F. for 45 minutes in convection oven or longer in regular oven, a little over an hour, or until the loaf tests as done.

Cool in the pan for 15 minutes, then turn out and cool completely before serving. Garnish with mint leaves. Wrap tightly to store.

It may be stored frozen or will keep refrigerated if well wrapped. Makes one loaf.

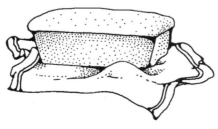

DATE & WALNUT LOAF

Birdie's Tearoom & Gift Shoppe – Lake Oswego, Oregon

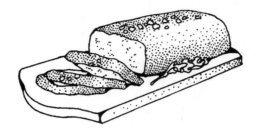

Years ago a friend of Birdie's owner Annette Suchy shared this recipe with her, and now she's sharing it with you here and in her popular tearoom. This loaf keeps well refrigerated or frozen, so it's nice to have on hand for unexpected tea parties – the best kind!

1-1/2	cups dates, chopped
3/4	cup water
1	teaspoon baking soda
2-1/2	cups whole wheat flour
3	teaspoon baking powder
1/2	teaspoon salt
5	tablespoons butter
1	cup sugar
1	cup chopped walnuts
1	large egg, beaten

Preheat oven to 300° F. Grease and flour one 2-lb. loaf pan.

Slowly bring dates and water to a boil. Remove from heat and add soda. Let cool.

Sift flour, baking powder and salt into a bowl. Cut in butter with pastry blender. Stir in sugar and nuts and add the date mixture, mix thoroughly. Spoon into prepared pan and smooth the top.

Bake in lower part of oven for 1 hour or until firm. Let cool in pan before turning onto rack. When cool, wrap and keep in refrigerator at least 2 days before slicing and serving.

Slice very thin and spread with a thin layer of cream cheese. Cut into bite size serving pieces.

SUGAR LADY'S PUMPKIN LOAF

Our friend Lucretia is not only a talented professional baker,
but she makes those adorable decorated sugar cubes
that TeaTime distributes to stores.

2	cups brown sugar
2	cups granulated sugar
1	cup vegetable oil
1	20-oz. can unseasoned pumpkin puree
1	teaspoon salt
4	teaspoons ground cinnamon
2	teaspoons ground cloves
2	teaspoons ground ginger
3	teaspoons baking soda
5	cups all purpose flour

Preheat oven to 350° F. Oil and flour a large loaf pan or bundt pan.

Mix all ingredients together and pour batter into pan. Bake for 30 to 40 minutes until loaf tests done. (Cooking time may vary depending on your pan size.)

LEMON PECAN TEA LOAF

The Wellington Tea Room – Seattle, Washington

*This recipe was created sixteen years ago by Benita Varnado,
the sister of the owner of the Wellington Tea Room.
It's been on the Afternoon Tea menu there for the past nine years.*

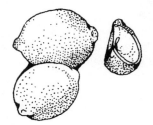

3/4	cup butter
3/4	cup sugar
2	eggs
1-1/8	cups flour
1/8	teaspoon salt
3/8	cup buttermilk
1/2	cup chopped pecans
	Grated zest of 1 lemon

For Glaze:	1-1/2	tablespoons lemon juice
	3/8	cup sugar

Cream the butter and sugar, add the eggs, mixing well. Mix dry ingredients in separate bowl and add to butter mixture. Add the buttermilk, pecans and lemon zest, mix well.

Pour into 9" x 5" loaf pan and bake at 350° F. for 30 – 35 minutes. When loaf tests done, remove from oven and cool briefly. Remove from pan while loaf is still warm.

For glaze: mix lemon juice with sugar. Spread over top of warm cake. You may also use granulated or powdered sugar to dust cake.

Place the loaf on your prettiest plate and garnish with sliced lemon twists all around it.

CARROT PINEAPPLE MUFFINS

I met a busy young mother at a book signing recently who seemed very wise. She told me that a cup of sweet milky tea and a muffin with her eleven-year-old daughter opened communication like nothing else. "Ask her how school went, and all I would ever hear was 'fine'," she told me. "But when I took the time to set a little tea out and sit with her, slowly the events of the day would emerge."

1-3/4	cups all-purpose flour
1	teaspoon baking powder
2	teaspoons baking soda
3/4	teaspoon cinnamon
1/2	cup dark brown sugar
1	egg
1/3	cup melted butter
1	20 oz. can crushed pineapple, drained
6	oz. pineapple juice (reserved from crushed pineapple)
1	cup shredded carrots

Cream cheese topping:

2	oz. cream cheese
1/4	cup sweetened condensed milk
2	teaspoon vanilla
1/4	teaspoon ground cardamom

Preheat oven to 375° F. In a large bowl, sift together the flour, baking powder, baking soda, and cinnamon. Mix in the brown sugar. In another bowl lightly beat the egg. To this second bowl add the melted butter and the pineapple juice. Mix in the crushed pineapple and the carrots. Pour this pineapple mixture into the flour mixture and mix by hand until all ingredients are blended.

Fill greased muffin tins (about 2/3 full) and bake about 19 minutes, or until the muffins are brown. Cool slightly and remove from the tin before topping.

While the muffins are baking, make the topping by blending the ingredients well. Spread it on the warm muffins. Makes one dozen.

"KEY LIME" MUFFINS

*I'll admit it. Given a choice between something chocolate or something
tartly lemon or lime, I'll always opt for the latter. I know that sounds
like heresy to you chocolate lovers, but I feel better for confessing.
Here's a tartly satisfying muffin that is so good when accompanied by a fruit
essence black tea, like ginger peach.*

2	cups all-purpose flour
1	teaspoon baking powder
1/4	teaspoon salt
	Juice from 3 limes
	Zest from 2 limes
2	eggs
3/4	cup sweetened condensed milk
4	teaspoons melted butter

Preheat the oven to 350° F. In a large bowl sift together the flour, baking powder, and salt. Squeeze the juice from the limes into a second, me-
dium-sized bowl. Add the lime zest and the eggs. Mix together, lightly
beating the eggs. Stir in the sweetened condensed milk and melted butter.
Pour into the flour mixture and stir until just moistened.

Fill greased muffin tins about 2/3 full. Bake for 15 to 18 minutes or
until they test done. Makes one dozen muffins.

FRESH STRAWBERRY-BANANA MUFFINS

Some things are just plain better in combination. It's hard to imagine peanut butter without grape jelly, for instance; or Matt Lauer without Katy Couric. I was unprepared for Doris Day without Rock Hudson, and what were The Mamas and the Papas without Cass anyway? Fish and chips, Lucille Ball and Desi Arnaz, hash browns and eggs, – all better in combination. Here's another.

3/4	cup butter, room temperature
2/3	cup firmly packed light brown sugar
3	ripe bananas
2	eggs
1	cup cake flour
1	cup all-purpose flour
3/4	teaspoon salt
1-1/2	teaspoon baking soda
1	teaspoon baking powder
1	cup sliced fresh strawberries (frozen will not work)
2	tablespoon granulated sugar

Preheat oven to 375° F. In a large bowl cream the butter and sugar. Puree the bananas in a food processor. Stir the pureed bananas and eggs into the butter mixture, beating until the batter is smooth.

In a medium bowl sift together the cake flour, the all-purpose flour, salt, baking soda and baking powder. Add the flour mixture to the batter and mix well. Fold in the sliced strawberries. Spoon the batter into greased muffin tins or foil baking cups. Sprinkle tops with granulated sugar and bake 20 minutes. Serve warm. Makes one dozen muffins.

ECCLES CAKES

The ovens of the village of Eccles in Lancashire, England gave birth to these traditional teatime treats.

1-3/4	cups all purpose flour
2-1/4	teaspoon baking powder
1	tablespoon sugar
1/4	teaspoon salt
1/4	cup butter
2	eggs, beaten
1/3	cup half and half
2	tablesoons currants
1	teaspoon butter
2	tablespoons sugar
	Ground cinnamon

Mix together the flour, baking powder, 1 tablespoon sugar, and salt. With a pastry blender, cut the 1/4 cup butter until the mixture resembles coarse meal. Set aside 2 teaspoon of the beaten egg and mix remaining egg with the cream. Make a well in the center of the flour mixture, add egg-cream mixture and stir until just blended. Turn dough out on a lightly floured board and knead lightly (about 15 times) until dough is no longer sticky.

Roll out dough to 3/4-inch thickness and using a biscuit cutter, cut 2-1/2-inch rounds and place them about 2 inches apart of greased baking sheet. Reroll scraps.

Poke a hole into the center of each round, fill with 1 tsp. currants and a pea-size dollop of butter. Pinch opposite edges of circle together in the center, enclosing currants in dough (dough will pull apart slightly while baking to form an 'X' on top.)

Brush tops of Eccles cake with reserved egg, and sprinkle with cinnamon-sugar. Bake at 450° F. for 12 minutes, or until golden. Makes 6 Eccles Cakes, which are best served freshly baked or warm.

SALLY LUNN BUNS

*"Soleil et lune" is French for sun and moon, so this bread with a celestial
name probably originated centuries ago in France. To the ear attuned
to English it sounded like "Sally Lunn," and that name stuck. British
settlers brought the recipe to the colonies and it is still a favorite
in the kitchens of southern belles. These rich rolls are a nice addition
to tea when served with jam and cream, or cut in half make
good shortcakes for berries. Served with butter, they even
make an excellent dinner roll.*

1	cup whipping cream
1/2	cup (1 stick) butter
1	package active dry yeast
1/3	cup sugar
1	teaspoon salt
4	large eggs
3-3/4	cups sifted all purpose flour

Heat cream and butter in a small saucepan over low heat until the
butter melts. Pour into a large bowl and let cool to a temperature of
about 110° F. Stir in the yeast, sugar and salt. Let mixture stand for
about 5 minutes until foamy. Beat in the eggs, one at a time. Add the
flour one cup at a time, stirring after each addition to incorporate.

Cover with buttered plastic wrap and place in a warm place to rise for
one and half hours or until the dough doubles in bulk.

Beat batter well to deflate it. Divide among 24 buttered or paper-
lined muffin tins, filling each about halfway. Cover with buttered plastic
wrap and let the buns rise in a warm place for about an hour, or until
doubled in volume. Bake in a preheated 375° F. oven for 12 to 17 minutes or until a toothpick inserted comes out clean.

*"Now for the tea of our host. Now for the rollicking bun. Now for the muffin
and toast. Now for the gay Sally Lunn!"*

Sir William Gilbert (1836-1911)

COOKIES
& BARS

CHOCOLATE TOP COOKIES

Fotheringham House Bed & Breakfast – Spokane, Washington

The aroma of this old-fashioned favorite wafting from the windows of the Fotheringham House must make the neighbors hope they'll be invited for tea. Three generations of the owner's family have won raves for these tasty bars.

1	cup butter
1/2	cup brown sugar
1/2	cup white sugar
2	egg yolks
1	cup flour
1	cup rolled oats

Topping:

6	oz. chocolate bar, melted
2	tablespoon butter
1/2	cup chopped nuts

Cream the butter and both sugars. Beat in the egg yolks. Add the flour and oats, stirring well.

Spread in a greased 13 x 9-inch pan, bake at 350° F. for 20 minutes. Cool for 10 minutes.

Melt the chocolate bar with the butter. Spread over the cooled cookie layer and sprinkle with nuts, and pat down gently.

Cut into 1-1/2-inch squares when cool.

CREAM-FILLED WAFERS

Lupine Cottage – Silverdale, Washington

*"'I can just imagine myself sitting down at the head of the table and
pouring tea,' said Anne, shutting her eyes ecstatically, 'And asking
Diana if she takes sugar! I know she doesn't
but of course I'll ask her'..."*
L.M. Montgomery
Anne of Green Gables

For the cookie wafers:

1	cup butter
2	cups flour
1/3	cup whipping cream
	Granulated sugar to sprinkle on

Cream filling:

1/4	cup soft butter
3/4	cup sifted confectioners sugar
1	egg yolk
1	teaspoon vanilla

Mix the cookie dough and chill for one hour. Roll dough 1/8-inch thick
on floured board. Cut into 1-1/4-inch rounds. Transfer to waxed paper and
turn to heavily coat both sides with sugar. Place on an ungreased sheet and
prick them with a fork. Bake in 350° F. oven for 7 to 9 minutes until
slightly puffy. Cool completely on rack.

Blend the cream filling mixture, color tint if desired. When the wafers
are cool, spread filling on one and top with another to make a sandwich
cookie.

Makes about 3 dozen

DOROTHY'S CRACKLE-TOP GINGER COOKIES

These were a favorite of mine while growing up. The recipe is from my mother's recipe box, and the card has the word 'excellent' printed neatly on it and underlined. The recipe was originally from my mother's dearest friend, Dorothy Wutzke, the wife of a Corvallis dairy farmer.
Try these with ginger peach tea.

1	cup shortening
2	cups brown sugar
1	egg
1	cup molasses
4	cups sifted flour
1/2	teaspoon salt
2	teaspoons baking soda
2	teaspoons ground ginger
1	teaspoon vanilla
1	teaspoon lemon extract

Cream shortening and brown sugar, and blend in the egg. Beat well. Add the molasses and beat together until light and fluffy.

Sift together flour, salt, baking soda, and ginger. Blend dry ingredients gradually into the creamed mixture. (Dough should be soft but not sticky or the tops won't crackle.)

Add the vanilla and the lemon extract, and chill about 4 hours. Shape into walnut sized balls with the flour-dusted hands. Do not flatten. Place in 350 ° F. oven on an ungreased cookie sheet for 12 to 15 minutes. Sprinkle with sugar, and cool on a rack.

SHARON CORY'S MACADAMIA COOKIES

Who needs to be on a first name basis with Mrs. Field when you have an old friend like Sharon Cory to make cookies that melt in your mouth?

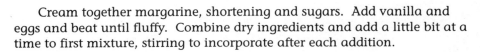

1/4	cup margarine
3/4	cup shortening
1-1/4	cups white sugar
1/4	cup brown sugar (packed)
1	teaspoon vanilla
2	eggs
1/4	teaspoon salt
1	teaspoon baking soda
2	cups flour
3/4	pound macadamia nuts (coarsely chopped.)
1	6 oz. package of chocolate chips.

Cream together margarine, shortening and sugars. Add vanilla and eggs and beat until fluffy. Combine dry ingredients and add a little bit at a time to first mixture, stirring to incorporate after each addition.

Stir in nuts and chocolate chips, then drop by tablespoonfuls onto ungreased cookie sheets.

Bake at 325° F. for about 12 minutes, watching carefully, until lightly browned. Best when served warm from the oven.

LEMON MADELEINES

I remember one Christmas Eve we were walking in Tucson. We picked a lemon off a tree, and it was so sweet you could eat it like an orange. I wish we could do that in the Pacific Northwest in the winter, don't you? Try these light treats instead.

2	eggs
1/2	teaspoon vanilla
1/2	teaspoon minced lemon zest
1	cup sifted powdered sugar
2/3	cup all purpose flour
1/4	teaspoon baking powder
1/2	cup butter, melted and cooled
	Powdered sugar

Grease and flour two dozen 3-inch Madeleine molds and set aside.

In a medium mixing bowl with an electric mixer on high-speed beat the eggs, vanilla and lemon peel for 5 minutes. Gradually beat in the powdered sugar. Beat for 5 to 7 minutes until the mixture is thick and satiny.

Sift together flour and baking powder. Sift one-fourth of the flour mixture over egg mixture, gently fold in. Fold in the remaining flour by fourths. Fold in the butter. Spoon into the prepared molds, filling three-fourths full.

Bake in 375° F. oven for 10 to 12 minutes until edges are golden and tops spring back. Cool in molds on wire racks for one minute. Loosen the cookies with a knife. Invert onto racks and cool. Sift additional powdered sugar over tops.

The cookies can be stored in an airtight container at room temperature for 2 or 3 days, or wrap and freeze for up to a month. Makes 24 cookies.

EARL GREY SHORTBREAD

Secret Garden Tea Company - Vancouver, British Columbia

Here's an unusual use for Earl Grey tea. Grinding the tea leaves finely is the key to the unique flavor it imparts throughout the smooth texture of the traditional shortbread.

1/2	cup butter, room temperature
1/4	cup sugar
3/4	cup sifted flour
1/4	cup Earl Grey tea, very finely ground
1/4	cup corn starch

Beat butter and icing sugar until light. Mix in flour, corn starch and tea until dough begins to hold its shape. Pat dough into 8 x 8-inch pan.

Bake 55 minutes at 375° F., cut into squares.

For a fanciful variation: Instead of baking in a pan, use a teapot-shaped cookie cutter and bake on an ungreased cookie sheet. Sprinkle with icing sugar.

LEMON SHORTBREAD COOKIES

Just Your Cup O' Tea – Bremerton, Washington

Does anything go better with tea than lemon? This English shortbread recipe traveled to Bremerton from the recipe box of a caterer's British grandmother.

1-1/2	cups butter, softened
2/3	cups sugar
2	teaspoons lemon extract
2	tablespoons water
4	cups flour

Mix all ingredients well. Shape into a log and wrap in waxed paper. Chill for two hours.

Cut into 1/4-inch-thick rounds. Bake at 350° F. for 10 minutes.

ROSEMARY SHORTBREAD COOKIES

The scent of rosemary is reputed to improve your memory. My memory of this shortbread recipe is extremely brief. They didn't last long at all.

1-1/4	cups all-purpose flour
3	tablespoons sugar
2	tablespoons snipped fresh rosemary
1/8	teaspoons salt
1/2	cup butter

In a medium mixing bowl stir together the flour, sugar, rosemary, and salt. Using a pastry blender or fork, cut in the butter until the mixture resembles fine crumbs and begins to cling. Form into a ball. Knead the dough in the bowl for about 1 minute until smooth.

On a lightly floured surface, roll dough to 1/4-inch thickness. Using desired cookie cutters or a knife, cut into 2 to 2-1/2-inch diameter shapes. Arrange on an ungreased cookie sheet.

Bake in 350° F. oven for 14 to 16 minutes until bottoms just start to brown. Remove from cookie sheet to wire rack, and cool.

Makes 12 to 14 cookies.

PEANUT BUTTER COOKIES WITH A CHOCOLATE KISS

Once upon a time, now in fact, in a drizzly rain forest of north central British Columbia there dwells an adorable school teacher who used to be a caterer. She's tired of frogs, it's time for the prince. In the meantime, have another cookie and we'll all live happily ever after.
(Thanks for the recipe dear Denise Davidson.)

1/2	cup butter
1/2	cup peanut butter
1/2	cup white sugar
1/2	cup brown sugar
1	egg
1	teaspoon vanilla
1-1/4	cup flour
3/4	teaspoon baking soda
1/2	teaspoon baking powder
	Pinch of salt

Hershey chocolate kisses

Cream together butters and sugars. Add egg and vanilla, stirring well to combine. Mix together dry ingredients, then add to butter-egg mixture a little at a time, stirring to incorporate after each addition.

Roll spoonfuls of dough into balls and slightly flatten. Bake at 350° F. for 8 to 10 minutes until lightly browned, remove from oven and immediately press a Hershey Kiss or chocolate wafer into the center of each cookie. Let cool, if you can stand to wait.

PUMPKIN BARS

2	cup sifted flour
2	teaspoons baking powder
1	teaspoon baking soda
1/2	teaspoon salt
2	cup sugar
2	teaspoons cinnamon
1	teaspoon pumpkin pie spice
1	cup vegetable oil
4	eggs, beaten
1	16 oz. can pumpkin puree
1	cup chopped pecans

Frosting:

6	tablespoons butter
3	oz. cream cheese, softened
2	cups powdered sugar, sifted
1	tablespoon milk
1	teaspoon vanilla

Combine flour, baking powder, soda, salt, sugar and spices. Pour oil into a large bowl. Stir in the eggs, then the pumpkin and nuts. Stir in dry ingredients. Pour into a 10 x 15-inch cake pan. Bake at 350° F. for 20 to 25 minutes.

For frosting, beat together the butter and the cream cheese. Then stir in the powdered sugar alternately with milk and vanilla. Frost bars when thoroughly cooled.

RUSSIAN TEA CAKES

Mon Ami – Florence, Oregon

Here's an authentic recipe from Russia that made its way to this Oregon Coast tea room. One of the owners' aunts was from Russia, and brought it with her generations ago.

1	cup (2 sticks) butter
1/2	cup powdered sugar
1	teaspoon vanilla
2-1/4	cups flour
1/4	teaspoon salt
3/4	cup chopped pecans
	More powdered sugar to coat them after baking

Cream together butter, sugar and vanilla. Work in flour, salt and nuts until dough holds together. Shape into 1-inch balls. Bake in a 400° F. oven for 10 to 12 minutes or until firm but not brown. Roll the hot tea cakes in powdered sugar, cool. Roll in powdered sugar again prior to serving.

WILLIAM OF ORANGE COOKIES

2-1/2	cups sifted flour
1/4	teaspoon salt
1/4	teaspoon baking soda
1	cup butter
1/2	cup white sugar
1/2	cup brown sugar
1	egg, beaten
2	tablespoons undiluted frozen orange juice concentrate (thawed)
1	teaspoon grated orange zest

Sift flour with salt and soda. In a large bowl cream butter and both sugars. Add the egg, orange juice and orange zest and mix completely. Gradually add in the flour mixture.

Drop by spoonfuls on ungreased baking sheet leaving 2-inches between cookies. Bake in a preheated 400° F. oven for 10 to 12 minutes until golden.

Makes about 40 cookies.

SARAH BERNHARDS

South Seattle Community College – Culinary Arts Program
Chef Jean-Claude Berger, Pastry Chef - Instructor

8	oz. almond paste
5	oz. powdered sugar
3	egg whites

Filling:

2	oz. bittersweet chocolate
1	pint heavy cream
1	oz. sugar

Garnish:

Pistachio nuts
Melted chocolate

Place the almond paste and sugar into food processor and pulse into coarse meal. Add the egg whites and mix until smooth.

Pipe the paste (about the size of 1/2 dollar) onto a sheet pan lined with parchment paper. Bake at 300 ° F. for about 20 minutes. Allow to cool completely.

Cut the chocolate into small pieces, place in a bowl and melt using a double boiler. Remove from heat. Whip the cream with 1oz. sugar to a soft peak. Add the cream to the soft chocolate and whisk well. Pipe the cream onto the almond paste tarts and refrigerate.

To finish, melt some chocolate over a double boiler. Remove from heat and dip the Sarah Bernhard into the chocolate. Place them on a cookie sheet and decorate the top with a pistachio nut.

SPICED SUGAR COOKIES

Market Spice – Seattle, Washington

1-1/3	cups shortening
1-1/4	cups sugar
2	eggs
3-1/2	cups flour
2	teaspoons baking powder
1	teaspoon salt
2-1/2	teaspoons Sweet Baking Spice (available at Market Spice)
1	teaspoon vanilla extract
1/4	cup milk

Cream shortening and sugar together. Beat in eggs until well blended.

In separate bowl, mix together flour, baking powder, salt and the sweet baking spice.

Blend the vanilla with the milk. Add the wet and dry mixes alternately to the shortening/egg mix. Mix well. Refrigerate covered for 30 minutes.

Form dough into 2 or 3 balls, roll on floured board and cut into desired shapes with cookie cutters. Bake on ungreased cookie sheet at 400° F. until lightly browned, about 10 minutes. Cool on rack.

(Also good frosted with icing if desired.)

Makes 3 dozen cookies.

VIENNA MOMENTS

Creative PossibiliTEAS – Portland, Oregon

3/4	cup margarine
1	cup all purpose flour
1/2	cup powdered sugar
1/2	cup cornstarch
1	tablespoon cocoa
1	tablespoon prepared Cafe Vienna instant coffee

Mix all dry ingredients and add cut up margarine at room temperature. Blend until all ingredients are moist, and press dough together to form a large ball. Refrigerate for 1 hour.

Roll approximately 1 teaspoon of the dough into balls by hand. Place the balls on an ungreased cookie sheet. Flatten with fork or cookie press.

Bake at 350° F. for 20-25 minutes. Let cool completely on wire rack.

Icing: Mix enough powdered sugar with prepared Cafe Vienna to form paste, (approximately 1/2 cup sugar to 1 tablespoon coffee)

Place tiny drop of icing in center of cooled cookie using spoon or pastry tube. Let icing harden before wrapping.

CAKES
& TARTS

APPLESAUCE SPICE POUND CAKE

Just Pretend – Port Townsend, Washington

Applesauce laces this pound cake from historic Port Townsend with homespun goodness.

1	cup butter or margarine (2 sticks), softened
1-1/2	cups firmly packed brown sugar
1-1/2	cups sugar
5	large eggs
1-1/2	cups applesauce
2	teaspoons baking soda
3	cups all-purpose flour, divided
1	teaspoon ground cinnamon
1	teaspoon ground nutmeg
1/2	teaspoon ground cloves
1/2	teaspoon ground allspice
1-1/2	cups raisins
1	cup chopped pecans

Beat butter in a large mixing bowl at medium speed of an electric mixer about 2 minutes or until soft and creamy. Gradually add sugars, beating at medium speed 5 to 7 minutes. Add eggs, one at a time, beating just until yellow disappears.

Combine the applesauce and soda and set aside.

Combine 2-3/4 cups flour and spices; add to butter mixture alternately with applesauce mixture, beginning and ending with flour mixture. Mix at low speed just until blended after each addition.

Combine remaining 1/4 cup flour, raisins, and pecans, fold into batter. Pour batter into a greased and floured 12-cup bundt pan.

Bake at 325° F. for 1 hour and 15 to 20 minutes or until a wooden pick inserted in center comes out clean. Cool in pan on wire rack 10 to 15 minutes. Remove from pan and cool completely on wire rack.

Yields one 10-inch cake

GERMAN APPLE CAKE

Hope Chest – Sherwood, Oregon

An old-fashioned delight that takes advantage of the bumper crop of apples every autumn….. if the deer leave us any.
Try this with apple-cinnamon tea for a real treat.

1	cup flour
2	teaspoons baking powder
1/2	cup milk
1	large egg
1/2	cup sugar
1/4	cup melted butter
2	apples, peeled and sliced
	Pinch of salt
1/4	cup sugar, mixed with
1	teaspoon cinnamon

Mix dry ingredients together. Add milk, melted butter and egg, mix well. Batter should be stiff. Pour into greased 8 x 8-inch pan.

Insert pared apple slices in rows into dough. Sprinkle with 1/4 cup sugar mixed with 1 teaspoon cinnamon.

Bake 30 minutes at 375° F.

Best served warm with whipped cream onto which you've sprinkled a little cinnamon or nutmeg.

LAVENDER CAKE WITH ORANGE GLAZE

Lavender Tea House – Sherwood, Oregon

A visual treat with orange slices and lavender from your own garden. Even nicer because it tastes so good served with an orange spice tea.

3/4	cup unsalted butter, room temperature
3/4	cup sugar
3	eggs, lightly beaten
1-1/2	cups self-rising flour
1	tablespoon dried lavender flowers
1/2	teaspoon vanilla
2	tablespoons milk
1	orange (sliced for garnish)
	Powdered sugar
	Freshly squeezed orange juice

Orange Glaze:

2	tablespoons orange juice
1	cup powdered sugar
	Zest from half an orange

Cream butter and sugar until fluffy. Add eggs one at a time until the mix is thick and glossy. Fold in flour, lavender flowers, vanilla and milk.

Preheat oven to 350 degrees. Lightly grease and flour 8-inch round cake pan with removable bottom. Pour mixture into pan and bake for 1 hour. Allow to sit for 5 minutes and then turn the cake onto a cooling rack.

Mix orange juice, powdered sugar and orange zest together to make glaze. When the cake has cooled completely, brush on orange glaze and sprinkle with lavender flowers.

Serve cake with orange slices and sprig of fresh lavender as garnish.

LINDA'S TEA & HONEY CAKE

*The late Linda Wexler was a highly respected California tea writer,
author of "A Spot of Tea." While we never met, our life paths crossed
when we both had guidebooks for tea released within a month of each other
without realizing the other was even working on the same project in 1996.
I intended to call and introduce myself, having heard so many nice
things about her, but she passed away. This was Linda's favorite tea
cake, reprinted here with the permission of her
husband, Dr. Howard Raff, as a special memorial to her.*

1	cup honey
2	eggs
1	cup brown sugar
1	cup strong brewed black tea
1-1/2	teaspoons baking powder
3	tablespoons oil
1/2	teaspoon plus 1 pinch baking soda
2	cups flour
1	tablespoon cinnamon

Preheat oven to 325° F. Grease and flour a 9 x13-inch pan.

Beat the honey and eggs together, add the sugar and mix again. Mix the strong tea with baking powder and oil and add to the egg mixture. Add the baking soda, flour and cinnamon and beat together well.

Pour batter into prepared pan and bake for 55 minutes to an hour, or until toothpick inserted in cake comes out clean.

JANE'S PUMPKIN CAKE

Pomeroy House – Yacolt, Washington

"Autumn nodding o'er the yellow plain
Comes jovial on."
James Thompson

Autumn is greeted very jovially at Pomeroy House where an annual Pumpkin Tea is held the last week of October. Jane Brink developed this recipe for that special event tea.

1	package lemon cake mix
4	eggs
1/2	cup sugar
1/2	cup canned pumpkin puree
1/3	cup oil
1/4	cup water
1	teaspoon cinnamon
1	teaspoon nutmeg
1/4	teaspoon cloves

Mix all the ingredients together and bake in a floured bundt pan for 35-45 minutes or until the cake tests done. Cool on a rack.

Glaze with your favorite powdered sugar glaze or dust with powdered sugar.

AUNT MARWAYNE'S TEACAKE

When my octogenarian father and his big sister Marwayne were 3 and 4 years old on the plains of Alberta, my aunt had a delicious trick she played on him. "Here, let me get that icky stuff off your cake for you," she'd coo as she scraped the frosting off his piece of cake and spread it on her own. For years he thought she was doing him a favor, and would wait patiently for her to fix his cake. She made a mistake one day and let him taste the "icky stuff."

2	cups granulated sugar
2	cups all-purpose flour
1	cup (2 sticks) margarine
4	tablespoons unsweetened cocoa
1	cup water
1/2	cup buttermilk
2	eggs, slightly beaten
1	teaspoon baking soda
1	teaspoon vanilla extract

Frosting Glaze:

1/2	cup (1 stick) margarine
4	tablespoons unsweetened cocoa
1/3	cup milk
1	16 oz. box confectioners sugar
1	teaspoon vanilla extract
1	cup chopped pecans

Preheat oven to 400° F. Combine sugar and flour in large bowl. Combine margarine, cocoa and water in saucepan and bring to a quick boil. Pour over flour-sugar mixture and stir well. Add buttermilk, eggs, baking soda and vanilla. Mix well.

Pour batter into 11 x 15-inch greased baking pan. Bake 20 minutes or until cake tests done. Prepare the icing 5 minutes before cake is done.

Frosting Glaze: Combine margarine, cocoa and milk in saucepan and cook over low heat until margarine melts. Bring to a boil and remove from heat. Add confectioners sugar, vanilla and pecans. Beat well. Spread on cake while it's still hot and in the pan. Serves 18.

VICTORIAN SPONGE CAKE

The Brits – Longview, Washington

This versatile sponge cake was a staple of Victorian tea tables and encourages kitchen creativity. Sliced horizontally, it can be filled with cream, fruit, preserves, curds, and any number of rich fillings. The Brits co-owner Pat Sprinzl provided this version from her treasury of English recipes.

2	eggs
1/3	cup sugar
1/2	cup self-rising flour

Combine eggs and sugar in a bowl, and whisk until thick and creamy. Lightly fold in the flour.

Place in a well-greased 8-inch cake pan. Bake at 350° F. for approximately 30 minutes.

When cool slice and spread with jam and cream or any filling that strikes your fancy.

LEMON PANCAKES

Fairgate Inn Bed & Breakfast – Camas, Washington

*"I believe it is customary in good society to take some slight
refreshment at five o'clock."*
Oscar Wilde
The Importance of Being Earnest

1/2	cup ricotta cheese
1/4	cup small curd cottage cheese
1/4	cup melted butter
1/4	cup + 1 tablespoon unsifted cake flour
2	tablespoons sugar
3	egg yolks
1	tablespoon lemon zest
3	egg whites
1/4	teaspoon cream of tartar

Blend cheeses, butter, flour, egg yolks, sugar, lemon zest, and salt. Process in bowl of food processor until batter is smooth.

In clean bowl with clean beaters, beat egg white until foamy. Add the cream of tartar. Beat until stiff peaks form. Fold the egg whites into the batter.

Heat your griddle to hot and lightly butter it. Pour batter into small rounds. Cook until golden brown, turn over, and cook for about 1 more minute.

Serve with fresh raspberry syrup.

LEMON CURD TARTLETS
South Seattle Community College, Culinary Arts Program

Jean-Claude Berger, Pastry-Chef Instructor at the prestigious Culinary Arts Program of South Seattle Community College allowed us to raid his recipe box for a favorite traditional tea treat.

Sugar dough:

1-1/2	cups pastry flour
3-1/2	oz. butter
2	oz. ground almonds
1/4	tsp. baking powder
2	oz. sugar
2	egg yolks
	Pinch salt

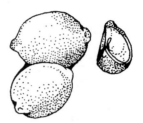

Filling:

4	lemons
1	lb. sugar
6	whole eggs
3	egg yolks
5	oz. butter

Place all dough ingredients into food processor, blend well and refrigerate overnight.

Peel lemons, avoid using the white part. Cut them in half and extract all the juice, keeping the pulp and pits with the juice.

Break eggs into a stainless steel bowl and add the 3 yolks, sugar, lemon juice, peel and pulp. Mix lightly. Place the bowl over a double boiler, the water simply needs to be hot, not boiling. With a whisk, gently mix the ingredients until the curd thickens, about 15 minutes. Remove from heat, add cold butter and mix until well blended. Put the curd through a fine sieve and set aside.

Line the tartlet shells with sugar dough. Bake about 5 minutes at 325° F. Fill each shell with the curd and bake the filled tartlets at 200° F. for about 10 more minutes. Remove from the oven and decorate each tartlet with a fresh raspberry and a sprig of rosemary.

CHOCOLATE WALNUT TORTE

Eden's Gate Farm – Applegate, Oregon

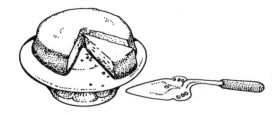

This rich torte, provided by caterer Diana S. Brent, is just one of the special goodies at Cathy Dunlap's Eden's Gate Farm tea parties in historic Applegate.

For the batter:

1/2	cup butter
1/2	cup light corn syrup
1	cup semi-sweet chocolate chips
1/2	cup granulated sugar
3	eggs
1	teaspoon vanilla
1	cup all-purpose flour
1	cup chopped walnuts

For the chocolate glaze:

1/2	cup semi-sweet chocolate chips
2	tablespoons butter
1	tablespoon light corn syrup
1	teaspoon vanilla

Butter and flour one 9-inch round cake pan.

In a saucepan, heat butter and corn syrup until butter is melted. Pour in the chocolate chips and stir until melted. Remove from heat and cool slightly. Beat sugar and eggs together. Blend with the melted chocolate mixture. Add the vanilla, flour and nuts mixing well. Pour batter into pan.

Bake in preheated oven, 350° F. for 25 minutes, or until center springs back when touched. Cool in pan for 10 minutes. Turn out of pan onto rack right side up. Allow to cool further while you prepare the glaze.

To make glaze, combine the chocolate chips, butter, and corn syrup in a saucepan, stirring over low heat until chocolate is melted. Remove from heat and stir in vanilla. Frost top and sides of cooled torte. Chill until set.

Garnish with 3 sliced strawberries or chopped walnuts sprinkled on top of glaze, or just try whipped cream.

WHITE CHOCOLATE BAVAROISE

The Sutton Place Hotel, Fleuri Restaurant
Vancouver, B.C.

This traditional Austrian/German dessert, a favorite of patrons of the Fleuri Restaruant, is a cross between a pudding and a mousse with a delicate white chocolate flavor.

	Nonstick vegetable spray
	Powdered sugar
1	cup milk
4	oz. white chocolate, shaved or finely chopped
2	egg yolks
2	tablespoons plus 2 teaspoons granulated sugar
2	envelopes unflavored gelatin
1/4	cup cold water
1-1/2	cups cream
	Fresh berries and chocolate leaves or curls
	for garnish.

Spray 8-inch bowl with vegetable spray and dust with powdered sugar, tapping to remove excess.

In a bowl, combine the sugar and egg yolks. In a small saucepan, bring the milk to a simmer. Slowly pour the milk into the egg mixture whisking constantly. Pour the mixture back into saucepan and continue whisking over low heat until the mixture thickens (mixture will coat the back of a spoon). Add white chocolate and whisk to melt. Soak the gelatin in cold water until softened, add to hot milk mixture and stir to dissolve. Cool.

Whip cream to soft peaks. Fold whipped cream into cooled milk mixture. Pour into prepared bowl and refrigerate overnight or until set.

To serve, unmold bavaroise onto a serving platter. Decorate with fresh berries and chocolate leaves or curls.

CHERRY NECTARINE TART

	All purpose flour for dusting
1	recipe Tart Shell Dough (see below)
1/3	cup sugar
1-1/2	tablespoons cornstarch
4	cups sweet Bing cherries, washed, pitted and halved.
1/3	cup + 1/4 cup cherry preserves
3	small ripe nectarines, pitted and sliced
3	whole sweet Bing cherries and mint sprigs for garnish

Divide dough into thirds. Dust with flour, three 5-inch round tart pans with removable bottoms. Press dough evenly over bottom and sides of tart pans.   Prick bottoms with fork and place in freezer 15 minutes. Preheat oven to 400° F. with rack on lowest level of oven.

In a bowl mix together sugar and cornstarch. Stir in cherries and 1/3 cup preserves until well blended. Spoon into prepared shells and place tarts on baking sheet. Bake 30 minutes, cover loosely with foil and bake an additional 10 to 15 minutes, until fruit is bubbly in center.

Cool tarts on wire rack.

Remove sides of pans and place on three serving plates. Melt and strain remaining preserves. Arrange nectarine slices in spiral over filling. Brush with preserves and top each with a cherry and a mint spring.

TART-SHELL DOUGH

A versatile sweet pastry shell for a variety of fillings.

1-1/4	cup unsifted all-purpose flour
1/4	cup confectioner's sugar
1/4	teaspoon salt
1/2	cup (1 stick) cold, unsalted butter, cut into pieces
1	large egg yolk mixed with 1 tablespoon ice water

In food processor, pulse the dry ingredients. Add butter, pulsing until mixture resembles small peas. Add egg yolk mixture and process until dough forms a ball. Press into tart pans, any size. Bake according to the directions in the included tart recipes.

STRAWBERRY-MANGO CREAM TART

	All purpose flour for dusting
1	recipe Tart-Shell Dough (see page 259)
1	envelope unflavored gelatin
1/4	cup mango, pear or apricot nectar
1-1/2	cup mango puree (from ripe mangoes)
1/2	cup heavy cream, whipped
2	pints small strawberries, hulled
1	small ripe mango, remove skin and pit, cut into 1/2 inch dice
1/4	cup strawberry jelly, melted

Dust a round 9-inch tart pan with removable bottom with flour. Press the dough evenly over bottom and sides. Prick bottom with fork and place in freezer for 15 minutes. Place oven rack in bottom position. Preheat oven to 375° F. Cover the tart shell with foil and fill with baking weights or dried beans. Bake 18 minutes. Remove foil and weights. Bake 14 minutes longer. Cool completely on wire rack.

Remove side of pan and place baked shell on serving plate. In a small microwave-safe cup, sprinkle gelatin over nectar. Let stand 2 minutes. Microwave on high for 40 seconds. Stir until dissolved. In a large bowl combine the gelatin mixture with the mango puree. Stir over bowl of ice water until mixture makes thick mounds. Fold in whipped cream.

Refrigerate one hour. When ready to serve, whisk filling to lighten; spread evenly with spatula in tart shell. Arrange strawberries and diced mango on top in any pattern, brush with jelly.

BLACKBERRY-KIWI LIME CURD TARTLETS

	All purpose flour for dusting
1	recipe Tart-Shell Dough (page 259)
2	large eggs, lightly beaten
1/2	cup (1 stick) unsalted butter, cut in chunks
1/2	cup sugar
1/4	cup fresh lime juice
1	tablespoon fresh lemon juice
2	teaspoons grated lemon zest
1-1/2	cups small blackberries
3	kiwis, peeled and sliced
	Strips of lime zest for garnish

Dust 16 mini tart pans (4-inch oval) with flour. With floured hands roll 16 tablespoons dough into 4-inch ropes. Press evenly over bottom and sides. Prick bottoms with fork and place in freezer for 15 minutes. On bottom rack of oven at 375° F., bake the shells 15 minutes on a cookie sheet. Cool on wire rack.

In saucepan, combine eggs, butter, sugar, lime juice and lemon juice and cook over medium-low heat, whisking until thickened. Pour into bowl, add zest, cover and refrigerate 2 hours.

Unmold the fragile shells. Fill with the lime curd, arrange blackberries and kiwi slices over tops. Garnish with strips of lime zest.

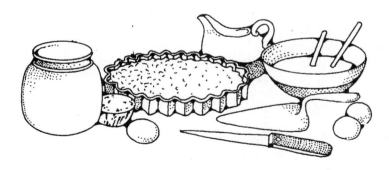

GRACIE'S OUTRAGEOUS ABC CUPCAKES

Our friend Gracie Adams-Hoke was born and raised in Ketchikan, Alaska. Before she was 24 she was panning for gold and staking mining claims; dispatching helicopters for search and rescue missions; and cooking on a rainy, remote island (with no store) for 60 hungry, cranky men in dripping tents. Nothing ever rattled her. One winter she spent with us in Utah, we came home to find her sitting cross-legged in coveralls reading from a how-to book on auto repair. Surrounding her in our garage were various important-looking greasy parts of her dismantled Datsun engine. "I figure it's alot like cooking," she explained as we gaped, "You just read the recipe and follow the instructions. How hard can it be?" The next day she drove the car to the library to return the auto repair book. Gracie's now a wife and mother living in Gold Hill, Oregon. Follow her directions to truly Outrageous ABC Cupcakes. After all, how hard could it be?

A)   Mix together:

1-1/2	cups all purpose flour
1	teaspoon baking soda
1/2	teaspoon salt
1	cup sugar
1/4	cup unsweetened dry cocoa

B)   Add these ingredients to A ingredients and stir to combine:

1	cup water
1/3	cup vegetable oil
1	tablespoon vinegar
1	teaspoon vanilla

C) Mix these ingredients in a separate bowl:

1	package of cream cheese (8 oz.)
1	egg, unbeaten
1/3	cup sugar
1/8	teaspoon salt

Place cupcake papers in muffin tins and fill 1/3 full with the A/B mixture. Drop 1 heaping tablespoon of the C mixture on top of it in the middle. Bake at 350° F. for 25-30 minutes.

Makes 20 cupcakes.

SWEETS

JENNIFER JAYNE'S MINI PAVLOVAS

Jenny, Ken's oldest daughter, is a a teacher in New Zealand and will be a first-time mommy by the time this book is in print. Let's celebrate the arrival with her favorite mini Pavlovas.

3	egg whites
1/4	teaspoon cream of tartar
1/8	teaspoon salt
1	teaspoon vanilla extract
1/2	cup superfine sugar
1	cup whipping cream, whipped
2	cups fresh fruit (kiwis, blueberries, strawberries, raspberries, blackberries, mandarin oranges)

Beat first 4 ingredients at high speed with electric mixer until foamy. Add sugar 1 tablespoon at a time beating until stiff peaks form and sugar dissolves. Drop mixture by rounded spoonfuls on parchment lined baking sheets. Spread into 2-inch circles, shaping with back of spoon to make shallow bowls.

Bake at 225° F. for 1 hour of until dry on outside. Turn oven off and let stand in closed oven 1 hour.

Spoon whipped cream evenly into meringues, top with a medley of fruit. Makes about a dozen.

GULAB JAMUN

Travelers Tea Bar – Seattle, Washington

A westernized recipe of a finger-licking treat from India, given to Travelers owner Allen Kornmesser. He suggests a cup of hot spiced chai to accompany these goodies.

1-1/2	cups powdered milk
3/4	cup biscuit mix
1	teaspoon ground cardamom
3	tablespoons ghee (clarified butter)
1/4	teaspoon baking powder
1/2	cup milk
4-1/2	cups sugar
6	cups water
	Vegetable oil for frying
	Rose water (optional - to taste)

Combine powdered milk, biscuit mix, cardamom, and baking powder in a bowl, mix well. Add ghee, (available at Indian markets) or use clarified butter, cut in evenly. Stir in milk to make soft, sticky dough.

Prepare syrup by boiling sugar and water on high heat for 5-10 minutes. Reduce heat and keep warm.

Heat vegetable oil (about 4" deep) to 325° F. Oil hands and roll dough into balls about the size of a cherry. Fry for about 15 minutes until golden brown. Drain on paper towel.

When cool, drop in the warm syrup and simmer gently 10 minutes. Leave them in the syrup, and refrigerate. These are really best after 1 or 2 days, and should be served warm with a sprinkling of rose water (optional).

BREAD PUDDING
WITH CARAMEL SAUCE

This dessert if a specialty of Summer Jo's Restaurant on the Rogue River. President Herbert Hoover loved fishing on the Rogue, and when criticized for wasting time, he engendered the everlasting goodwill of sportsmen everywhere when he retorted, "The hours a man spends fishing do not count against his total lifespan." I like that though so much I vote we change it to "the hours spent at teatime..."

6	cups cubed sourdough baguette
3/4	cup diced dried apricots
1/4	cup cranberries
4	cups milk
2	cups heavy cream
4	egg yolks
7	whole eggs
1	cup sugar
2	teaspoons vanilla extract
	Caramel pieces

Spread baguette pieces, apricots and cranberries evenly in a buttered 13 x 9 x 2-inch glass baking dish.

Bring some water to a boil, which will be poured into another pan to serve as a bath when pudding is ready to bake.

Heat milk and cream on stovetop, simmer only. Whisk egg yolks, eggs and sugar in large bowl, slowly add hot milk mixture whisking constantly to avoid curdling. Add vanilla extract.

Strain though a wire sieve onto bread and fruit in pan, press down with a large spoon to ensure that all bread is moistened.

Place pudding pan into a larger pan and fill larger pan with hot water to about half way up pudding pan. Bake in preheated 350 degree oven for 40-50 minutes, until center is set.

Melt caramels. Place slice on a pool of melted caramel and heat in microwave for 1 minute.

KAREN'S CHOCOLATE BREAD PUDDING

Exhibitor's Mall Tea Room – Puyallup, Washington

This definitely qualifies as "comfort food."

4	oz. unsweetened chocolate
1/2	cup semi-sweet chocolate chips
2	tablespoons butter
1-1/2	cups sugar
6	cups french bread cubes, 1/2-inch
3	cups whipping cream
2	teaspoons vanilla
9	eggs
1	teaspoon cinnamon

Warm chocolate and butter on low heat until melted, stirring constantly.

In a large bowl beat together the eggs, cream, sugar, cinnamon and vanilla until just combined. Gradually add the cream mixture to the chocolate stirring constantly.

Fold in the bread cubes, and pour into 8 x 11-1/2-inch greased baking dish (2 quart). Bake about 1-1/4 hours or until knife inserted in the center comes out clean. Cool slightly before serving.

Makes 12 servings

GREEN TEA FROZEN YOGURT

1	cup water
4	green-tea bags
1/2	cup sugar
1	16-oz. container plain fat-free yogurt

Several hours before serving, prepare the green tea with boiling water and sugar in a medium sized bowl. Set aside to cool, stirring occasionally, then cover and refrigerate at least 1 hour. Remove and discard tea bags, squeezing to release liquid. Stir yogurt into tea until well mixed. Transfer to an airtight container and freeze 1 to 2 hours. Serve in chilled parfait dishes.

JASMINE TEA AND PEAR SORBET

Here's an interesting palate cleanser for between courses or as a light, refreshing dessert.

1-1/4	cups water
2	tablespoons jasmine tea leaves
1	pound ripe Bosc pears
4	tablespoons fresh lemon juice
6	tablespoons sugar

Pour boiling water over tea leaves and let steep 20 minutes, then strain.

Peel, core and chop pears then put into small pan with lemon juice. Turn pears in lemon juice to prevent discoloration.

Add sugar to the tea and bring to boil with the pears, stirring until sugar dissolves. Simmer 20 minutes. Pour mixture into blender and puree.

Taste and add more lemon juice and/or sugar if needed. Spread in glass pan, cover and freeze about 4 hours.

Makes about 1 quart.

HIGH TEA FRUIT SALAD

Pleasant Times – Endicott, Washington

8	oz. cream cheese
2	tablespoons mayonnaise
2	tablespoons sugar
2	14-oz. cans Ocean Spray Cranberries
2	cups crushed pineapple, drained
2	cups fresh strawberries, if available
2	cups Cool Whip

Mix together cream cheese, mayonnaise and sugar. Add 2 cans cranberries, mix well. Fold in the Cool Whip, pineapple and strawberries. Freeze until firm.

Before serving, allow to soften enough to scoop with ice cream scoop, about 30 minutes, or cut into squares to serve.

"Many other fruits can be substituted for one of the cans of cranberries, so experiment," is the advice of owner Jean Cisneros.

SWEET SPICED PECANS

I think when "visions of sugarplums danced in their heads" these festive
Sweet Spiced Pecans were doing the Macarena too.

1	cup sugar
1-1/2	tablespoons ground cinnamon
1	teaspoon ground cloves
1	teaspoon salt
1	teaspoon ground ginger
1/2	teaspoon ground nutmeg
1	egg white
1	tablespoon cold water
1	pound pecans

Preheat oven to 250° F. Butter a large jelly roll pan.

Mix together thoroughly all dry ingredients. (May be done in food processor.) Beat egg white with cold water until frothy but not stiff. Add spiced sugar mixture and stir well. Add nuts; stir well to coat.

Spread nuts in pan, place in oven and bake for 1 hour, stirring to separate every 15 to 20 minutes. Remove from oven when dry and toasty.

Cool. Store in airtight container. Makes 16 one-ounce servings.

SPREADS & CONDIMENTS

ANGELINA'S CHAMPAGNE JELLY

Angelina's French Tea – Aurora, Oregon

More and more people are discovering the delights of the French approach to tea. Here is an elegant condiment of the Regency era.

4	cups sugar
1	cup white grape juice
1	cup brut Champagne
1/4	teaspoon citric acid powder
3	oz. liquid pectin

In a deep saucepan, combine the sugar, grape juice, Champagne, and citric acid. Cook, stirring constantly over medium high heat, until it comes to a full boil that cannot be stirred down.

Add pectin and bring to a full boil once more, stirring constantly, and continue boiling for one minute longer. Remove from heat and skim off foam. Pour into containers following usual canning procedures for preserves.

LEMON CURD

Country Tea Garden – Selah, Washington

"I'll be with you in the squeezing of a lemon."
Oliver Goldsmith

5	eggs
1	cup sugar
2/3	cup fresh lemon juice
1/2	cup butter
	Lemon zest

Melt the butter. Blend the eggs, sugar and juice in a blender and add melted butter while blending. Cook on stovetop over low heat stirring constantly until the mixture thickens enough to mound. Pour into containers and cool.

Serve with scones and Devonshire cream or use as a filling for tarts.

HUMMUS BI TAHINI
Morning Glory Chai – Seattle, Washington

Here's a free form recipe from a free-wheeling spot for good chai in Ballard. The recipe originated, in the words of owner Jessica Vidican, "somewhere in the Fertile Crescent of Mesopotamia."

1	can of garbanzo beans, drained
	Lots of fresh garlic, to taste
3	tablespoon tahini (available at middle-Eastern markets or ask your grocer)
	Lemon juice to taste
	Sufficient olive oil to provide moistness
	Middle Eastern spices to taste – experimentation is the key
	Salt and pepper
	Coriander
	Paprika

Combine all ingredients in a bowl and stir well. Spoon into a food processor and add sufficient water to create a smooth fluffy pate. Adjust spices to taste.

Serve with warm pita bread, good crackers or bagels chunks. Garnish with sprouts, olives and peppercorns.

JUDY'S CHEESE SPREAD
I don't know how she does it, but my friend Judy Carroll has a real knack for combining flavors into something uniquely her own. This simple spread is great on crackers or crusty toast points.

1	4-oz. can chopped green chiles
8	oz. cream cheese, softened
1	cup mayonnaise
1	cup shredded Monterey Jack cheese

Place all ingredients in the bowl of a food processor fitted with a steel blade. Process until smooth. Store covered in the refrigerator.

ROSE PETAL JAM

Gearhart Gallery and Gifts – Gearhart, Oregon

In my husband's native Liverpool slang, to be extremely lucky is to be "jammy." I think we should all count ourselves jammy with this elegant recipe from Carol Cox, owner of Gearhart Gallery and Gifts.

1/2	cup dark rose petals
1	lb. sugar
5	cups water
	Juice of 2 lemons

Snip the light-colored triangles from each rose petal base and discard. Tear the remaining colored petals into small shreds. Sprinkle enough sugar over them to cover, and leave overnight. (This intensifies the fragrance and darkens the crimson of the petals.)

Dissolve the sugar in water and lemon juice over low heat. Stir in the sugared rose petals and simmer for 20 minutes. Bring to a boil, and boil for about 5 minutes, until the mixture thickens.

Pour into containers and store in the conventional manner.

Place a small dish of jam on a doily and garnish with fresh rose petals.

Glossary of Tea Terms

Agony of the leaves - Tea tasters expression descriptive of the unfolding of the leaves when boiling water is applied.

Assam - High grade tea grown in Assam Province in Northeast India.

Aroma - Denotes that both the tea leaf and infusion have one of a certain number of smells which are highly valued. Such aroma is connected with flavor and is highly fragrant.

Autumnal teas - Term applied to India and Formosa teas, meaning teas touched with cool weather.

Biscuity - A pleasant aroma associated with a well-fired Assam

Black tea - Any tea that has been thoroughly fermented before being fired as opposed to green or Oolong tea.

Blend - A mixture of different growths.

Body - A liquor having both fullness and strength as opposed to a thin liquor.

Bright - Sparkling red liquor. Denotes good tea which has life as opposed to a dull looking infused leaf or liquor.

Brisk - "live" not flat liquor. Usually of pungent character.

Caffeine content - In a cup of tea, less than 1 grain; in a cup of coffee, 1.5 grain.

Ch'a - (Char)(Chai) Chinese. Tea.

Color - Color of liquor which varies from country to country and district to district.

Darjeeling - The finest and most delicately flavored of the Indian teas. Grown chiefly in the Himalayan Mountains at elevations ranging from 2,500 to 6,500 feet.

Even - Tea leaf which is true to grade and consisting of pieces of roughly equal size. When applied to infused leaf it is usually combined with bright and coppery.

F **Fermented (black) tea** - Chinese refer to black tea as "hong Cha" or "Red tea" because when it is brewed it takes on a reddish-orange color. More popular often among Westerners than Chinese. Often used to make specialty blends with the addition of Jasmine blossoms or spices.

Full - Strong tea, without bitterness, having color and substance as opposed to thin and empty.

G **Garden** - Used interchangeably with "plantation" in some tea countries, but usually referring to an estate unit.

Garden mark - The mark put on tea chests by the estate to identify its particular product.

Goddess - A semi-fermented tea. Has a stern taste and is credited as an aid to digestion.

Green tea - Tea leaves that have been sterilized either in live steam, hot air, or hot pans, whereby fermentation is prevented, and then rolled and dried.

H **Handkerchief tea** - From the island of Formosa. It gets its name from the fact that Chinese tea growers bring down from their little gardens or farms very tippy teas, often of the highest quality, in large silk handkerchiefs.

I **Ichiban-Cha** - Japanese for "first tea," or first plucking.

M **Malty** - Slightly high-fired tea, like Keemun

Mature - No flatness or rawness.

Monster - Dutch for "sample."

N **Nose** - The aroma of tea.

Oolong - From the Chinese wu-lung meaning "black dragon." A semi femented tea of fine quality, hand rolled and fired in baskets over pits containing red-hot charcoal. Originally shipped principally from Guanzhou and Amoy in China, the production of Oolong was introduced more than a century ago to Taiwan.

 Sappy - Full juicy liquor.

Scented tea - Made in China and Taiwan by introducing jasmine, gardenia, or yulan blossoms during the firing and packing process.

Self drinking - In tea tasting, a tea is said to "stand-up" when it holds its original color and flavor.

Smoky - Tasting of smoke, used interchangeably with the term "tarry."

Standing up - In tea tasting, a tea is said to "stand-up" when it holds its original color and flavor.

Stand out - Liquor above the average.

Stewy - Soft liquor, lacking point.

Strength - Thick liquor, pungent and brisk.

Sweet - A light, not undesirable liquor.

 Tea - Tea is the tender leaves, leaf, buds, and tender internodes of different varieties of Thea sinesis prepared and cured by recognized methods of manufacture.

Tip - The bud leaf of the tea plant.

Tippy tea - Teas with white or golden tips. (See handkerchief tea.)

 Well twisted - Leaf which is tightly rolled or twisted which is indicative of ideally withered tea.

Websites for Tea

I didn't see The Computer Age coming. It sneaked up on me when I was hunched over the typewriter slathering White-Out on a carbon copy. I was just beginning to recover from the trauma of transitioning from the comforting 'clackity-clack' of a manual typewriter to the fast-talking smoothie ways of an electric. Now this.

Nonetheless, fascinating new websites for tea, food and hospitality are appearing daily on this magic box, and now I too am entangled in the Internet. Some of these are commercial sites of tea merchants, some are personal home pages of tea lovers. In addition to the sites listed for the tea rooms in this book, here are a few more notables you may enjoy exploring over a pot of tea:

www.harney.com - excellent tea advice, teas and supplies

www.republicoftea.com - ask Madame Oolong for a tea leaf reading

www.livingvictorian.com - resource for Victorian elegance

www.afternoonteaparty.com - a marvelous home page of a tea lover

www.theteachest.com - teaware and handcrafted gifts

www.victorianaonline.com - informative site for lovers of the era

www.wayoftea.com - commerical site that invites your participation

www.teatimegarden.com - fresh herbals and tea gifts shipped locally

www.teatimeinthenorthwest.com - our own personal site coming mid-2001

www.homearts.com - recipes and household tips

www.sallys-place.com - food and travel, recipes from around the world

www.victoriamagazine.com - the glorious magazine goes online

www.todd-holland.com - commerical site featuring rare teas

www.teaquotes.com - new tea quotes being added all the time

www.someplaceintime.com - teawares and adorable Victorian goodies

www.catteacorner.com - vegetarian cat-lover with a tea chat room

www.tea.com - with links to many tea sites including Tea, A Magazine

www.urasenke.org - learn about the Japanese Tea Ceremony

www.northwest-gourmet.com - home to Northwest Gourmet Guides

www.foodtv.com - link to that television network's recipe box

www.celestialseasonings.com - commerical site with goods and goodies www.teatalk.com - the "Tea Man" educates and informs

www.svtea.com - commercial site with many teas, coffee and wares

www.gourmetreats.com - tea treats and speciality foods delivered to you

www.learn2.com - learn about anything and everything, including tea

www.marthastewart.com - America's queen of lifestyle holds court

www.stashtea.com - commercial site with a virtual tour of a tea estate

www.nuttysites.com - need a smile? Crazy, silly and goofy site

Tea Rooms Anticipating Opening in 2001

In addition to superlative hospitality skills, the new tea room owner needs patience and nerves of steel. Side roads along the path to their gentle vision include building inspections, parking areas, plumbing glitches, loan officers, leasing agents and lots of people wielding hammers. Look for the possibility of tea to come through the following locations in 2001 if their path is smooth. We hope it is.

The Arbor Tea Room at Faded Elegance
2112 Hewitt Avenue , Everett, WA 98201
It's tea time amid yesteryear's glories.

Carnelian Rose Tea Room
1501 Columbia Street, Vancouver, WA 98661
Opening early 2001. A Northwest style tea room serving heartier fare.

La-Tea-Dah
904 Main Street, Tillamook, OR 97141
Opening spring 2001. An English country style tea room and gift shop in the heart of dairy and cheese country.

The Resort at the Mountain
68010 E. Fairway , Welches, OR 97067
Tea with a country European flair and close-up views of Mount Hood. What on earth could be nicer?

The Sycamore Tree
2108 Main Street , Baker, OR 97814
Tea and upscale gifts with a backdrop of historic Baker sounds delightful.

Victorian Threads Tea Room
207 N. Meridian , Puyallup, WA 98371
Tea adjacent to a cozy needlecraft shop.

Recommended Tea Reading

The New Tea Lover's Treasury by James Norwood Pratt

The Agony of the Leaves by Helen Gustafson,
    Henry Holt & Company, 1996

The Book of Coffee & Tea by Joel, David & Karl Schapira,
    St. Martin's Press, New York, 1982

Tea Gardens by Ann Lovejoy,
    Chronicle Books, San Fransciso, 1998

The Charms of Tea by Victoria Magazine-The Hearst Company,
    William Morrow & Company, New york, 1991

If Teacups Could Talk by Emilie Barnes,
    Harvest House, 1996

The Pleasures of Tea by Victoria Magazine-The Hearst Company,
    William Morrow & Company, New York, 1999

Tea Celebrations by Alexandra Stoddard,
    William Morrow & Company, New York, 1994

The Book of Tea by Okakura Kakuzo,
    Charles E. Tuttle Company, 1967

All About Tea by William H. Ukers, Volume 2,
    Westport Hyperion Press, 1994

The Classic of Tea by Lu Yu, translated by Francis Ross Carpenter,
    The Ecco Press, 1997

Tea Resources

Angelina's French Tea
P.O. Box 254
Aurora, OR 97002
503-221-3794
mail order, wholesale & retail
elegant teas from France

The Art of Health
321 S.W. 4th Avenue #200
Portland, OR 97204
800-816-8174
503-224-8411
E-Mail:
laurawashing@earthlink.net
wholesale therapeutic and
healthful herbal teas by mail
order

Barnes & Watson Fine Teas
270 S. Hanford Street #211
Seattle, WA 98134
wholesale only

Blue Willow Tea Company
911 E. Pike - #204
Seattle, WA 98122
wholesale only, emphasis on
organics, new tearoom in Seattle

Camellia Tea Company
P.O. Box 8310
Metairie, LA 70011-8310
800-863-3531
mail order retail

Celestial Seasonings
4600 Sleepytime Drive
Boulder, Co 80301
800-2000TEA
www.celestialseasonings.com
mail order retail

The Collector's Teapot
62-68 Tenbroeck Avenue
Kingston, NY 12402
800-724-3306
mail order retail, teapots and
accessories

Golden Moon Tea
P.O. Box 1646
Woodinville, WA 98072
wholesale

Grace Tea Company
50 West 17th St.
New York, NY 10011
212-255-2935
mail order wholesale and retail

Harney & Sons Fine Teas
P.O. Box 638
Salisbury, CT 06068
888-HARNEYT
www.harney.com
mail order wholesale and retail
fine teas and nice people

High Tea
Center Village, Box 902
Harrisville, NH 03450
800-587-9595
mail order retail teas, pots and
books

Market Spice
P.O. Box 2935
Redmond, WA 98073
425-883-1220
E-Mail: mktspc@juno.com
wholesale and retail hand-blended
teas and spices

The Perennial Tea Room
1910 Post Alley
Seattle, WA 98101
888-448-4054
www.perennialtearoom.com
marvelous repository of teas, pots,
and knowledge, mail order and
store in Seattle

Rather Jolly Tea
J.G. British Imports, Inc.
7933 Pinegrove Court
Sarasota, FL 34238
941-926-1700
E-Mail: jgbrit@aol.com
mail order wholesale and retail

Teatime in the Northwest

The Republic of Tea
8 Digital Drive, Suite 100
Novato, CA 94949
800-298-4TEA
www.sipbysip.com
wholesale only

Senok Tea (USA)
126 S. Spokane St.
Seattle, WA 98134
877-736-6583
E-Mail: admin@senoktea.com
importers and merchants of Ceylon
teas, wholesale and retail

Stash Tea Company
9040 S.W. Burnham St.
Tigard, OR 97223-6199
800-826-4218
www.stashtea.com
mail order retail

Tazo
P.O. Box 66
Portland, OR 97202
503-231-9234
wholesale only

Tea, A Magazine
P.O. Box 348
Scotland, CT 06264
860-456-1145
E-Mail: teamag@q.continuum.net
bimonthly glossy magazine by, for,
and about tea lovers

The Tea Council of the USA
230 Park Avenue, Suite 1460
New York, NY 10169
212-986-6998
excellent source of information
regarding the health benefits of tea

The Teacup
2207 Queen Anne Avenue North
Seattle, WA 98109
206-283-5931
mail order retail and quarterly
newsletter

Tea Talk
P.O. Box 860
Sausalito, CA 94966
415-331-1557
"a newsletter on the pleasures of
tea" published quarterly

TeaTime
298 W. Parkside Drive
Camano Island, WA 98282
wholesale tea distributor, decorated sugars and tea-related gifts

Tea Time Garden
P.O. Box 34
North Lakewood, WA 98259
360-652-8488
www.teatimegarden.com
herbals and handicrafts by mail
order retail and wholesale

The TeaTime Gazette
P.O. Box 40276
St. Paul, MN 55104
E-Mail: lleamer@aol.com
a nifty "Newsletter for English Tea
Lovers," and British tea tours

Todd & Holland Fine Teas
7577 Lake Street
River Forest, IL 60305
800-747-8327
www.todd-holland.com
rare and very special teas mail
order retail

Water and Leaves
380 Swift Avenue - Unit 6
South San Francisco, CA 94080
415-952-4503
E-Mail: wayoftea@aol.com
wholesale only

Windham Tea Club
12 Wilson Road
Windham, NH 03087
800-565-7527
tea-of-the-month club, mail order

Index of Tea Rooms

Index of Tea Rooms

Index of Teatime Recipes

Index of Teatime Recipes

TEATIME IN THE NORTHWEST
THIRD EDITION

REPORT FORM

This book was conceived to fulfill two yearnings. We set out to encourage people in the Northwest to take time from busy agendas to simply slow down for tea. In doing so, it's our belief that you can better collect your thoughts and really make a connection with your world. Cup by cup, the Northwest is becoming a more thoughtful place for it. Additionally, we wanted to thank those who have created a business plan based upon providing havens from life's stresses for the rest of us - tea businesses. Often we must rely on our readers to let us know when a new one opens, or if we've left your favorite one out of this edition. Either way, we love to hear from you, so please take a minute to give us your opinions and insights:

Name of new tea room, tea caterer, or tea merchant:

_____

Address:

_____

Phone or email:

_____

Your comments

_____

_____

_____

Any comments about any tea businesses listed in this edition, or about the book itself?

_____

Your name and address

_____

Your input to TeaTime in the Northwest makes future editions possible. Thank you. Please mail to: Sharon & Ken Foster-Lewis 298 W. Parkside Drive, Camano Island, WA 98282 or email: teatimenw@juno.com